The Politics of

BLACK

Empowerment

African American Life Series

A complete listing of the books in this series
can be found at the back of this volume.

General Editors

Toni Cade Bambara
Author and Filmmaker

Wilbur C. Rich
Wayne State University

Geneva Smitherman
Michigan State University

Ronald W. Walters
Howard University

The Politics of
BLACK
Empowerment

THE TRANSFORMATION
OF BLACK ACTIVISM
IN URBAN AMERICA

James Jennings

 WAYNE STATE UNIVERSITY PRESS   DETROIT

Library of Congress Cataloging-in-Publication Data

Jennings, James, 1949–
    The politics of Black empowerment   :   the transformation of Black
    activism in urban America / James Jennings.
        p.   cm. — (African American life series)
    Includes bibliographical references and index.
    ISBN 0-8143-2317-0 (alk. paper)
    1. Afro-Americans—Politics and government.   I. Title.
    II. Series.
    E185.615.J46   1992
    323.1'196073—dc20   91–25944
                                                                         CIP

Book design by Joanne Elkin Kinney

Contents

To my parents, James Jennings, Sr. and
Natividad Baez Jennings

Acknowledgments

This manuscript expands my earlier writings that focused on the political experiences of Blacks in urban America. I base my analysis on critiques of the germane theoretical and empirical literature, my own activist experiences in Boston and New York City, and the reported experiences and ideas of activists across the country. Between 1987 and 1990 I interviewed several Black activists around the country for this study. Careful reading of this manuscript and encouragement of this undertaking by friends and colleagues at various points was crucial for the development of my ideas. My accomplishment of this completed manuscript is due, in part, to the input and reactions of several individuals; I am most grateful, therefore, to Martin Kilson, Lucius J. Barker, William E. Nelson, Hanes Walton, Jr., Mack H. Jones, Eugene "Gus" Newport, Bette Woody, William Fletcher, Marilyn Frankenstein, Meizhu Lui, and Mary Ann Crayton, who played a critical role in encouraging me to complete the manuscript and helping me strengthen its early drafts.

Geneva Smitherman and Wilbur C. Rich were extremely helpful as editors of the African American Life Series sponsored by Wayne State University Press. Their comments considerably strengthened the study and ensured its final publication. I also wish to thank Alice J. Burnette, Eugene Rivers, Diana Yin, Benita Rheddick, Karen Hull, and Ileen Carver for various kinds of editorial and research assistance. Vivien Morris and April Taylor, activists in their own right, were helpful in arranging and conducting interviews with Black activists across the

United States. The community activists who trusted me and allowed interviews played a key role in my research and writing.

Thanks and appreciation must be extended to my colleague and former director of the William Monroe Trotter Institute at the University of Massachusetts/Boston, Wornie Reed, for his continual support of this study and effort. A grant from this organization allowed me to complete this undertaking.

Finally, my most special thanks to Lenora, for her continual support and inspiration.

Introduction

Arguably, one can detect two distinct strands in studies of Black political activism: one approach focuses on behavioral aspects, that is, individual and group characteristics of voting/nonvoting and elections; other writings include more fundamental philosophical and cultural questions regarding Black politics. To analyze current Black political activism both strands must be examined. This study represents a theoretical reexamination of Black politics since the late 1960s.

Based on interviews with Black and Latino activists in several big cities as well as review of the literature and Black newspapers around the country, this study analyzes how the "traditional" face of Black politics and electoral activism interacts with a growing "progressive" face of Black politics. While traditional Black political activists seek access or political incorporation, another group aims for power sharing. The traditional approach, seeking a "piece of the pie," is sometimes satisfied with merely replacing white politicians with Blacks, but the progressive constituency focuses on fundamentally changing the whole economic and political pie.

Current literature on Black politics has not fully examined the significance and implications of progressive Black political activism. Coverage of political efforts of Blacks who seek access into the social, economic, and electoral arena—indeed a major part of Black politics in this country—dominates the literature. Most Blacks vote the Democratic party loyally; they seek opportunities to show white voters that they can operate within the system as effectively as any other group. Unjustifiably,

9

however, many writers on this topic have presupposed that all Blacks participating in the electoral arena reflect the same values that character- ize the culturally dominant society. And in the popular literature and media, many have suspected that the 1990 election of L. Douglas Wilder, Virginia's first Black governor, or Norm Rice, the first Black mayor of Seattle, sounded the death knell of either a Black political activism at- tuned to new political values or political processes more responsive to Black aspirations.

There are interesting political rumblings in Black urban America. Blacks are exhibiting political preferences and behavior that have yet to be fully analyzed or explained by efforts in either academe or the main- stream media. The political agenda for Black America is changing, and new Black actors are participating in the local electoral arenas of urban America. One can sense a rebellious mood, usually associated with social change, in the Black community. This is the case even among Black voters who are not new in the electoral arena. For example, political scientist Lucius J. Barker writes, "Success of Jackson's 1984 campaign indicates that black voters and other minorities, no longer satisfied to remain clients whose benefits would still be determined largely by white patrons, may be on the verge of participating more directly in American pluralist politics"[1] A mood of rebellion and increasing political participation is reflected in a range of political developments at both national and local levels.

This represents a qualitative change in Black activist circles from the end of the 1970s, a period described by Black poet Gil Scott-Heron as "Winter in America."[2] Another Black activist, John Trice, wrote in the earlier part of the 1980s: "Many of the black activists of the late 1960s and early 1970s have shied away from serious political involvement. . . . Others have drifted into disillusionment with the two party system."[3] There may still be much Black disillusionment with national party poli- tics, but there are indications that a new kind of political activism is beginning to emerge, especially at the local level in urban America.

Two major propositions underlie this study. First, Blacks have utilized the electoral arena for the pursuit of "divisible" benefits, primarily; this parallels the goals of early European immigrant groups settling in urban America. Today, however, the goal of access is giving way to goals of social protest with implications for the structure of wealth and power. Thus, the philosophical basis of Black politics is beginning to change, a development noted in some political occurrences in cities like Boston, Detroit, Chicago, and Milwaukee. Unlike the recent past, Black activists of the 1990s who are involved with protest are beginning to use the electoral arena to a far greater extent than in the 1960s and 1970s.

Second, and related, the Black electorate is undergoing major changes as a result of demographic developments and the introduction of new kinds of actors into the electoral arena. The Black electorate is increasingly differentiated into several sectors that must be mobilized differently. Although a traditional core of Black voters continues to participate electorally, many new Black actors and voters are being pulled into the electorate by leaders who are advocating an agenda of political "empowerment" rather than access. The usual calls for electoral participation based on civic responsibility are ineffective with this sector.

Political activism oriented towards access generally refers to goals, preferences, and behavior aimed at economic accommodation with existing structures and distribution of wealth, including land. The rules of the game, or the position of interests with significant economic power, are not challenged. Empowerment activism, on the other hand, is more militant in terms of style and substance. Here Blacks seek more than just a "piece of the pie"; instead, Black activists seek to determine the size and flavor of the pie, as well as who the baker is and how the economic pie actually will be cut and shared. In the last few years, both these faces of Black political activism have utilized the local and national electoral arenas to win adherents.

Until recently the major ideological challenge to liberal America in the local and national electoral arenas came from the right wing of this country's political spectrum. Since 1980 the conservative challenge has effectively changed public debates regarding major domestic policy and initiatives. The right on the American political map has successfully mobilized a sizeable portion of the electorate to support its programs and symbolism. The Democratic party has responded to this challenge from the right by attempting to capture that part of the electorate that has supported America's rightward shift. Several political developments in the Black community, however, represent yet another challenge to the Democratic party. The seeds of these challenges were contained in the 1984 and 1988 presidential campaigns of Jesse Jackson, but a growing number of local political events also portend philosophical difficulties for the Democratic party. These developments include incorporating new kinds of Black voters and actors in the electoral arena and instituting policies and programs that question economic arrangements in the American city.

Although a Black presence in national politics has been significant, especially after the Second World War, it has usually been characterized as an integral—if not fully equal—part of what liberalism has come to mean in American national politics. One political scientist contends that this means "the activities of the political leaders of the Black underclass from the time of Reconstruction to the era of the 'new right' have been, *seriatim*, marked by patronage, clientelism, and civil rights rather than by power politics. The struggle was designed to gain acceptance by Blacks into the mainstream of power but Blacks were destined never to fully share it."[4] Many Black leaders and organizations are politically entrenched in the liberal and welfare state coalition established and maintained by the administrations of New Deal, Fair Deal, and Great Society.

In the Black community another, more "nationalist," strand of social activism has always existed to continually challenge the Black integrationist framework, but its political saliency was periodic. The level of efficacy for the more nationalist strand has depended on overall social and economic conditions facing the Black community. During periods of progress, the nationalist strand has not been as popular as in times of Black social, educational, and economic retrogression.[5]

There are indications that the more nationalist, even separatist, or radical strand is reemerging, but an especially noteworthy and significant development in the last decade is the emergence of this strand in the electoral arena. Notwithstanding the electoral victories of Blacks such as Tom Bradley, L. Douglas Wilder, and other "moderates," this radicalism promises a wide-ranging impact on both national politics and the competitive relationship between the two major American parties. The latter strand, the progressive face of Black activism—what I refer to as "empowerment" politics—will have the greatest impact on the relationship between the Black community and the major parties; it will determine the direction and viability of the Democratic party in this country. A few examples of politicians who have attempted to operate under this framework include the former Mayor of Berkeley, California, Eugene Newport, Boston-based activist Mel King, the late Ken Cockrel of Detroit, and Al Vann, state assembly-representative from Brooklyn, New York.

Organization of the Study

This book begins with a general definition and description of the characteristics of Black empowerment activism in urban America. I discuss several major political developments within the Black community such as a growing ideological bifurcation and the synthesis of protest and electoral activism. I also argue that Black empowerment activism represents a social movement in America in the same vein as the earlier Black political mobilization of Garveyism and the civil rights movement.

In chapter 2 I discuss Black empowerment activism in relation to the contemporary American political spectrum and illustrate the range of ideology in the Black community. I present one strand of Black activism as a philosophical and political challenge to both liberalism and conservatism—a very important growing third force on the national political landscape. The weaknesses of pluralist literature in analyzing current developments regarding Black political activism is examined as well.

Chapter 3 gives a brief overview of Black politics and shows its orientation changes from a focus on "access" into America's mainstream institutions to more of a "power" orientation in the current period. I present information showing how increasing numbers of Black activists are seeking new kinds of public policy demands. Some of these demands could be described as populist, but I also examine major differences between Black and white populist politics.

Chapter 4 examines continuing racial and class tensions in the American city and proposes that the traditional political and economic approaches of big city mayors and politicians can no longer respond to such tensions. Here I argue that the "executive coalition" and "urban political managerialism" evolving through several national administrations is no longer effective in controlling or directing Black activism that threatens the power status quo.

Chapter 5 describes and analyzes the patterns of responses of corporate leadership to the emergence of a political activism that moves beyond merely calling for a Black economic "piece of the pie" in the American city. Here I propose that corporate leaders of major cities may be increasingly concerned with Black empowerment activism that they may perceive as radicalism because of potential confrontation regarding systemic values and economic interests and institutional arrangements. While the corporate sector seeks a policy framework characterized as "growth ideology" during periods of economic expansion or the "austerity state' in response to fiscal crisis, many Black activists are calling for programs that elevate the needs of people and neighborhoods over corporate interests. Both "growth ideology" and "austerity state" benefit corporate interests over neighborhoods; the former suggests that local governments should do everything possible to let big business and financial interests flourish, even at the expense of poor and working-class people. The latter term suggests that during periods of fiscal crisis social and human services should be cut from local budgets before benefits to business and developers, and that corporate taxes should also be reduced, rather than increased.

The conclusion presents the major points regarding growing differentiation within the Black urban electorate as well as the shifting ideological transformation suggested in the rise of Black empowerment activism. By proposing that the Black electorate can generally be divided into three types—the politically-divorced, the participatory voter, and the selective voter—I offer a useful framework for analyzing the nature and potential impact of the Black electorate on national and local politics.

CHAPTER ONE

Characteristics of Black Empowerment Activism

Winds are blowing . . . that have not stirred American politics just this way in a half century, . . . one system of politics is giving way to another still unnamed, unshaped. . . , What rolls loose now in American politics are forces of emotion and resentment completely outside the conventional old political system.

Theodore White (*New York Times*, February 5, 1984)

Cities such as Boston, New York, Philadelphia, Chicago, Detroit, Cleveland, Washington, D.C., and Milwaukee indicate that certain kinds of Black political goals are emerging that reflect neither traditional liberal nor traditional conservative agendas. Furthermore, Black activists associated with these new kinds of political goals are using the electoral arena. In fact, two strands of Black political activism can be detected in many cities where the size of the Black population is relatively large in comparison to the total population.

The ultimate goal of one kind of Black activism is political incorporation into current social and economic arrangements, while the challenging Black activism seeks to rearrange social and economic systems to enhance the position of the poor and the working class and promote neighborhood interests. Thus, one strand of Black political activism has emphasized access to a given power structure, but the other has sought power sharing or community control. The traditional face of activism has relied on the electoral arena; however, the new face reflects a synthesis of the electoral arena with protest and grass-roots mobilization around

15

specific issues. Traditional Black activism has represented an important political support for the welfare state in its measured redistribution of wealth; the other activism seeks a more radical redistribution. Although the more traditional Black activism in the electoral arena has relied heavily on coalitions with liberal whites, the other primarily focuses on mobilizing poor and working-class Blacks. The major actors in the former style are liberal whites, "participatory" Black voters, and civic leaders; in the latter case, political activists are more prominently new Black voters who have not represented the normative participants in the electoral arena.

There are several reasons for the emergence of a new Black political activism, more militant in style and substance than traditional electoral activism in this community. The explosive growth of an impoverished Black *lumpenproletariat* in the last twenty years, concurrent with a rightward drift of American society and a marked deterioration in living conditions for poor and working-class sectors in the Black community, partially explains the emergence of Black "empowerment" activism. This activism has been reflected in the 1986 and 1988 Mandela referenda in Boston, seeking to establish a Black city within that city, the call for an autonomous Black school district in Milwaukee, the founding of the Harold Washington party in Chicago in 1988, the call for a national reparations bill by Rep. John Conyers (D-MI) in 1990, and a growing number of Black-led boycotts of white businesses in Kentucky, Mississippi, and New York City in 1988.[1] Such activism is also apparent in the same year in the Black-led threats to close down the construction of the Dan Ryan Expressway in Chicago, similar roadways in East St. Louis,[2] and the Bradley Center in Milwaukee.[3] It also includes growing Black-led protests about housing issues and the homeless in cities like Philadelphia, Chicago, and Atlanta.[4]

The political mobilization of Blacks in Brooklyn, New York, led by independent Black electoral officials such as Al Vann and Roger Green and community activists like Sonny Carson and Jitu Weusi, could also be included in this category of activism. It is also reflected partially in the political pressure applied from Black activists to the 1988 Jackson campaign to use the mobilized Black electorate to challenge the agenda of the Democratic party. This pressure was reflected in two rallies held in Atlanta the day before the Democratic 1988 National Convention opened. Both the Association of Community Organizations for Reform Now (ACORN) and the Nation of Islam publicly called on Jesse Jackson to continue forcing the leadership of the Democratic party to adopt a progressive agenda. The call by Minister Louis Farrakhan for an independent Black political thrust has been joined by many Black activists and intellectuals covering a wide political spectrum, such as theologian and activist Cornel West, Lenora Fulani of the New Alliance Party, as well as journalist Tony Brown, recognized as a Black conservative by many activists.[5]

Journalist Rob Gurwitt points to the 1989 election of Michael White as mayor of Cleveland as perhaps an example of a new kind of Black political activism. He suggests that Michael White's election "had successfully blended two currents that have begun to nudge the course of black politics in new directions." These currents not only embrace themes of "inclusion and racial unity," but they also challenge the alliance that has emerged in some cities between a Black political establishment and downtown business interests. Rob Gurwitt continues, "Neither of these developments is strong enough yet to justify a conclusion that black politics has entered a new era, but there is little doubt that this is a time of transition. White and his allies in Cleveland are members of a new generation that is just starting to flex its muscles, and there is little question that it holds the potential for radically altering the black political landscape."[6]

The kind of Black activism and elections described above, although disparate, disjointed, and sporadic, may be suggesting a resurgence of Black protest. But there are differences with the Black protest of a few decades earlier. As Rob Gurwitt suggests, the resurging Black protest may not be completely defined in terms of a racial agenda. In the 1960s Black protest was based primarily, although not completely, on a racial agenda. For instance, Joe Darden and others write about a local situation in Detroit:

> In 1968 the Reverend Albert Cleage, Jr., a major leader of the Group on Advanced Leadership (GOAL), one of several black nationalist groups in Detroit, stressed the importance of black political power in areas where blacks were in the majority. . . . Blacks would soon be a majority in Detroit, the Reverend Cleage stated, and "by voting black we can elect a black mayor, a black council and a black school board." A black candidate's only necessary qualification, according to Cleage, was that he be "devoted to the black nation, putting his dedication to black people first."[7]

The racial agenda, however, is shifting; Black populist economics is growing in importance. And yet some Black activists are concerned that Black nationalism could negate the strides made in political mobilization. For example, Shafik Abu-Pahir, an activist in Philadelphia with the New African Voices Alliance expresses concern regarding race loyalty as the primary political consideration of sections of the Black electorate in this city: "Many of our people are biologically entrapped—equating 'Black' with 'progressive.' Often cities need the experience of going through the biological stage before the residents are able to examine the program of political office seekers. This process is beginning to happen in Philadelphia."[8] It is suggested by this and other Black activists that an exclusive racial mobilization could in fact hinder the development of a populist, people-oriented economic orientation. The call for Black capitalism, for example, or the historical example of Booker T. Washington's accommodationism, were based on a limited racial conceptualization.

Although some instances of Black activism and political behavior are molded primarily by a strong nationalist sentiment, the call for economic approaches that challenge downtown interests is also growing. The development of a populist economics may be more significant than any change in the racial style of new Black politicians and activists. The latter may in fact depend on the kind of constituency one is trying to mobilize or reach. For example, while Douglas Wilder became the first Black governor of Virginia partially due to his style of racial "moderation," the mayor of Detroit won a fifth term despite running a campaign that emphasized race. Although Wilder's and Young's campaign styles were different, this was merely a function of the kind of constituencies each had to attract to win election. But their economic orientations, however, are quite similar; both pursue a framework of economic activities that represents the concerns and interests of "downtown" businesses.

Public policy and the private sector's role in urban America are being approached differently by leaders reflecting the more progressive Black urban activism. The agenda of certain Black activists and leaders is changing in terms of rejecting the traditional liberal framework and values for making and implementing such policy.

Furthermore, as suggested earlier, Black nationalist and separatist sectors that participated in the protest activities of the 1960s were neither supportive nor convinced of the saliency of the electoral arena; these sectors may have voted at times, but only sporadically and temporarily. This separatism led Martin Luther King, Jr., to urge the union of these two kinds of Black leaders who suffered from a "unique and unnatural dichotomy."[9]

This separation can be witnessed in the growing Latino urban concentrations as well. Ruben Martinez has pointed out that a division is emerging between establishment Latino politicians and community activists. He describes one instance:

> Indeed, the clearest division found among Latinos this election year is the rift between the 'establishment' politicos and the community-based activists. Although both of these groups grow out of the Chicano/Latino explosion of the 1960s, the distance between the two has grown steadily. The

majority of Latino establishment politicians lined up early behind Gov. Michael Dukakis rather than swing to the left of the party, which was represented by Jesse Jackson.[10]

The Jesse Jackson campaign, the Harold Washington and Mel King campaigns in Chicago and Boston, and the establishment of the Unity Party in New York under the leadership of activists like Jitu Weusi reflect a marriage between these two orientations in the Black community.

Although the upsurge or groundswell of Black political activism does not yet consistently threaten those interest groups that have wielded economic influence and political power in the last few decades, it seems that this activism is moving away from the traditional arrangements of power and wealth that characterize major urban centers. Some evidence for this shift includes the way new actors and first-time Black voters are being mobilized by community activists. The language used for this mobilization defies the political and economic establishment; the rhetoric that seems to attract many people to various campaigns and rallies could be considered anticorporate or even fundamentally anticapitalist.

Activists espousing separatism, self-determination, or cultural reawakening in the Black community may seek to enter the local and national electoral arena—a sign of this anti-establishment mobilization. Leftist activists in the Black community have also sought to use the electoral arena in the current period. Many surveys show the strong populist leanings and sentiment in the Black community, another suggestion that new kinds of systemic challenges may be emerging in the Black community. The growing calls for Black agendas that include principles for action demanding power sharing, rather than access to the corporate or governmental sector, may also indicate new winds blowing in Black politics. Thus, it may no longer be accurate in all cases to differentiate between politics and protest, as did Bayard Rustin in the mid-1960s.[11] Nevertheless, this differentiation continues: consider, for instance, Lucius J. Barker's "Jesse Jackson's Candidacy in Political-Social Perspective: A Contextual Analysis," where the author makes a conceptual difference between politics and protest as a means to achieve political objectives.[12]

I do not suggest here that protest and electoral activism are coming together to challenge the system for the first time. In fact, the Black Panther party sought to infuse the local electoral arena with radical, anticapitalist candidacies in the late 1960s and early 1970s. Several members of the Black Panther party ran for office in Oakland, Milwaukee, and Chicago. In Oakland, Huey P. Newton ran for mayor, and Bobby Seale also pursued electoral office as a national leader of the Black Panther party. The Black Panther party endorsed many activists for political office to the Oakland City Council. A former member of the Black Panther party, Bobby Rush, serves on Chicago's City Council. In Milwaukee another, Michael McGee, presently serves as a city alderman; McGee, furthermore, believes that the self-defense advocated by the Black Panthers is still necessary and has called for the development of a Black militia.[13]

Black activists have made several local efforts to use the electoral arena as an extension of protest and progressive demands on city government. For example, Imamu Amiri Baraka mobilized Black activists and potential voters to elect Kenneth Gibson as the first Black mayor of Newark, New Jersey. Similarly, the Congress of African People organized the Black community and the Black Political Convention to participate in the 1971 mayoral election in Philadelphia; this convention's endorsement of Black activist Hardy Williams was a first step toward the election of Wilson E. Goode twelve years later. Political scientist Thaddeus P. Mathis writes that the Black United Front, another protest organization, also played a significant role in mobilizing the Black electorate a few years after the first Black Political Convention: "The Black United Front, under the initial direction of David Richardson and Falaka Fattah, issued a call for reconvening of the Black Political Convention to develop a human rights agenda for the 1979 elections and to serve as a vehicle for encouraging mass participation by black Philadelphians in the upcoming elections."[14]

Different today is the increasing number of Black activists using the local electoral arena to raise new kinds of political and policy issues; furthermore, Black activists who take issue with the major political and economic institutional arrangements, and the policies and values that are reflected therein, are beginning to build local power bases. Some of these activists include Mel King in Boston, Al Vann in Brooklyn, New York, the late Harold Washington in Chicago, and others. In New York City, activist and political scientist Basil Wilson believes that the expansion of the number of seats on the city council will give rise to a cadre of Black nationalists who previously did not rely on the electoral arena.[15]

The conjoining of protest, or what some might describe as racial militancy, and the electoral arena in the Black community reflects an activism that has not been analyzed fully by the major pluralist, conservative, Marxist, or populist paradigms related to race. The pluralist literature does not reflect this new development because its underlying assumption is that all "noise" produced by Black interest groups concerns inclusion within a given economic and social status quo. Pluralists assume that political noise made by an out-group focuses only on entry into a given arrangement of economic and political power. Writers in this school have generally dismissed the political impact and potential of

Black activism that does not automatically opt for economic integration and political inclusion into the mainstream American polity.

The Failure of the Pluralist Explanation

One concise statement describing the notion of pluralism in American politics is offered by political scientist C. V. Hamilton:

> One of the most prevalent interpretations of the American political system concerns the purpose and function of groups within that system. According to this "pluralistic" interpretation, groups organize in response to perceived self-interests and then bargain, negotiate, form coalitions, and inevitably compromise their goals. The result is policies that often feed back into the system to form another round of group interaction. It is assumed that no group obtains all it wants at any given time but that all groups engaged in the process can achieve some of their goals. It is also assumed that no one group can sustain enough strength permanently to dominate the others.[16]

Political activist Sheila Collins described pluralism in another, but similar, way:

> The central tenet of pluralist politics is that political power in the United States is more or less evenly allocated among blocs of competing voluntary associations or interest groups. The implication is that while groups may vary in the amount of power they wield, no one group exercises sufficient power to bar others from entrance into the political arena. The government's role is to mediate these competing centers of power, which work out their differences in a rational way through negotiation, compromise, and coalition-building, thus averting the need to resort to extra parliamentary, violent, or disruptive means of making one's voice heard.[17]

But Black political history in America cannot be thoroughly analyzed within the traditional pluralist framework as described in the literature.

Pluralist literature posits that Black politics represents a process of making noise to gain equality as participants in a given system of power and wealth. Hanes Walton, Jr. suggests that pluralism, as a political school of thought, reflects a serious bias in approaching Black politics by identifying the major or perhaps only issue as who votes and who doesn't.[18] The literature generally has not captured certain critical developments in Black political activism. For example, it has underestimated white resistance to Black political incorporation; it has not focused enough on the significance of a growing nationalist sentiment in the Black community, a sentiment not necessarily inconsistent with an expanding class-based Black political agenda. As does much of the mainstream media in the late 1980s, and early 1990s, pluralists writers seem to propose that the only significant movement or activism in the Black community is represented by the moderate style of someone like the first Black governor of Virginia, Douglas Wilder. The media has especially been notorious in declaring the end of the era of Black militancy.

Many studies that use a pluralist framework and focus on the election and presence of Black mayors have overlooked some important questions regarding the impact of Black nationalism and its value as a critical resource for mobilizing voter support. Black nationalism, while certainly a factor that shielded some Black mayors from criticism, can also set a foundation for radical political activism. Perhaps the best example of how this can happen is represented in the political development of Malcolm X, who on the basis of Black nationalism, evolved and developed his ideas into a clear radical critique of the U.S. political economy. The force of Black nationalism, along with the limits of the civil rights movement, also moved Martin Luther King, Jr. toward a radical critique of this society.[19] Black nationalism has led to a bifurcation of leadership that has not received much or serious attention in the scholarly literature. In a study of the election of a Black mayor in New Orleans, political scientists Huey L. Perry and Alfred Stokes write that "in a city where poverty is rampant among blacks, it has been a source of pride among blacks to have a black serve in the highest position in city government." This observation suggests Black mayors have translated nationalist sentiment as a political resource; this idea should be explored further.

In one article political scientist Bruce Ransom examines the first successful mayoral election of Wilson Goode. But here only slight reference is made to the potential impact of Black nationalism. Ransom discussed the bombing of MOVE and nearby homes: "Some residents left homeless by the fire, admitted a mistake was made, but there was a reluctance to criticize Mayor Goode, and some praised him."[20] Race apparently played a part in muting criticism of the mayor, as Margot Harry points out: "If the assault had been carried out under the administration of a white mayor, the response of these sectors clearly would have been different. But a Black man sat in the mayor's chair. . . . From this perspective, any exposure or criticism of Wilson Goode's role in the massacre was viewed as gravely detrimental to the strategy of 'Black Empowerment.'"[21] A Black activist in Houston and member of the Ida Delaney Justice Committee, Rose Upshaw, also implied that this dynamic was evident in that city when Black clergy and elected officials refused to criticize Black police commissioner Lee Brown.[22] Despite mobilizing a grass roots effort to protest police killings of two Blacks within a period of a month in late 1989, some Black clergy and elected officials felt that they should not criticize a Black governmental official.

But is the impact of Black nationalism in the political arena static? Is it possible that this same sentiment could be the basis of major dissatisfaction with a Black mayor? Philadelphia activist and director of the Money for Neighborhoods Coalition Joyce Brooks describes the changing sentiment among Black poor and working people toward Mayor Wilson Goode: "The Black community's first response was that even though he [Wilson Goode] didn't come from among the community, it should 'give him a chance.' . . . Experience has been a good teacher to our community and people are realizing the tools that are used to disenfranchise us. People now want to know why our neighborhoods are deteriorating."23 This change in support shows a possible redirection of Black nationalist sentiment, a possibility overlooked in some literature focusing on Black and urban politics.

Can Black nationalism be viewed as a major factor in Black politics today? How is it being manifested in the local political arena? And what is its potential impact on a city's politics and public policy agenda? Does Black nationalism mean that Black mayors and elected officials will have an easier time managing cities, or because they are Black, will more difficult problems be posed to these elected officials as a result? These questions are increasingly important in understanding Black political activism today. But pluralist literature falls short of investigating seriously these questions and related issues. Some Marxist and populist writers share this weakness with the pluralists. They too have overlooked the political significance of Black nationalist activists. Many times, Black nationalists like Louis Farrakhan, Al Sharpton, and Sonny Carson are dismissed by some Marxists and populists as insignificant figures or even charlatans, unworthy of serious consideration in a study of Black political activism.

Pluralism as a social and political theory that presents local government as neutral arbiter of competing interests is not adequate for fully explaining Black political participation, behavior, and preferences in urban America. Black political participation suggests not an interest-group behavior, similar to white political behavior, but participation as a distinct racial group, which then raises both divisible and indivisible issues. Many instances illustrate, furthermore, that local government has postured itself as an interest opposed to full Black participation in the supposedly open and democratic pluralist arena.

One can note several characteristics from a brief historical overview of recent Black politics to illustrate this argument. The historical role of Black politics in producing social change must be appreciated fully. The significance of Black political activism will not be captured if Blacks are approached as merely another special interest group. Black political activism, even that reflecting America's liberal agenda, has had major implications for both fundamental social questions and the very direction of American society. That is, the systemic and social consequences of Black success had political, economic, and cultural repercussions for the broader society.

Perhaps the expansion of democratic rights for all Americans as a consequence of the civil rights movement best exemplifies the widespread impact of Black political success. The development of public education and public works in the Reconstruction South provides a good historical example. W. E. B. Du Bois contended that public schooling for everyone—even the children of poor white farmers—was a consequence of Black governmental innovations to help former slaves.[24] Because Blacks are on the bottom of America's social and economic ladder, to use activist and writer James Boggs's metaphor, as living conditions for Blacks improve, it elevates conditions for others on higher steps of the ladder.[25] No other interest group in American society can claim that its successes or failures have had such profound effect and impact on American politics and culture.

The Committee on Policy for Racial Justice has described how Black activism in America has had far broader consequences than the usual activism of interest groups in the American polity:

> Black Americans have been at the helm of a profound social revolution. Since World War II, we have engineered the demise of a rigidly segregated society, used nonviolent action and litigation to compel the protection of basic rights, expanded the American society's conception and application of equality, made dramatic gains in political participation and leadership.[26]

The success of Black activism such as A. Philip Randolph's threatened march on Washington in 1941 and the civil rights and Black power movements in the 1960s and 1970s, in other words, has changed the very nature of American society by forcing it to be more democratic and participatory. Thus, analysis that conceptualizes Blacks as just another interest group in a pluralist America is inaccurate.

Another characteristic of Black political history not fully acknowledged within traditional pluralistic literature is that social progress realized by Blacks was not necessarily institutionalized within the political and economic fabric of America. This major point does not fit well with the ways that some have used pluralist-based analysis to explain urban political developments. For the Black community, progress in one period, however limited, did not necessarily lead to political or economic progress in subsequent periods. Hanes Walton, Jr., specifically focused on political participation; he argues cogently that Blacks have experienced various stages of political participation, including "nonparticipation," "limited" or "moderate" participation, and "full" participation.[27] Stephen Thernstrom has shown that, even after Blacks surpassed white immigrant groups in terms of schooling, economic progress and its continuation were tenuous to a much greater extent for the former than the latter groups.[28] Unlike white ethnics Blacks have not experienced a linear progression in achieving higher levels of political participation, with resulting social acceptance and economic benefits. Enjoying full participation in one period, Blacks could readily revert to "limited" participation or even "nonparticipation" in succeeding periods, owing to the economic and political needs of white interest groups in America.

Thirdly, Black political behavior essentially represented a response to racism. Regardless of region or city, Black political strategies and tactics responded and reacted to the physical and social limitations placed upon Blacks as *Blacks* according to Walton. Although some groups within the Black community have won acceptance as an interest within American's pluralist arena, such progress has not altered a rigid racial hierarchy, with its historical roots, that continues to exist today.

This racial hierarchy, founded upon white racism and economic privilege, was in operation as Blacks migrated to the big cities in large numbers during the first half of the twentieth century. A racial hierarchy separated ideologically and substantively the formative political experiences of Black and white ethnic groups. As Martin Kilson has written, "Of all the variables governing Negro city dwelling outside the South, preeminent were those associated with white racism. No other major American immigrant community—Irish, Jews, Italians—faced such systematic and hateful restrictions upon its urban adaptation as did the Negro."[29] Blacks and other minorities have been forced to respond to an American ideology of white racism.

Although the "value of white supremacy" in this country has been long-lived and pervasive, an "animating feature of Americans and their governmental policies throughout our history," this reality has received relatively little attention under pluralist analysis.[30] Race has been acknowledged as an important factor in American political behavior in some pluralist studies, but the role or impact of racism as a critical factor in analyzing local and national politics has been unreasonably minimized; pluralist analysis tends "to threat all groups as both equal and similar, neglecting the patterns of consistent dominance by some groups or coalitions rather than others."[31] Racism, as a matter of fact, is at times reduced to merely a temporary and isolated social aberration rather than

a persistent and fundamental facet of American society. Pluralist literature does not consider seriously the existence of persistent and institutionalized racism.

Today pluralist politics lack the capacity to respond to the needs of
poor and working-class Blacks and Latinos and their heightened political
mobilization to seek redress for such needs. The social and economic
conditions of masses of Blacks and Latinos reflect a failure of American
pluralist politics and the resulting policy agenda for these communities.
As a theory, pluralism is inconsistent with an urban politics "fraught with
some of the most perplexing and intractable issues that confront a liberal
democracy; namely, racial segregation, social exclusion, and political
fragmentation." As Joel Lieske and Jan W. Hillard point out,

> These issues now appear to challenge a key objective of the pluralist dream;
> i.e., the development of an integrated society cemented by the bonds of eco-
> nomic self-interest and material progress. For instead of emphasizing the
> economic and social problems that residents share in common, much urban
> politics revolves around the racial, ethnic, and cultural divisions that sepa-
> rate them.[32]

The gulf between Blacks and whites described here is also evident in the
political attitudes of both groups.

A survey of Black and white elected officials in the mid-1970s reported some interesting data regarding attitudes about socialism and
capitalism. Of the Black elected officials who were surveyed 42 percent
agreed that "the Country is moving dangerously close to Socialism," but
of white elected officials 66 percent agreed with this statement. More
than one-third (36 percent) of the Black elected officials in the survey,
compared to just 18 percent of the white elected officials, agreed that
"the Country is moving dangerously close to Fascism." This and other
surveys indicate a substantial ideological gap between Blacks and whites
in American society. In a 1984 survey Blacks and whites were asked if
they agreed with several statements: "The government must see to it
that everyone has a job and that prices are stable, even if the rights of
businessmen have to be restricted." "It is the responsibility of the government to meet everyone's needs, even in the case of sickness, poverty,
unemployment, and old age." "Personal income should not be determined solely by one's work. Rather, everybody should get what he/she
needs to provide a decent life for his or her family." The responses to
these kinds of questions could have implications for the types of public
policies supported by Blacks and whites. On the first question 67 percent
of Blacks with incomes over $15,000 surveyed agreed, compared to 33

percent of whites in agreement. Although 79 percent of Blacks in this income category agreed with the second question, only 50 percent of whites with incomes over $15,000 did so. In response to the last question, 30 percent of Blacks agreed, but only 22 percent of whites did so. This survey also showed that Black-white attitudinal differences exist even when income is controlled.[33]

Similarly, a survey of delegates to the Democratic and Republican party national conventions also suggested budding ideological differences between Black and white delegates. Significant differences appeared between both Democratic and Republican Black and white delegates regarding the following issues: "U.S. business out of South Africa," "Busing for school desegregation," "Increase in defense spending," and "U.S. negotiation with the PLO in Arab-Israeli conflict."[34]

As whites in some big cities may come to feel "surrounded" by increasing numbers of Blacks, the racial divisions suggested above may intensify. According to one activist in Boston the continuation of two societies, with different social concerns and political attitudes generates mistrust; this development poses serious problems to American democracy.[35] Many Black activists across the country have also voiced concerns regarding a potential wave of white political backlash as a result of the increasing potential of Black political influence.

One journalist reported that in 1987 the "off-year contests confirmed that there is a growing polarization of the electorate. And this trend reinforces blacks' suspicions that whites are conspiring to retake control of many cities now under African-American leadership."[36] This fear is fueled by white-led attempts to unseat Black elected officials across the nation. One such attempt involved Buffalo, New York, City Councilman James Pitts who many Blacks believe was targeted in 1988 because he had a good chance of becoming Buffalo's first Black mayor.[37] These kinds of concerns have also surfaced in Washington, D.C., where Mayor Marion Berry stated before his indictment on drug charges that some Blacks and Hispanics "feel there is some kind of conspiracy on the part of some people somewhere, to put them out of the city and to move in and take over the city."[38] Developments such as the mayoral recall campaign organized by whites in Denver, Colorado, also contribute to a growing sense that Black and Latino electoral gains are in danger of being derailed. A few months after Federico Pena's reelection as mayor of Denver in 1987, voters, primarily from the affluent and mostly white southeast section of Denver, sought to recall the city's first Chicano mayor after alleging his fiscal mismanagement. It was reported that "the leaders of the anti-Pena campaign are right-wing forces from affluent, white Southeast Denver.

Marge Doty, their spokesperson, also led the opposition to divestment of the city retirement funds from South Africa. Joining them were some disgruntled ex-city employees who benefited from the patronage system of previous city administrations."[39]

Following the suspension of three Black community development officials for allegedly mismanaging federal funds, twenty Black ministers formed the Toledo Coalition for Economic Justice; the president of the Toledo chapter of the NAACP stated that "across the country right now, there is a conspiracy where it relates to Black leadership."[40] The bombing and killing of civil rights and NAACP officials has led NAACP President Benjamin Hooks to raise similar concerns.[41] On this issue, Clarene Royston, a St. Louis-based activist, stated: "There has been an increase in the number of Black elected officials since the 1970s. The white political right wing is taking note of this and rising Black political power and they want to keep us in our place. Just as they had to box in Adam Clayton Powell, they have to box in new Black officials."[42]

Many activists feel that sectors of the federal government are supporting and orchestrating a white backlash to Black electoral gains. The National Council of Churches reported that there are "increasing and disproportionate attacks on African American elected officials, and other persons and organizations of conscience by law enforcement agencies across this country. Federal law enforcement agencies are engaging in specious sting operations that target 'Black' and elected officials."[43] Congressman Mervyn Dymally has also stated his belief that Black elected officials have been targeted by the FBI under the "Fruhmenschen" program.[44]

Harassment against Black elected officials may effectively dampen or dilute the kinds of demands on government and the private sector that would reflect the interests of poor and working-class Blacks. As the Black population grows, demands for local public services will rise along with the cost of these services. Whites, especially those unable to move to the suburbs, may not support taxation policies geared to paying for these services, even while living conditions in Black residential areas deteriorate. This situation points to "zero-sum" politics between downtown business interests and Blacks in the electoral arena.[45]

Black elected officials and activists must be effective in obtaining important social and economic concessions by playing the game of pluralist or else their constituents' sense of efficacy for participation in American local politics may deteriorate. This is a real possibility; one observer points out, "Whether black officials can continue to satisfy the black and white communities is uncertain. If the economic and social gaps between gaps between the races cease to converge, black citizens will spurn political leaders whatever their color."[46] As a consequence of such disillusionment Black activists are questioning the economic and political arrangements and values that have become associated with pluralism and the liberal public policy agenda.

Clarence Stone and others who have proffered a "revisionist" theory of pluralism still fall short of developing an analytical framework for fully understanding recent Black efforts toward empowerment in urban America. Revisionist critiques have focused on the weaknesses or urban systems in responding equitably to the needs of various groups within a context of racial and economic hierarchy. But these critiques have overlooked emerging challenges suggested by several political events in the Black community. Such oversight may be understandable upon noting how Blacks encounter massive historical and current resistance even to mere participation in the electoral arena, a fact that has obscured ideological challenges and differences among Black urban activists.

The general refusal to allow Blacks use of the system's resources on an equal footing with other interests has been adequately documented. Again, Stone describes the situation: "Most efforts to mobilize slack resources and bring about change encounter deep resistance. Incumbent political leaders and positionally advantaged groups are not apt to respond lightly to a threat to established power relationships, and they are likely to have very substantial resources that can be used to preserve these existing relationships."[47] But Stone discusses what happens when Blacks seek entry into a given structure of power, with a given set of personal and organizational relationships. For instance, Stone focuses on conflict between the business community and former Atlanta Mayor Maynard Jackson. This resistance did not emerge because the mayor offered a program of social change or fundamental economic rearrangements; rather, the business community resisted the "new person on the block." In fact, Mayor Jackson's public policy and political agenda was quite modest; it did not go much beyond gaining the business leadership's acceptance of his authority as mayor and obtaining incremental benefits, primarily access to appointments and business contracts, for individual Blacks.

Mayor Jackson did not seek to challenge Atlanta's big business community despite the tension exhibited by this sector to immediate Black economic and social interests. As Adolph Reed, Jr., writes,

> Despite the rhetorical tempest, Jackson's record gives no reason to suspect that he ever would have considered breaking the longstanding

public/private marriage that defined Atlanta's development policy. He un-
hesitatingly supported the implementation of the major development initiatives that his administration inherited, . . . and he was an avid proponent of
the general framework for downtown development and revitalization. Indeed, even when Jackson sought, during his second term, to concentrate his
energies on the problems of poverty and unemployment in Atlanta, his dis-
position was to define these problems in ways that confirmed to the agendas
of development interests.[48]

Mayor Jackson sought only a "piece of the pie," access to the development agenda; this is the case despite the volatile rhetoric exchanged
between the mayor and the business sector during his first administration.

In 1989 Maynard Jackson again ran for mayor and was challenged by
civil rights activist Hosea Williams who decided to run as a candidate of
the poor, "not one of the black elite."[49] According to activist Marian
Petty, who worked for Hosea Williams, he decided to run on the basis of
issues like homelessness, job discrimination, and police brutality.[50] Although Maynard Jackson refused to debate Hosea Williams, the latter
obtained 20 percent of the vote. But the issue's of Atlanta's alliance
between the Black middle-class and downtown interests and its implications for the poor and working-class sectors were effectively muted. Perhaps this was a reason for the low turnout of voters (38 percent) in the
mayoral general election.

Political theorists generally have not differentiated among the range
of Black demands for access; they do not distinguish traditional Black
political activism in the electoral arena from more fundamental Black
demands for systemic change due to a tendency to conceptually separate
Black protest from more acceptable forms of political participation such
as voting and support for political machines. Earlier writers noted clearly
the differences between Black leadership seeking incorporation in the electoral arena and those relying on social protest. As Anthony Oberschall
has noted, "The political power of the black population will continue to
increase in the 1970s, and with it, that of the black politicians and officials at the expense of the civil rights leaders and the black militants." He
commented further on the ascendency of electoral participation: "Within
the black community the militants will keep losing power."[51]

This rivalry between Black politicians and Black militants has a long
history. In a review of the development of the 1972 National Black Political Convention in Gary, Indiana, Ronald Walters observed the juxtaposition of these interests: "In some states, the process of organizing delega-
tions according to the requirements contained in the *Call* that they should

be broadly representative of the Black community, was controlled by youthful Black nationalist groups, while others were dominated by professional politicians. This led to some friction between these two dominant forces."[52] Walters provides several examples of the hostility generated by these two factions toward each other during this convention. One prominent example of this hostility was the walk-out by Mayor Coleman Young because he and his Michigan delegation were challenged as unrepresentative of Black grassroots interests.

In an important essay, Ron Daniels outlined various organizational attempts to develop a political agenda based on unity between these two sectors; he described the fissure that occurred even as late as the 1970s. This activist has pointed out that the differences between the "nationalists" and the more "moderate" activists, including many elected Black officials as late as the mid-1970s, were almost irreconcilable. They were reflected in the changes of the National Black Political Assembly, born out of the 1972 National Black Political Convention. He notes the diverging interests:

> There was also the seemingly irreconcilable tensions between independent Black politics, and a commitment to the Democratic Party; and between electoral politics and protest politics. By 1974 at the Little Rock Convention, Richard Hatcher and State Representative Hannah Atkins and Lois Deberry were the only elected officials in top positions in the NBPA.
> Though there were a number of elected officials still in the NBPA, "prominent" elected officials and notable national leaders had become noticeably absent. Community activists, nationalists, grassroots leaders, and progressive intellectuals were clearly the dominant elements within the NBPA as 1975 approached.[53]

He suggests a separation between those Black leaders pursuing electoral positions and influence and those community activists or "militants," to use Anthony Oberschall's terminology.

This separation was again analyzed and emphasized, albeit erroneously, in the National Research Council's study of the status of Blacks in America. According to this study,

> Since the early 1970s, the base of black leadership has been undergoing a major transformation. . . . The breakthroughs in the politics of rights inspired a major debate over the question of alternative strategies and alternative leadership frameworks for the pursuit of the politics of resources. In an influential article, Bayard Rustin . . . argued that the era of protest was over and had to be succeeded by an era of black advancement through electoral politics. Similarly, Kilson . . . argued that "the decline of civil rights groups is both inevitable and functional," and he agreed with Reed . . . that black

elected officials are destined to become the most important source of black political leadership. . . . In contrast, Carson . . . and Nelson . . . argued that the protest movement was part of a long historical process of institutional development in the black community and stress its continuity with the strategy and tactics of black politics throughout the century. According to their view, social movement activity will continue to retain an essential role in black politics in the years to come.[54]

This presentation is anachronistic in that it overlooks the possibility of a Black social movement tradition merging with electoral activism. These two areas are merging, a fact partially reflected in new political actors and candidacies in the electoral arena. The summary is also inaccurate, however, because both Martin Kilson and William E. Nelson have discussed the possibility of these two Black political strands synthesizing in the electoral arena.[55]

It is no longer accurate to describe Black leadership and activism along a divided continuum of activism and electoral activity. The so-called activists are using and exploring the potential of the electoral arena for social change in America. Note that a leading theoretician of Black cultural nationalists in America, Ron Karenga, has embraced the potential of electoral activism. One observer described Karenga's shift in focus: "Once a foe of electoral politics, for example, he was one of candidate Jesse Jackson's strongest supporters in the 1984 and 1988 presidential campaigns."[56] Similarly Jitu Weusi, a long-time New York-based activist reflects on his changing views on electoral work: "Twenty years ago I said electoral politics was a waste of time, but by 10 years ago I was deeply involved in electoral politics. Now I feel the street has much value, and we must continue to protest in the street, but we must also play all over the board. In Zimbabwe, the folks came out of the bush and ran for office. We need to have that same kind of flexibility."[57] The implications of this kind of change in tactics on the part of Black activists for major American cities with sizeable Black populations could be powerful in terms of impact on the nature, direction, and style of political participation.

Presuming that electoral activism is a totally different category from protest activity obscures the vision of how the former has become part of the latter. Today, it may be erroneous to describe Black "politicians" as if they formed a category different from Black "militants," as was suggested by political scientist James Q. Wilson in his work *Negro Politics: A Search for Leadership* and most recently by Dale Marshall et al., in *Protest Is Not Enough*. Cornel West's lament regarding electoral activism may also not be justified in the current period of activism. In a reported interview he stated: "Louis Farrakhan of the Nation of Islam and Rev. Al

Sharpton, and other charlatans are seemingly the only black people with extrapolitical thrusts. I'm not saying we should neglect our electoral responsibilities, but I think the emphasis on political matters has siphoned off too much of our very limited resources."[58] This remark implies that electoral activism and "extrapolitical thrusts" are separate roads to group goals. The electoral arena is a crucial battlefront today—a place where certain kinds of ideological challenges can be raised and where mass mobilization of the Black community can take place for strategic and sometimes policy gains. Alabama-based activist Gwen Patton agrees: "The court system no longer offers remedy for civil and political rights. [Affecting] public policy via elected office is more key. . . . Public policy is set in the electoral arena."[59]

The New Face of Black Politics:
Black Empowerment Activism

Recently social historian Harold Cruse lamented the state of affairs of Black political activism in America: "There's nothing new being done, because no one knows what to do."[60] The frustration suggested in this claim is understandable given the deterioration of social and economic living conditions for most Blacks in America. It may be correct to claim that no one knows what to do about this continual deterioration; new answers to poverty and social inequality are needed. But these answers cannot be confined by the traditional liberal and neoconservative ways of thinking about race and politics. Black empowerment represents a brand of activism that may provide some political responses and strategies to stop the continual economic deterioration of Black communities.

The term "empowerment" has been used in different, even contradictory ways. In some discussions it refers to a sort of psychological liberation; that is, someone has been "empowered" to act on his or her own behalf. In other discussions it may refer to the capacity of individuals or a group to pursue an economic agenda free of interference from excessive government. This is how a conservative Black Republican senatorial candidate in Maryland used the term in his campaign. Candidate Alan K. Keyes stated that his campaign is "based on empowerment for the people. . . . And insofar as we support some type of government action to help folks, it has to be with a view to empowerment, giving them a new power over their own affairs."[61] But eliminating "excessive" government does not necessarily change the nature of the political and economic arrangements underpinning government. As an adequate response to social inequality Blacks must seek to eliminate and change in particular political and economic arrangements, both private and public. They can only do this if their level of power—the capacity to change social relations and the ownership, management, and distribution of wealth—is enhanced. Genuine change will not occur simply by making government smaller.

Some have used the term Black empowerment to mean only electoral activism. For example, Margot Harry writes:

> In the 1960s, the absence of Blacks in key political positions helped to fuel the ghetto uprisings of that period. . . . One of the things done in the effort to remedy that situation has been to foster the election of Black mayors and their Black officials. . . . These officials have also been able to serve as living examples of the "success" Black people are said to have achieved through traveling the electoral road to "Black empowerment."[62]

In this study I used the term Black empowerment much more precisely than Harry suggests in her definition.

Black empowerment activists distinguish between "access" to the powerful and actual "power"; they believe that only the latter can make a difference in social and economic conditions for the majority of Blacks. Black empowerment suggests that power relations between Blacks and whites must change before the economic conditions facing Blacks can be improved. Several social theorists have already proposed this idea. Sociologist H. Edward Ransford has written:

> In most multiracial societies racial groups are found in a hierarchy of power, wealth and prestige. The most important of these variables is differential power. . . . The dominant stratum is that power hierarchy that has the most immediate access to the means of force (such as monopoly on the use of weapons), to the technology and to the control of economic institutions and the mass media. When we speak of racial stratification, it is important to note that we are referring to a system of power inequality.[63]

He continues, "We view power inequality as the key variable for distinguishing strata in an ethnic-race hierarchy. That is, power inequality comes first, is the primary mover of the system, and determines the distribution of economic privilege and prestige [social honor]."[64]

Political scientist Theodore Cross offers a similar conceptualization of power in his work: "For all groups in a given society, the prospect for improved incomes, greater holding of property, and more favorable life chances generally is profoundly influenced by the group's relationship to the instruments of power." As is the case with several observers, for Cross the word "power" means the ability to use all those sanctions, rewards, inducements, and methods that people in an advanced society use to control their environment and influence the behavior of others.[65] Sociologist Mancur Olsen declares that most writers consider power "the ability to affect social activities."[66] We can define power, therefore, as simply a group's capability of changing, maintaining, or managing social relations. Another way of defining and describing power is by pointing out that prevailing social relations in American society reflect the actual distribution of power. Amos H. Hawley wrote, "Every social act is an exercise of power, every social relationship is a power equation, and every social group or system is an organization of power. Accordingly, it is impossible to transpose any system of social relationships into terms of potential or active power. Perhaps such a transposition is nothing more than the substitution of one terminology for another."[67] Generally the distribution of wealth—and its accompanying benefits such as income, information, and technology—maintains the hierarchy of power and determines social relations in modern societies.

The particular systemic and policy framework and its accompanying institutional arrangements, in which wealth, technology, and information are produced, collected, organized, managed, and distributed should be viewed as the major obstacles to adopting public policy that could qualitatively change social relations between Blacks and whites. Without an exertion of power—that is, changing or successfully challenging the ownership, accumulation, and management of wealth—government cannot be expected to produce public policies that would fundamentally change social relations between Blacks and whites.

Changes in power relations usually involve some type of confrontation. This was pointed out by Martin Luther King, Jr., when he argued that only Blacks' exertion of power will improve living conditions; the forces that maintain the ghetto must be challenged by more powerful forces seeking to change life in the American ghetto.[68] But King did not confine his definition of power merely to Black voting. Regardless of the level of political participation in the electoral arena, voting by itself cannot substantively change social relations. Mack Jones points out that "voting in itself is not power; having a Black majority in itself is not power; nor is having black elected and appointed officials power. These phenomena become power only when they can be used to influence and affect the behavior of other actors—principally white individuals and groups."[69] Voting and other modes of political participation should not be, ipso facto, equated with power. Voting is but a tool that can be used for the aggrandizement of power, just as money, wealth, information, and position are also merely tools for the acquisition of power. Other observers and analysts of Black politics have also argued against defining voting as synonymous with power.[70]

Despite this caveat, the importance of certain approaches to electoral activism as a key component of social change can still be proposed today. We can begin by pointing out a basic fact: the accumulation, maintenance, and distribution of wealth in modern society is directly related to governmental actions. Economist Charles E. Lindbloom argues:

> Some people believe that wealth or property is the underlying cause of power. But property is itself a form of authority created by government. Property is a set of rights to control assets; to refuse use of them to others, to hold them intact, or to use them up. Property rights are consequently grants of authority made to persons and organizations, both public and private and acknowledged by other persons and organizations. The wealthy are those who enjoy larger grants of authority than most people do. Just as ecclesiastical authority sets limits on secular authority in medieval Europe, entrepreneurial authority today in the form of property rights limits governmental authority. But that is because governments authorize such an arrangement.[71]

This view is also supported by social scientist Ralph Miliband, who claims that it is

> the case that advanced capitalist countries now have an often substantial "public sector," through which the state owns and administers a wide range of industries and services, mainly but not exclusively of an 'infrastructural' kind, which are of vast importance to their economic life; and the state also plays in all capitalist economics an even greater role by way of regulation, control, coordination, "planning," and so forth. Similarly, the state is by far the target customer of the "private sector"; and some major industries could not survive in the private sector without the state's custom and without the credits, subsidies and benefactions which it dispenses.[72]

Hence, the fact that wealth is fundamental to understanding social relations establishes rather than diminishes the primacy of the struggle for control of government.

The pursuit of political access, rather than power, may mean that Blacks are not confronting the very institutional arrangements and values that maintain racial and economic hierarchy in America. Access separated from the notion of power almost always results in public decisions and practices that make it more difficult for Blacks to challenge their depressed social and economic status. This argument is developed in Mack Jones's case study of Atlanta. Examining the years between 1965 and 1975, he points out that Black leadership was effective with some issues but it still could not address the fundamental problems facing the Black community. Black leadership could effectively coalesce with other groups, but it was incapable of raising issues or public policies representing alternatives to the priorities established by the white civic-business elite.[73]

Thus, rather than realizing Black political power, leaders settled for mere association "with those who exercised power," in the hopes that this proximity would permit influence to determine public policy. This association did produce some limited benefits, to be sure, specifically with minority participation in city contracts. But, as Jones confirmed, these "significant accomplishments . . . were made in the face of inconsiderable opposition." He concluded: "Yet they do not represent a reordering of the city's priorities, but only a more equitable share for the Black community within existing priorities. To the extent that the inequitable position of Blacks in Atlanta and other cities are at least partially a function of existing priorities, these conditions cannot be redressed through politics as the games is currently played."[74] It becomes difficult, perhaps even unthinkable, for Black leadership concerned with access, rather than power, to explore public policy alternatives outside the established priorities of the private economy and powerful local government actors.

A political strategy that emphasizes only access, without seeking to change power relations between Blacks and whites, also deepens the status and class schism within this group. Those relatively few Blacks in positions to take advantage of opportunities arising from policies of access, may improve their economic well-being, and as individuals they may experience equal social relations with whites; simultaneously, however, economic conditions for the majority of Blacks worsen, and depressed social relations with whites become more rigid. Allowing a few Blacks to make it economically and extending the opportunity of participatory rights to all Blacks may have the ironic but still functional effect of legitimizing further racial and economic arrangements that perpetuate hierarchy and unequal social relations.

Black political activism based on seeking access into the corridors of powerful interests is divisive in several ways. Chicago activist and civic official Howard J. Stanback explains this: the Black middle class, with a political program focusing on access rather than power, could be used not only to derail political movements spearheaded by Black working-class and poor sectors but also to maintain socially regressive, but profit-healthy political administrations.[75] Abdul Alkalimat, another Chicago-based activist and political scientist, echoes this sentiment: "The Civil Rights movement won and created a Black middle class. Whenever the middle class gets the masses behind them, they make a gain. In some instances this represents a real gain—the number of Black middle-class elected officials increases. What we need to start talking about is restructuring the state and exposing this government as corrupt. Our gains must be measured by how we develop structures that mobilize and democratize a movement."[76] New Black middle-class political partners to corporate-based leadership could be used, according to Stanback, "to manage the oppression of other national minorities in the U.S. such as Puerto Ricans, Native Americans and Chicanos."[77] Jitu Weusi provides an example from New York City Democratic party politics: "Once we go outside the democratic party we can have qualitatively better unity with Hispanics and other people of color. Blacks and Hispanics are played off each other inside the Democratic Party. . . . I'll give you an example. To avoid giving the Education Committee Chair [of the New York State Legislature] to Al Vann who deserved it based on seniority and knowledge, the chair was given to a Hispanic moderate. This was done to blunt Black outcry."[78] Today, then, one sure way of stopping local drives for Black empowerment is to undermine any independent leadership that has garnered mass support by supplanting it with leadership that is financially controlled and supported by corporate-based leadership. But, Jitu Weusi adds, part of the formula for success also includes racial and ethnic competition between poor and working-class people.

In the 1960s some leaders and activists called for Black Power—a concept both explosive and threatening to established civil rights leaders and their white allies. The significance of the call was the realization that only substantive and systemic change in social and economic arrangements could produce equal social relations between Blacks and whites in America. Black power advocates did emphasize access; but in other ways they began to focus, more clearly than the established civil rights movement leadership, on changing the wealth and power relationships in American society.

Today the concept of power is emerging as most critical in understanding future directions of Black politics. Whether Black politics can result in more elected or appointed positions, or greater effective implementation of affirmative action, or greater levels of city hall–controlled patronage is certainly important, but it is not necessarily fundamental in changing social relations. Black politics does not mean merely influence in certain policy arenas or accessibility to decision makers; rather power itself and the ability to hold accountable the decision makers and their processes can alter the relative social and economic position of Blacks as a group in the urban polity. Political participation may be directed at either structural change in distributing wealth and power and therefore social relations or maintaining the status quo. The latter is characterized by limited flexibility (liberalism) or resistance (conservatism); both approaches, however, emphasize maintaining social continuity and political stability.

There are clear differences "between having power and being associated with those who have it, between participating in the decisional process and actually influencing the outcome of that process, and between the symbolic trappings of political power and political power itself."[79] Activists whose orientations and issues reflect the emergence of Black empowerment are focusing on power, that is, the capacity to question and upset the ownership, management, and distribution of wealth in both public and private sectors. This is a much more important political resource than proximity or access to public and private decision makers— no matter how liberal or supportive they may be about issues of concern to Blacks.

Various features of leadership associated with Black empowerment activism differentiate it from traditional Black political leadership in urban America. Elected Black leaders who have mobilized Blacks around calls for power rather than access include Mel King in Boston, the late Harold Washington in Chicago, Al Vann in Brooklyn, the former mayor of Berkeley, California, Gus Newport, and Jesse Jackson (on a national level). Although these individuals have employed traditional methods by which to gain office, their programs and political strategies also raised issues of power sharing between Blacks and the corporate sector.

Several events reflect momentum for the nontraditional face of Black electoral activism; consider, for example, the electoral foray of Louis Farrakhan and the Nation of Islam in the 1984 endorsement of Jesse Jackson as well as other Black candidates for public office, the precipitous increase of Black voter registration in the early 1980s, the use of the electoral arena by community activists and protest leaders, and the introduction into the electoral arena of first-time Black voters. These occurrences point toward the emergence of a kind of Black activism, unfolding in the electoral arena and reflecting the historical quest for social change. This is what we call Black empowerment activism.

Black empowerment activism differs from traditional Black political activism, therefore, in several ways:

- The use of the electoral arena by new Black actors
- The emphasis on power sharing, rather than access to decision makers as an ultimate goal for mobilization
- Direct political challenges to the accumulation and distribution of wealth in America as well as challenges to institutional arrangements

that maintain such distribution (rather than accommodation or integration into such institutional networks)
- The control of territory or land
- The development of independent organizing strategies outside Democratic party–based political structures
- The revitalization of nationalist and separatist sentiment in the Black community for mobilizing potential Black voters
- The call for Black "self-determination"
- The promotion of neighborhood interests over "downtown development" interests
- The rejection of "progrowth" or fiscal austerity strategies as a response to local fiscal crisis or economic development
- The acknowledgement of linkages between domestic and international issues.

Although each characteristic has appeared earlier, in the current period these features are becoming more evident in activism and with the kinds of issues raised in the Black community.

The "metropolitan establishment" and Black leaders who are part of the dominant urban political, economic, and social networks are now being confronted by this new mood of Black urban activism. In Los Angeles, for example, some black city council members and "long-time Mayor Tom Bradley, who in many ways established the model for today's non-racial black politicians, [have] come under fire recently from within the black community for failing to steer resources to poor black neighborhoods."[80] And in San Francisco, activist Susan Anderson commented that a confrontation between Black leaders representing the interests of the Black community and economic powers is necessary to revive the hope of Black politics: "If there is to be a renewal of black politics, it will depend upon the ability of leaders to embrace the cause of the poor, and in so doing challenge the economic order, which creates poverty as casually as it amasses wealth."[81] The political confrontation between Blacks pursuing a populist economics and downtown business interests may also be unfolding outside the bigger cities.

There are also examples of a changing Black political agenda or orientation in rural sections of the country, as suggested in one study of the politics of several Southern rural towns. Minion K. C. Morrison has perceived some change in the Black political agenda since the 1960s in these locations.

> While much of the change in the late 1960s and 1970s was symbolic, the active focus was the redress of past racial exclusion. . . . It is argued that consistent with a mobilization that began in the 1960s in the rural South,

blacks not only acquired the trappings of political office, they also sought to redefine the task of governance and to create an essentially new kind of community. . . . In this context, the assumption of political power was not merely that of "equals" trading spoils; it was rather a highly mobilized group displacing what was seen as an oppressor class.[82]

Another example of this kind of political development is provided by Gwen Patton: "In Lexington, Mississippi, Blacks went to the water board about the high water prices. On the day of the elections the grassroots people voted themselves onto the Board.[83]

Hanes Walton, Jr., has pointed out that Southern victories of access have not been as numerous and lasting as in the North: "Black activism here [South] is still trying to achieve access—the right to participate. . . . In the North, . . . black politics have moved beyond the beginning access stage. Entrance is not crucial. Yet, in many areas of the south—'entrance' is still where the problem is."[84] Elaine Dillahunt, a North Carolina activist and educator, supports this view: "One big issue in the south is challenging gerrymandering. In much of the south there are areas where despite the high numbers of Blacks there has been no Black elected official, and it is important to exercise the democratic right to run [for office] and win. The immediate goal is to 'make history' by getting a Black elected."[85] Some regional differences apparently depend on the degree of political and economic incorporation for the Black community. But as Blacks gain access victories, Black politics may move from access to power, a trend in some American cities.

If indeed the new political mood in Black America is moving away from traditional liberal coalition and toward a more radical position, then it almost certainly portends a significant meaning for race relations in America as well as for other economic and political questions. For instance, how should the city be governed? What interests will gain or lose benefits? And what should the political role of private capital be in the development of the city? This development also has several important implications for national politics. The rise of Black empowerment activism explains, in part, some success in Jesse Jackson's presidential campaigns, but, more important, the Black activism seriously challenges the center-oriented national image of the Democratic party. As this kind of Black political activism grows and develops an agenda that diverges from the traditional liberal agenda, it pressures the Democratic party to move to the left of the political spectrum. Such pressure, however, presents a dilemma for the Democrats: if the party responds to Black political pressures by moving left, then it may continue to lose the allegiance of conservative white voters. Barker points out that Blacks and whites continue to differ fundamentally regarding certain social and economic issues; this division means continuing strife within the Democratic party. He offers this insight:

> Blacks and whites continue to differ sharply on the role of government in solving these problems. . . . They also continue to differ sharply on issue priorities that disproportionately affect blacks. For example, blacks ranked government programs to help the poor as the fifth most important problem, but it ranked fifteenth among whites. Similarly, blacks ranked civil rights sixth, but whites ranked it near the bottom of their list of priorities, nineteenth. Overall then, these continuing sharp policy differences between blacks and whites portend problems enough for party leaders without open attempts to court whites and effectively ignore blacks, a strategy guaranteed to increase rather than lessen divisions within the party.[86]

Thus, the Democratic party must continue to balance the political agenda of Black activists who seek social change with the view of conservative whites who feel the party has already given too much to Black Democrats.

This balancing act makes it difficult for the Democratic party to present a center-based political alternative to the Republican party. Some Black activists feel that the Democratic party has already opted to favor its conservative wing. The president of the National Black United Front, Conrad Worrill, states: "I disagree that progressives are having a positive impact on national politics. Instead, Jesse Jackson is working to build the Democratic Party. He met with moderates and conservatives in Louisiana. Also, Ron Brown [Chair of the Democratic National Committee] rebuked Gus Savage after Savage exposed Israeli PAC money. Ron Brown also endorsed Richard Daley. The white power establishment is chilling out radicals and progressives and is saying that we'll accept you if you become a 'cross-over Negro' "[87]

Activist Jitu Weusi sees the possibility of a locally based movement that would challenge the Democratic party and thus continue to pressure it ideologically and politically. He contends that the possibility of a major, national third party is growing.

> On a local level, we have a chance to make a breakthrough with party building. There is a lack of participation by Blacks in electoral politics as it is now constituted with the Democratic versus Republican parties. 53% of the Black registered voters voted for Dinkins—and that was the highest we've ever had in a primary. The norm is 13% of Black registered voters to vote in a primary. So with very few votes, a Democratic candidate can get in office since in New York City to win the Democratic primary is to get the seat because this is an overwhelmingly Democratic city. If we had another

party, we might be able to upset some of these people who win the democratic primary with very few votes. This would stimulate the folks to come out to vote. The other reasons for starting on a local level is because there are so many gut issues like housing, recreation, gentrification—on a national level, these issues may not stimulate people as much.[88]

In response to this kind of pressure emerging from some of America's bigger cities, the Democratic party must consider its future directions carefully. If the Democrats move to the left in response to Black activism, then the Republican party can continue to hold the conservative wing and make even greater gains among white voters. But if the Democrats ignore the growing numbers of and pressure from Black activists, especially as they realize gains at the local level, then its traditional electoral base will continue to be seriously weakened. As described, Black empowerment activism not only changes the face of local politics, but it also exposes the Democratic party to questions and contradictions of race and class on the national political terrain.

Only a few studies have examined an analyzed the reaction of government and corporate-based leadership to demands and activism associated with emerging Black empowerment politics. Studies have focused on explanations for varying levels of minority mobilization in different cities; for example, one study sought "to explain why minority groups mobilized so much more vigorously in some cities than in others."[89] These authors deemphasized particular political agendas or specific ideological issues reflected in different kinds—or, levels—of minority mobilization; they also noted the government's and private sector's reactions to these different political and social agendas. This question, however, will increase in prominence as a politics based on Black empowerment activism rather than Black liberalism wins the attention of Black leaders and activists around the country.

Both examining the ideological thrusts of a more radical Black political activism than the one associated under a liberal coalition and studying relatively powerful interests in the private sector as they react to this shift may shed light on the limits of urban activism within the current social and economic framework of American democracy. Analyzing these boundaries or the conceptual parameters of what is, should be, or should not be in the realm of public policy is a crucial topic—especially in reference to Black politics. According to Ira Katznelson,

> Analysis of games or contests, political or otherwise, must do more than describe the players and their adversary play. They must also say something about the boundaries of the contest, which define its limits prior to the playing of the game itself. Such boundaries are an integral part of the rules

of the game: they determine who may participate, what identities participants may assume, what they may legitimately do, and so on. Such rules
preclude certain outcomes and make other improbable.[90]

The bounds of public policy and the political relationship between corporate leadership of big cities and Black urban leadership are important
because they not only determine the prevailing economic policies and
practices of urban America but also raise questions regarding conflict and
consensus in this society. Furthermore, because "cities are obviously the
location of key production and distribution activities in Western economics,"[91] what occurs in cities socially and politically does have an
impact on the wider society.

Another reason for the importance of this new kind of Black political
activism involves American demography and its political implications. In
the twenty U.S. cities with the highest Black population, their numbers
are projected to either grow significantly or increase considerably their
portion of the total population by the year 2000.[92] In these same cities
the Latino population is also projected to grow significantly. Note Table
1, which shows the percentage of Black population in 1980 and its
projected proportion for the year 2000, in selected big cities in America.

One immediate question prompted by this kind of demographic development is the relationship between the rise of Black empowerment
activism and the Latino community. Kenneth M. Dolbeare asks,

> What will it mean, for example, to have predominantly black and Hispanic
> populations in almost all the major cities, with nearly all-white surrounding
> suburbs? Hispanics include different groups with different economic and
> political interests, and they are highly concentrated in a few states. Is it rea-
> sonable to expect working coalitions between Hispanics and blacks? We
> know that there is a high potential for new minority political power, but
> not much about its prospects for realization.[93]

This is a major query for the political and economic management of
America's largest cities.

One general direction points to increasing racial and ethnic tension
between communities of color. It is relatively easy to build a Black political foundation that is regressive with respect to this question; Black political activism could conceptualize Latinos, or people of Asian descent as
competitive ethnic groups rather than important allies with similar social
and economic concerns. Traditional Black political activism has reflected
this divisive tendency in many instances. The hostility between certain
Black and Puerto Rican leaders regarding the selection of a mayoral
candidate to run against Mayor Ed Koch in New York City in 1986 was

TABLE 1 Proportion of Blacks in Total Population for Selected Central Cities in the United States, 1980 and 2000 (in percentages)

	1980	2000
New York	24	25
Chicago	40	41
Philadelphia	37	40
Detroit	63	72
Cleveland	44	46
Baltimore	54	57
St. Louis	44	48
Milwaukee	23	30
New Orleans	55	62
Indianapolis	21	24
Dallas	29	31
Memphis	47	52
Jacksonville	25	27
St. Louis	44	48
Atlanta	66	73
Oakland	46	52

Source: This table was derived from census data projections and reported in Ebony (April 1989), p. 88.

one example of how Black political activism seeking access, rather than power, can be divisive. Rather than selecting a mayoral candidate on the basis of issues and a common agenda with the city's Latino population, some Black leaders instead opted for a candidate who would not disrupt the political and economic status quo, although it meant snubbing another major group of citizens of color.[94]

The potential for hostility between Blacks and other groups of color is great, a strong possibility that could dilute the influence of all these groups. Ethnic hostility among nonwhite urban residents was witnessed in Cleveland, Ohio, where a group of Palestinian store owners accused some Black leaders of racism when they called for a boycott against the merchants; the boycott followed the fatal shooting of a Black man by a Palestinian store owner after an argument. In Philadelphia, by the late 1980s, fights between Laotians and Blacks started to increase. Similar racial conflict has erupted in New York City between Blacks and Koreans and in Washington, D.C., between Blacks and Chinese residents.[95] By focusing on an agenda of power—not access built on the backs of the next lower group—Black empowerment activism can overcome some of this political divisiveness. The call for power thus questions a social and economic system historically built on pitting one group against another.

The evolving Black political activism is also significant because of the social role of urban governments in American society and political stability. "On the one hand, urban governments must be responsive to the infrastructural and service requirements of capital accumulation, and to changes in these requirements generated by economic growth. On the other hand, they must also manage political participation among the masses of the urban population who do not control capital accumulation and may not benefit from it either."[96] Thus, urban governments have a dual, sometimes contradictory role: to oversee healthy environments for business development, and simultaneously to provide public services to the general citizenry. Local government has served as a buffer between private-sector leadership and interests and the citizenry at large. But this separation does not imply a neutral position on the part of government in mediating conflicting social interests.

The governmental arena is neither politically nor socially neutral. Clarence Stone argues,

> In contrast to the pluralist position that officials are relatively uncommitted to any one segment of the population, the argument here is that officials, even those who hold major elected posts, may not serve as impartial arbiters of group conflict. They may play a role other than that of neutral broker. In short, they may be consistent advocates of some interests at the expense of others. And, to the extent that public officials perform an interest-advocacy role, policy-making may not be a matter of bargaining, negotiation, and neutral accommodation. It may be a process in which the not-so-fine arts of deception and manipulation are practiced in order to manage conflict on behalf of certain favored groups and objectives.[97]

Stone used Atlanta as a case study to illustrate the above paradigm linking government, public policy, and political conflict in favor of the well-to-do.

Even when a particular public policy is presented as an advantage to poor and lower-income groups the systemic boundaries reflected in Stone's statement prevent these groups from reaping any substantive benefits. A case in point is the failure of casino gambling in Atlantic City to alleviate the social and economic problems of the poor in that city. The *New York Times* appraised the situation in Atlantic city:

> Ten years after the first of a dozen casino hotels opened in Atlantic City, it is clear that they have failed to be the "unique tool of urban redevelopment" the New Jersey Legislature envisioned. The casinos have made fortunes and

have transformed the Boardwalk into a glittering strip of towers; they provide thousands of jobs and pay hundreds of millions of dollars in taxes. But
much of Atlantic City is still blighted, with dilapidated housing, boarded-
up businesses and unkempt vacant lots where buildings were razed for development that hasn't occurred.[98]

Some local and state governments have been willing and cooperative
partners in assisting casino interests at the expense of poor and working-
class people. They have represented the organizational interests of the
casinos far more effectively than those of the citizenry. The governments
justify this behavior by claiming that nurturing a healthy environment for
casinos and related businesses will in turn strengthen the local economy,
thereby benefiting the general citizenry.

David Greenstone and Paul Peterson examined five major cities and
reported that local government in New York, Philadelphia, Detroit, Los
Angeles, and Chicago have their proper organizational, electoral, and
ideological interests that many times are closely aligned with business
and other powerful and entrenched interests. Local government action,
therefore, often involves a consideration of how electoral, organizational,
and even ideological interests interact with those of these entrenched
groups.[99] But this does not mean that local government and its apparatus, ipso facto, always reflect the concerns and whims of more powerful
private interests. It does mean, however, that local government and its
apparatus should not be viewed as either neutral voices regarding ideological challenges or passive listeners regarding calls for a governmental
role in redistributing wealth in local areas or regions. Local government
and its service bureaucracies, in other words, reflect both a political and
service agenda. This political agenda usually reflects the interests of
wealthy and powerful developers, not those of poor and working-class
neighborhoods. Again Joyce Brooks speaks about Philadelphia: "We had
two demonstrations about development of the waterfront. The waterfront
had been desolate; now 25% of it is a tourist attraction. Private developers got 10 million dollars seed money from HUD for a private yacht
club—is this trickle down? This obviously angered the Black community.
The response of the city government is that we should be happy that the
developers are giving us jobs.[100]

The City of Mandela: Black Empowerment Activism

The call by several Black community activists and others for the in-
corporation of a predominantly Black and Latino neighborhood from the
City of Boston in 1987 illustrates some of these ideas. In many ways, the
"Mandela" nonbinding referendum in 1986 and 1988 not only reflected

aspects of the changing Black political activism in urban America, but it also illustrated that local government's primary political and economic agenda often differs from an agenda of Black empowerment.

Mandela was an empowerment issue because its goals were presumably major redistribution and control of wealth rather than a "developmental" or "allocational" programs. Boston activist and former mayoral aspirant Mel King claimed that Mandela offered a challenge to "the status quo and raises the issue of power over the land and resources of the Roxbury community."[101] The redistribution of resources and influence would occur by virtue of incorporating the land area containing the majority of Black and Latino residents in the city. This episode suggested that some Black activists no longer considered mere access to or even accountability by public institutions in the Black community the most important political goal.

Mandela, perhaps in a manner more crystallized than ever in Boston, also raised issues of governance and legitimacy of given political arrangements as they affected Blacks. This urban protest movement incorporated three themes identified by Manuel Castels as major in such movements: "collective consumption," "cultural identity," and "political mobilization."[102] But a large part of the struggle for Mandela took place in the electoral arena; this does represent something new in urban politics. Mandela was not simply a militant call for political access into the power corridors of Boston; it rejected mere access into the power corridors of Boston; it rejected mere access in favor of the opportunity to build an alternative power structure.

While the Mandela referendum was defeated both times when presented to the voters, it nevertheless represents a significant political development—and realization. In 1986 the referendum was defeated by approximately 23,000 votes out of about 47,000 total votes cast in the areas of the city included in the secession plan. In this election about one-third of the electorate voted in favor of secession from the city of Boston. In the 1988 election, approximately 11,000 out of 32,000 total voters— again, slightly more than one-third of ballots cast—favored secession. Despite the almost nonexistent debate on Mandela in the 1988 election and its defeat, this issue forced into the public arena certain ideological questions regarding race relations, government, and the corporate sector. Mandela illustrated the kind of challenge that will increasingly be directed at local government—even if controlled by Blacks—by Black grass-roots activists.

The Mandela issue and similar issues throughout the country like the call for a Black-controlled independent school district in Milwaukee, or the establishment of an independent municipality for East Palo Alto,

California, reflect a growing realization that the attainment of independent political power—rather than mere proximity to interests with power—is fundamental in responding effectively to the social and economic crisis faced by masses of Blacks in urban America. This means that Black activists now are beginning to understand that "wealth and success are not only a product of diligence and ambition to get ahead, they are the result, too, of seniority agreements, government franchises, mineral grants, work permission cards, farm allotments, interest-free loans, and protected employment. Political power, regrettably, is one of the major driving forces of the American economy."[103]

> No one offered the black housemaids of New York or Chicago a minimum wage until government commanded it. The end of racially segregated schools, all-white primaries, and race discrimination in credit and employment was never the natural outcome of an easy and automatic evolutionary process. In each case, these gains were the result of intense political pressures. In every instance, things got better because people—particularly black people—struggled to make them better"[104]

As this realization continues to grow, local governments must manage political and social disruption that may occur as a result of the negative fall-out from citizens—especially Black poor and working-class citizens—in need of ample and high-quality public and municipal services.

Now, what would happen if urban government were controlled by Black activists and allies who reject the notion that pursuing a healthy business environment—or to use the term of planners, "growth ideology"—should or must have primacy over the goals of basic, dependable urban services for the poor and working class? And what would be the reaction of corporate-based leadership deciding that, for whatever reasons, it would not want to relocate to "friendlier" locales? Gregory D. Squires and his colleagues raised similar questions:

> What will happen should private capital feel threatened by public sector and community-based efforts to guide private investment and capital allocation decision-making? Such infringements on what is firmly believed to be management prerogatives will, or course, be strongly resisted. Will the financial community threaten to undermine the solvency of the city as happened to Cleveland under Dennis Kucinich? Will more businesses simply choose to leave Chicago? Can capital go on strike?[105]

These questions may become more urgent and politically salient as Black activists who have adopted progressive urban agendas seek to control electoral structures and processes of local government.

CHAPTER TWO

Black Empowerment and the American Political Spectrum

The struggle for black liberation is alive and well. To the extent that we make progressive movements forward, we will help others in the process. . . . We must forge ahead and hope that those in the progressive community will support that struggle but grant us the self-determination to develop our own leadership, our own goals, and our own methodology.

Rev. Benjamin F. Chavis, Jr., *Black Voices*

Ideologically, Black empowerment activism cannot be placed within the standard American political spectrum of left, center, and right. Although it is not yet fully clear that what is considered Black empowerment activism represents an ideological alternative to American liberalism or conservatism, there is some indication that the philosophical basis is different. Black political thought, and the ideological range within the Black community, should no longer be described as simply "integrationist" or "separatist," although Black political thought has basically been put into one of these two categories. On a philosophical level Black empowerment activism offers elements different than traditional liberalism and conservatism in American politics. As Gerald Horne points out, the Black community has at various times exhibited a "leftist tilt."[1] Although Black empowerment rejects, in part, the integrationist orientation of the civil rights movement, it cannot be classified as separatist.

50

The American Political Spectrum and Black Empowerment

Major characteristics of liberalism within the American political spectrum include political rights for the minority or individual point of view, the right of individuals to pursue property interests, the belief that the market requires periodic adjustment to meet the needs of American society, and the belief that democratic values and culture can hold accountable the administrative behavior of the state. The conservative end of the American political spectrum also reflects some of these values and beliefs, but those conservatives would not fetter free market forces. Conservatism also posits that governmental interference in social policy is inefficient and harmful to the development of entrepreneurial initiative.

Robert R. Alford and Roger Friedland define liberal politics as those "attempts to solve problems by transforming unmet social needs into marketable commodities (health services to be bought and sold, housing subsidies) and by assuring that all people will be able to participate equally in the labor market whether through the elimination of racial and class barriers to occupational mobility or through special training or education."[2] And politics that reflects conservative thinking considers the

> operations of the markets as self-regulating and attempts to limit the scope of state intervention in the belief that such interventions tend to undermine the efficiency of the market. Government efforts to support household incomes not only divert societal resources from more productive uses but encourage state dependency on the part of those who would otherwise work at lower wages. . . . The conservative ideology holds that people make their own choices to participate in the political and economic markets.[3]

Kenneth Dolbeare has up-dated these two philosophical outlooks; he describes the current national political and economic competition as rivalry between Yankee Capitalism and Cowboy Capitalism.

To a certain degree, the former corresponds to American liberalism, while the latter reflects conservatism. Dolbeare expands on these terms:

> Cowboy capitalist proposals call for restoring investment, productivity, and growth through freeing those with capital to follow the incentives of the economic marketplace. They also intend to free business from regulation and taxation as another means of promoting productivity and growth. I use the characterization "cowboy" to suggest a widely shared nostalgic attachment to the idea of individual responsibility in a private enterprise system as well as the geographic, nationalist, and militaristic orientation of many supporters for these proposals.[4]

Yankee Capitalism, however, calls "for an active government role in helping the nation's leading industries to greater profitability and growth, based on a new system of cooperation in which business dominates the other major 'partners,' government and labor."[5] Despite the electoral competitiveness of the two major parties representing these two orientations, their commonalties may be more important. Both the Democrats and Republicans believe that economic and social advancement depends on a healthy environment for investment and profits; the difference between the two revolves around methods, not goals or values.

Advocates of both orientations would also "agree on the need for a rollback of the welfare state with its limits on business freedoms, expensive social programs, and resulting need for tax revenues. They also agree on the need to reduce the power of trade unions, redirect capital from consumption to investment, and expand American military capabilities."[6] These two philosophical and economic orientations have competed continually during the last several decades, but there is yet a third orientation, which Dolbeare describes:

> Economic democracy proposals accept the private corporate system less willingly than the others, preferring to view it as a temporary reality or perhaps a transitional necessity. The market is rejected entirely as either an efficient allocator or an equitable means to achieve income distribution. Economic Democrats see the economy as a set of social relationships among people rather than an aggregate of mechanical forces working on each other; they condemn the present character of the economy as wasteful, alienating, and destructive. Instead, they would set the entitlements of people at the center and try to run the economy—and the society—in a completely democratic manner.[7]

This range of economic policy orientations has been reflected in intense political struggle and debate regarding various kinds of public policy issues and social controversies across urban America. This orientation is also found within the framework of Black empowerment activism. For example, the outline of "economic democracy" appeared in the Harold Washington administration, the Mel King for Mayor Campaign, and to a certain extent the presidential campaigns of Jesse Jackson.

These three orientations undergird increasing conflict in the American city. In those cities with significant Black populations political conflict has pitted certain sectors in the community against powerful business interests or white ethnic groups. Although the issues involved with such controversies may be quite specific and localized, the implications for the general direction of the city's economy and social landscape are enormous. On one side of urban America's political economy is the big business sector. Generally speaking, this sector and its allies and beneficiaries adopt the position that American cities can be revitalized by attracting developers and a middle-class citizenry.

In Detroit, for example, this position is reflected in what planners there have dubbed the "get smart" strategy, essentially an attempt to move toward a more "technology intensive and high skill manufacturing economy."[8] But this kind of strategy has depressed other sectors of the economy:

> Victims of industrial crisis and reorganization include unskilled workers who often suffer long-term unemployment and downward mobility into low-paying service work. But many skilled workers—welders, painters, tool and die makers—are also displaced by computers and robots. Victims too are new entrants into the labor force for whom opportunities for gainful employment have dried up.[9]

The conflict is reflected in the tension arising from gentrification of city land, which usually pits higher status whites and relative newcomers against those who wish to preserve the physical status of a city and Blacks seeking to maintain affordable housing.[10]

Tension may also be reflected in the struggle over the direction of economic development and use of public dollars. Many large American cities with sizeable Black populations display examples of community-based groups and coalitions that have attempted to use local government as a platform from which either to extract benefits from the private sector or to stop the private sector from taking land away from Black residents. In Philadelphia, for instance, protests in 1987 surrounding the use of Urban Development Action Grants exemplify this conflict. Philadelphia's Money for Neighborhoods Coalition has challenged the Goode administration to spend a larger proportion of the grants on neighborhood revitalization.

According to activist Joyce Brooks, this neighborhood coalition "came out of the knowledge that there was a major trend nationally to destroy neighborhoods, the need to move to linkage of the central city and neighborhoods, and the need to go thru the City Council to get legislation to get developers to put resources into the neighborhoods."[11] This community organization is also challenging the corporate leadership to share some of its resources with neighborhood groups. Philadelphia community activist Michael Blackie lamented the neighborhood plight: "The developers have gotten tens of millions of our tax dollars to build commercial properties downtown, but our neighborhoods are going ignored."[12] This coalition is seeking a "city ordinance that would link downtown commercial development to neighborhood revitalization." This attempted redistribution would share some profits realized by downtown developers with neighborhoods for social expenditures. The Money for Neighborhoods Coalition has demonstrated against the city's mayor for allowing public funds to be used for a luxury development rather than neighborhood housing; while the former reflects the vision of the high-powered developers and the "get smart" people, the latter reflects Black activists seeking to strengthen community-based initiatives and neighborhood infrastructure.[13]

This new theme and political struggle in major cities is spearheaded by Black activists. Partially as a result of strong grass-roots support in Boston's Black community, that city has now adopted a linkage program. Rather than seeking access to corporate leaders who have invested profitably in urban locations, Black leadership changed the rules of the game in terms of investment practices and expectations through linkage policy.

In Milwaukee two community activists stated that "downtown interests don't give a damn about the Black community here." Andrew Walker, chair of the NAACP's Discrimination Committee in that city, suggested that Blacks must begin to challenge the corporate sector because so much housing and land use is affected by their decisions. He felt that downtown businesses and Marquette University, in particular, should be forced to give back the housing that it eliminated for both Black and white working-class citizens of Milwaukee.[14] The gentrification generated by Marquette's decision to take over YMCA facilities to house its students led to the formation of the Task Force on Emergency Shelter and Relocation, which called for a boycott of all Milwaukee YMCA health clubs.[15] This group has obtained the support of some Black elected officials in this action.

The city of Houston offers yet another example of how this dynamic is growing among Black political activists at the neighborhood and city level. Houston's city government proposed to tear down rather than renovate the Allen Park Housing Development in order to allow investors to rebuild and sell it at higher prices. These increased costs would have displaced the development's Black poor and working-class residents. The move was resisted by mobilizing grass-roots organizations and their constituents; the late Congressman Mickey Leland first supported the plan to raze Allen Park Development, but the community's furor forced him to change his position in favor of the Black community.[16]

In Atlanta, which has the highest per capita income of all major American cities, political tension between City Hall and the Black community is intensifying, despite the presence of a Black mayor with nationally recognized civil rights credentials. In 1988 Mayor Andrew Young characterized the growth of Atlanta's economy as "all blessing and no curse."[17] But Michael Lomax, elected chairman of the Fulton County

Commission, the legislative body that includes Atlanta, explains that this growth means that "one group winds up living in a twilight zone of privilege and affluence and the other in a kind of inferno of destructiveness and blight." This is "extremely destructive," according to Commissioner Lomax.[18] The growth ideology described earlier, therefore, has not and perhaps cannot produce success without also maintaining significant poverty, urban blight, and economic misery.

This failure is partially motivating growing numbers of activists who identify with Black empowerment to reject both Yankee and Cowboy capitalist visions and policy responses to the nation's urban problems. As one Black labor activist based in Albany, New York, put it, these choices sound like "one kind of garbage in terms of the interests of poor people and Blacks, versus another kind of garbage."[19] Since the 1960s there have been numerous instances of what can be considered neighborhood-based political rejections of these economic visions. But today, such rejections are becoming more ideologically and socially crystalized. Thus, more and more Black neighborhood activists are concluding that present political and social arrangements and access to them are no longer enough to guarantee a certain quality of life in their communities. This was a major theme reflected in interviews with many Black activists in Los Angeles, Detroit, Philadelphia, New York, Atlanta, Chicago, and Boston.

Historian Carl Boggs has suggested that for many sectors in American society liberalism as a political philosophy and the current social arrangement is not as salient as in earlier periods—but the greatest potential for effective rejection of liberalism is still based in the Black community. Although Boggs ignores the possibility of Black rejection, his statement about liberalism is important and relevant:

> Liberalism, which in one guise or another has shaped the European and American political tradition for more than two centuries, today stands far removed from the orbit of the new movements. A hegemonic ideology well into the postwar period, liberalism has since the 1960s steadily disintegrated in the wake of the Vietnam defeat, the new left, economic stagnation, expansion of the authoritarian state, and cold war mobilization. By the 1980s it had degenerated into a corporate liberalism, the main function of which is to legitimate an outmoded power structure.[20]

The rejection of liberalism is an especially significant development for Blacks, and consequently for urban politics in America, because until now much of this community's political leadership defined its goals and activism within the framework of liberalism or Yankee capitalism.

Alford and Friedland elaborate on this idea:

> Liberal politics dominated the 1960s and the early 1970s in the United
> States. Large parts of the civil rights movement and the women's movement
> were liberal politics. . . . At a partisan level, liberal Democrats—like Ken-
> nedy and Johnson between 1960 and 1968—pushed through various gov-
> ernment programs to make the market work as it ideally should. . . . The
> code word that symbolically unified this politics was "equal
> opportunity"—opportunity for all individuals to compete equally and
> freely in the market place without regard to parentage, race, or gender.
> Equality would allow economic markets to operate more efficiently as
> well.[21]

Although in earlier periods pluralism may have been a viable claim to
mute the emergence of a crisis of legitimacy owing to a relative abundance
of economic resources, today "the political system is no longer blessed
with the economic abundance of an earlier time," according to Charles V.
Hamilton. But another observer also believes that the white liberal sector,
in order to remain politically dominant in American politics, dropped
matters of race from its agenda.

Gary Orfield writes,

> White liberalism turned its back on the problem of the ghetto, despite
> abundant signs that social and economic conditions in the ghettos had dete-
> riorated rapidly and severely, even amid the unprecedented prosperity of the
> 1960s. . . . Once they abandoned an analysis rooted in an understanding of
> the history of white prejudice and the need for fundamental change in the
> ghetto system, the ground shifted in the entire debate. . . . When Blacks
> asked for more, they were accused of ingratitude.[22]

Liberal interest groups, while willing to accommodate—somewhat—the
political demands of Blacks for inclusion in the liberal, New Deal agenda,
were unwilling to either give up power or share wealth through its redistribution. The social and economic demands of Blacks after the civil
rights movement's victories increasingly pointed toward civil and systemic tensions; such tensions could be accommodated temporarily while
it was possible for the economy to expand and incorporate some of these
demands as occurred during the New Deal with other groups.

As suggested earlier, absent an expanding economy, this accommodation represents a major strain on the capacity of the U.S. pluralist system:

> Politics in America has been greatly aided by economic resources. This is
> not to deny or to mitigate commitment to ideology and principle; it simply
> stresses that such commitments are challenged less in situations of eco-
> nomic abundance. New political groups will make demands on the govern-
> ment to do more and for longer periods of time. The working partnership

of an earlier time between government and the private sector does not seem as promising, at least in the short run. Invariably, this partnership will involve a zero-sum game in the politics of scarcity. Again, pluralist politics is familiar with this, but it has usually had more resources. It would not be an exaggeration to say that . . . the assumptions of pluralist politics in the United States will receive, in the next several years, their most serious challenge.[23]

This theme is repeated by Herbert Haines who agrees that one major factor, "conducive to pro-civil rights reactions in America" during the 1960s, was the ability of the economy to expand and incorporate the demands of Blacks to a certain degree. He expands on this view:

A favorable economy undoubtedly had an effect on both policy enactment and financial support. During periods of affluence, it might be expected that those in positions of power would be less inclined to guard jealously the privileges of dominant groups. In other words, it is easier to talk about equal access to jobs, decent education, income security, and the like, and to make policies which ensure such access, during times when the goods can be delivered without seriously depriving dominant groups.[24]

The economy's continuing inability to respond to the needs of increasing numbers of Blacks, coupled with growing Black political activism, increases the instances of systemic rather than reformist challenges to traditional pluralist arrangements and values.

It is logical that groups in American society positioned differently in terms of wealth and social status have certain interests and needs that are not conciliatory toward each other. As illustrated by sociologist Ralf Dahrendorf groups hold different positions of socioeconomic influence, status, and authority; those dominant groups have interests that contradict those of nondominant social groups.[25] Political scientist Mack Jones extends this thesis and argues that "it is theoretically useful to conceptualize Black politics as a power struggle between whites bent on maintaining their position of dominance and Blacks struggling to escape this dominance."[26] This tension can be reduced, at times, if the Black demands do not question the foundation of power and if the system is elastic enough to provide minimally satisfactory responses to actual and potential Black insurgents.

Ultimately, despite a group's liberal or conservative tendencies, the more powerful must ensure that those groups without access to power do not present threats to social, economic, or political arrangements that may disrupt the hierarchy of power. Systemic restrictions are placed on urban political activism that points to social change. Studies have described systemic restrictions on urban leadership that attempts to develop public policies and alternatives for Blacks that challenge power and wealth. Some of these policies include fiscal restraints, dependency on the federal government, state legislative restrictions, programmatic cooptation of leadership, and the particular political structure of city government.

One activist believes that change in campaign financing "is the next phase of electoral reform." The high cost of running electoral campaigns denies Blacks and the poor access into political structures. Therefore, Gwen Patton stated, "Elections are not free in this country. Elected officials are often beholden to the fat cats. We need public financing of campaigns. [Private financing] makes a mockery of voting rights."[27] Most grass-roots candidates either cannot afford to run for office, or they must accept large campaign contributions from interests protecting the economic arrangements that are being challenged.

Another kind of restraint has attracted much attention from writers such as E. E. Schattschneider, James Boggs, C. W. Mills, and, more recently, urban analysts such as Roger Freidland, Francis Fox Piven and Richard Cloward, Ira Katznelson, and Hanes Walton, Jr.[28] These observers have suggested that the parameters or conceptual boundaries of public policy disallow urban leadership to consider, let alone use, certain kinds of public policy and social welfare approaches or innovations. This is related to an observation of labor activist William Fletcher: "Except for places with left wing histories like Vermont or Santa Monica, left candidates can't get a hearing. They can get a hearing only in an alliance with non-left candidacies that appeal to larger progressive constituencies."[29] This carryover of cold war politics and "red baiting" prevents all ideological points of view from receiving a fair hearing in electoral politics. In various ways the social structure of the city and region do not allow the emergence of public policies that challenge traditional systemic values or institutional arrangements protective of the economic and, at times, the political status quo.

This can be true even when a city is politically controlled by a Black mayor. Certain systemic values and practices favoring those interests with both wealth and access to powerful decision makers discourage using public policies that overregulate the private sector's responses to the social and economic needs of local citizenry. The debates about particular public policy positions are not as significant, furthermore, as are the conceptual boundaries that either shape these debates or exclude certain kinds of policies from even being raised for public discussion. The boundaries that shape policy debates are molded significantly by how influential private groups perceive their own interests. A review of literature on business and urban policy describes the phenomenon: "These studies indicate that business participation is often instrumental in shaping a broad policy consensus in which later decisional conflicts are fought out."[30] Although corporate-based leadership may lose decisions on some conflicts, this sector cannot afford to allow either the development or public discussion of public policy that may question the social, economic, political, or cultural boundaries supporting corporate America.

Regarding this issue of moneyed interests Norman Fainstein and Susan Fainstein write, "State solutions . . . must not impede the accumulation process by burdening profits with taxes, and they must not threaten directly the character of control over production to which a national business class has become accustomed."[31] Studies of business participation have shown "the role of business participation in setting agendas—producing some local issues and preventing the production of other local issues"; that is, the business sector cannot be perceived as a neutral player in either setting or vetoing certain public policies or approaches to public problems.[32]

A few have suggested that this kind of constraint is a particular problem for urban Black leadership. Political scientist John Howard has written, for instance, "There are a variety of constraints confronting urban Black leadership in terms of the development and implementation of meliorative policy with regard to the ghetto problems. Among these constraints are . . . the political (and moral) inaccessibility of certain policy approaches theoretically available to white leadership."[33] But around the country there are enough white neighborhood groups offering alternative public policy approaches to make us cautious of identifying this solely as a problem for urban Black leadership. Those interests most threatened by different responses to the social and economic needs of the citizenry are as threatened by white-led populism as they are by Black political activists with progressive agendas.

Another major restraint on urban Black leadership, however, dictates a different response by the corporate leadership to white populist versus Black demands: institutional racism supports an economic, racial, and cultural hierarchy. White-led populism can be presented in ways that compel greater responsiveness from the private economy without substantively changing long-standing racial and cultural hierarchy. In fact, certain expressions of white populism support a racial status quo where whites enjoy benefits to a greater extent than Blacks. Political scientist Joseph McCormack offers an example: "One of the greatest ironies of Cleveland's politics is that the one politician in recent times, Dennis

Kucinich, who made the effort to forthrightly address many of Cleveland's nagging fiscal problems by challenging its corporate community, failed because of his inability to transcend the sort of racism that he had helped to foment in the 1960s."[34] This theme is repeated by other observers and activists.

A few historians and political scientists have argued that reformist elements in the white community have utilized race as a divisive political resource; populist whites cannot be spared from this criticism.[35] The inability of even reformist whites to confront racism supports and maintain a racial and cultural hierarchy in America but also benefits economically and politically the interests controlling wealth in the United States. This is a major factor in making cities profitable for the owners and managers of wealth. One study pointed out:

> The urban question, in central cities, continues to be shaped by the racial and ideological fragmentation of the working class in confronting the forces of accumulation. As a consequence, low-income populations find themselves squeezed between the suburban ring and the expanding case in a period where public housing programs have dwindled almost to nothing. The position is particularly excruciating for blacks, whose race continues to exclude them from the suburbs. Conversion is thus a double triumph for capital, for it weakens political opposition through dispersal and it takes the problems of race and poverty out of the public view.[36]

This characteristic and the historical subdominant status of the Black community allow for the possibility that Blacks—perhaps to a greater degree than any other ethnic or racial group—continually pose potential ideological confrontation to the political and economic status quo.

Jane Bayes has suggested that the minority's situation depends on five major factors:

> Strategic position of any minority group depends upon (1) a degree of social disruption and displacement in the society, which creates disaffection and uprootedness; (2) the international political situation; (3) the content of the dominant political ideologies; (4) the ideological and political preparations that minority leaders have made in developing and articulating their own consciousness in light of the dominant ideologies; (5) the political skill of minority leaders in achieving symbolic as well as token material and legal concessions that can provide a stronger strategic base for raising consciousness in the future.[37]

Structural confrontation is not typically reflected in Black political demands for access into the corridors of power. It is reflected when Black activists question the values and institutional arrangements that underpin the private economy. The leadership of the corporate sector may not continually react adversely to calls or programs for Black participation in the given political and economic structures of the big city. This same leadership, however, will react adversely to calls in the Black community for different social and power relationships between Blacks and the private sector.

In support of this proposition it is interesting to note that the corporate sector generally did not attempt to curtail the emergence or growth of antipoverty programs in the late 1960s. Whether accurately or inaccurately, such programs were perceived as politically beneficial to Blacks and Latinos, but, more important, they were socially functional for corporate interests. The major opposition to the emergence and spread of antipoverty programs did not emerge from the corporate sector. As Greenstone and Peterson have written, "The major opposition to Black efforts came not from businessmen antagonistic to changes in class relationships nor from white groups resisting racial equality. In the large cities, businessmen were largely uninvolved in the anti-poverty programs."[38] The corporate reaction to Black control of antipoverty programs differs from its reaction to a radical Black activism, which questions the economic and political arrangements perceived as beneficial by powerful interests. Antipoverty programs involve a relatively small and confined political arena; it merely questions how the system might accommodate Black demands. Urban radicalism, however, questions the legitimacy of the system and its particular institutional arrangements and systemic values.

In some cities Blacks have captured positions of significant electoral influence, but that does not necessarily lessen the potential for structural confrontation with powerful private-sector groups. But the capture of electoral influence by Blacks may be important in managing potential conflict between economic and social interests with different goals and needs; this, in fact, has been a major social function of electoral processes. Many on the American "left" have pointed to precisely this function in proposing that electoral activism is not a reliable tool for social change.

In the late 1960s one activist declared that "dabbling in elections in the pretext of 'organizing and educating' is an unnecessary waste of scarce resources. This activity may inflate egos, but it does little to build a mass-based organization."[39] This statement echoes the sentiment of activist Shafik Abu-Pahir:

> In Philadelphia, there is very little confidence in Black elected officials. The more elected officials [we have] the more demobilized the community becomes. The people are angry about decreased services and deteriorating neighborhoods, but Black elected officials say "this is not our fault." Then

they don't want to criticize the democratic state government, so all criticism goes to the national level to the Bush administration. But they still don't call for national reprioritization. They are afraid of a mobilized constituency. If they were to mobilize [their constituency], the anger of the community would lead to replacing them with new leadership.[40]

Another prominent activist declared, "No less naive is the dream of Black liberation through the election of Black politicians. Black politicians continue to delude themselves. . . . Every economic, social and legislative concern won by Blacks in this country has been the result of independent Black struggle outside the electoral arena."[41] The theme that the left must be cautious with electoral activism was repeated in several workshops focusing on electoral activity and social change at the Eighth Annual Meeting of the Socialist Scholars Conference in New York City (1988). Most interesting about this discussion is the fact that historically white ethnic groups did not generally debate this matter. Old-time ward bosses in these communities showed that electoral gains, once achieved, were a salient tool to actualize socioeconomic mobility for significant numbers of the group.

Clarence J. Mumford claimed that "there is a growing realization among American Blacks that Marxism-Leninism provides humanity with universal principles of social transformation." Although Mumford's sentiment is a bit strong, and perhaps even inaccurate, it does seem that activists reflecting Black empowerment are pursuing a political and economic orientation beyond programs based on access into American institutional arrangements.[42] At this stage, however, Black activism does not seem to reflect a conscientious aim of class transformation in the power hierarchy of American society. This may be evidenced in the lack of widespread Black voter support for leftist parties, such as the New Alliance party that provided the Black community with an opportunity to support the independent presidential candidacies of Daniel Serrett in 1984 and Lenora Fulani in 1988. As Ronald Walters has pointed out, voting for the Democratic party is still the major form of political expression for the overwhelming proportion of Blacks.

Some activists are attempting, nevertheless, to change or alter given political arrangements and social relations between Blacks and whites by challenging the social structure and distribution of wealth and power rather than merely reforming the system of redistributive benefits. A certain brand of Black social and political activism, one that questions the legitimacy of the governing political system is becoming more prevalent and noticeable in urban America. There is an ideological basis in the Black Community for the emergence of this kind of political activism, as is suggested by labor activist William Fletcher: "Black radicalism is a credible tendency within the Black community—whether the number of radicals is large or small. It intersects with progressives and sometimes has an electoral force."[43]

Although the ideological diversity and orientations found in Black urban communities have been noted, primarily by a few Black scholars, this topic has generally been ignored by many urban researchers analyzing Black politics. In *Protest Is Not Enough,* political scientists Rufus P. Browning, David H. Tabb, and Dale R. Marshall offer explanations of local mobilization in the Black community, but they fail to explore fully the role of either group consciousness or Black nationalism. They explained, "We posit nine factors of resources, opportunity, and incentive that might explain levels of local mobilization, . . . size of minority population, socioeconomic resources of the minority population, political resources outside the group itself, organizational development through demand protest, group competition and modeling, resistance of the dominant coalition, size of city, socioeconomic inequality, and structure of government."[44] Black nationalism has been noted as a major resource and continues to have significant ideological impact on the political behavior of Blacks. Yet this study, like some others before it, has overlooked this most important factor.

Hanes Walton, Jr. addresses this problem in the relevant literature: "Traditionally, political ideologies in the black community have been looked at as curious or as perhaps historically interesting but not as motivating forces. Many social scientists study black political ideologies to see why people adhere to them rather than to see how they affect and shape black political action." But a major national study reported that "the long history of discrimination and segregation produced among blacks a heightened sense of group consciousness and a stronger orientation toward collective values and behavior than exists generally among Americans, and group consciousness remains strong among blacks today." This same study continues:

> Probably no other aspect of black political behavior is so thoroughly misunderstood by the broader society as black nationalism. . . . Yet black nationalist movements have played leading roles in the election of such blacks as former mayor Kenneth Gibson of Newark, New Jersey, and former [the late] mayor Harold Washington of Chicago. Nationalist sentiments have also been instrumental in black protest and lobbying campaigns, conflicts over community control of schools and housing authorities, and most recently in the 1984 and 1988 presidential campaigns of Jesse Jackson.[45]

Mack Jones's criticism of discussions of Black politics on the part of mainstream political scientists as "atheoretical" is appropriate here. He points out that inquiry of political processes nationally and internationally has been appreciative "of the need for appropriate conceptual schemes or frames of reference to guide empirical inquiry" and "the need to distinguish between having power, political and otherwise, and being associated with those who have it; between participating in the symbolic trappings of political power and political power, itself." Jones adds that "when the issue is black political power in America, critical discrimination is often dropped."[46] This observation may partially explain why both the range of ideology in the Black community and its impact on political behavior have not been studied as seriously as they deserved.

Noting the ideological diversity and characteristics of the Black community is important in understanding the emergence of Black empowerment activism and its movement away from a liberal policy agenda. A major presumption regarding race relations has been that Blacks seek or engage in political participation primarily to gain access to a given system of values—economic and social power controlled by whites. But, as several opinion surveys confirm, Blacks and whites differ on some fundamental political and economic matters. These differences include attitudes regarding not only the role and responsibilities of government in the area of social welfare but also the existence and extent of racism and discrimination. Blacks seem more politically conscious and concerned about the need for an activist government that constrains the excesses of the private sector, to a far greater extent than the majority of whites.[47]

Black Empowerment and the "Black Body-Politic"

Reginald Gilliam, Jr. has argued that, given the historical and racial experiences of Blacks, the "black body-politic" does not fit into what is usually considered left, moderate, or right.[48] Political scientist Jane H. Bayes has similarly argued that the experiences of minority groups are not consistent with major ideological patterns in this country.[49] Two other authors write that "in the political scientists' sense of ideology, all ideologies are presumed to fall somewhere within or between conservatism and liberalism." Charles P. Henry and Lorenzo Morris also suggest that discussions of American politics and ideology have generally overlooked specific Black ideologies or group orientations that diverge conceptually from standard left and right ideology.

> Where the conservatism-liberalism distinction is given the broadest interpretation, namely support for the status quo in America against advocacy of societal change, there is some theoretical significance for black politics. The significance is, however, rather low because it leaves the whole of black politics on one side, the liberal side. When the distinction has been made more specific in terms of political objects which cut across the American polity, it has become almost irrelevant to black politics.[50]

In the Black community of this nation various ideological strands go beyond the white American ideological spectrum and also affect Black political behavior.

Attempts to study Black political behavior without factoring the interplay of various and at times contradictory ideological leanings in the Black community result in incomplete political analysis and sometimes erroneous conclusions about current political and social tendencies among Blacks. For example, Walton writes that few scholars have "bothered to analyze the role that black nationalism plays in black politics or how it translates itself into political action in the black community. In fact, most scholars have argued that black nationalism is *apolitical*. They fail to see the different manifestations of black nationalism as both a force for separation and a politically motivating vehicle."[51] Failure by the scholarly community and mainstream media to accept the significance of Black nationalism as a major mobilizing political force is interesting in light of the work of several Black writers who argue otherwise. Robert Allen, for example, states that although Black nationalism is "invisible" to most whites, it nevertheless is the "insistent motif" in Black political life.[52] Black nationalism is fundamentally responsible for not only the heightened political activism of Blacks at the local and national level but also the movement away from the liberal policy agenda. Much literature, however, has acknowledged Black nationalism only as a limited factor, a view contributing to the inadequacy of some analysis in dissecting Black empowerment activism.

An example of how Black nationalism has been treated as insignificant is offered in an essay by Ralph J. Bunche. In a memo to Gunnar Myrdal, "Conceptions and Ideologies of the Negro Problem,"[53] Bunche attempted to describe the black ideological spectrum in the 1930s and 1940s by dividing different ideological leanings into two general categories. He argued that "roughly speaking all Negro ideologies on the Negro question fall into one or the other of two rather broad, arbitrary categories: accommodation, and release or escape."[54] Bunche described accommodation as entailing an "adoption of white conceptions" and believing in "gradualism and conciliation." These categories are too broad to capture the presence and impact of various Black ideologies. Bunche also argued that ideology was significant only for the "articulate Negroes." As he stated, "the ideologies on the Negro problem about which we can speak are those which are the products of the articulate Negroes—the intellectuals, professional men, the Negro middle- and upper-class; the expressions of the 'talented tenth.'" A couple of decades after this statement historian Howard Brotz reported the presence of various kinds of group orientations among Blacks. His collection of primary source materials was based on the perennial question confronted by Blacks: What is the future of the race in America? He identified four basic conceptualizations including, "Emigration," "Assimilation," "Accommodation," and "Cultural Nationalism."[55]

C. V. Hamilton listed several themes associated with Black political thought: "constitutionalism," "plural nationalism," "sovereign nationalism," "leftist thought," and "Pan-Africanism."[56] He argued that at various times any one of these ideological orientations could be dominant in helping to shape the political activism of Blacks. Gilliam expanded this by discussing specific group orientations reflected in the Black community. His list included the following:

Traditional Integrationist
Black Moralist
Alienated Reformer
Alienated Revolutionary
Black Anarchist[57]

He proposed that these orientations may be useful in understanding philosophical directions of Black politics in America. Furthermore, all the orientations "have a vast constituency within the black populace, which are simultaneously operating on virtually all political issues affecting blacks" and continually interacting and molding a "silent black majority," to use C. V. Hamilton's phrase.[58] Among Blacks there is constant movement and fluidity between these orientations.

Although the silent Black majority is not tied specifically to a definitive ideology, this sector reflects strong nationalist sentiment. It can support both Black power and integration within a nationalist framework. The popularity of Gilliam's specific orientations and their potential impact on Black political behavior depend on its changing linkages with the silent black majority. Others have proposed various terms to capture the ideological diversity of the Black community, but the Gilliam approach satisfactorily makes the point that recent Black political activism is reflecting more than merely the traditional integrationist, or Black moralist beliefs. Owing to worsening social conditions for many in the Black community, nationalist sentiment is increasing. As nationalism grows leadership based on more systemic and aggressive challenges to America's economic and political mainstream institutional arrangements will emerge.

Toward a New Black Agenda?

What kinds of political developments reflect Black empowerment? Salim Muwakhil, a long-time observer of Black politics, has noted a growing trend for some Blacks to organize around political and economic issues shrouded in the terminology of self-determination, nationalism, and empowerment:

> Boston and Milwaukee are just two of several cities that have experienced major encounters with this developing black strategy. Others—including East Palo Alto, California, Brooklyn, New York, and Columbia, Maryland—have had similar, though less publicized encounters. The details vary in every situation, but the theme of self-determination is constant. And the rationale grows increasingly compelling as the economic picture bleakens.[59]

Black empowerment activism is thus also associated with calls for self-determination.

The call for reparations on the part of some Black activists and elected officials is another example of the political agenda shifting from a liberal tradition to a focus on power for the Black community. Underlying the idea of reparations is the need for distributing wealth in America to reflect the historical and current economic contributions of the Black community according to well-known Black activists for this issue, such as Imari Obadele, Chokwe Lumumba, and Ron Karenga, of the Institute of Pan African Studies in Los Angeles. These activists use the example of "The Japanese Reparations Act" passed by the United States Congress in 1988 as one kind of model that could be used for a program of Black reparations.[60] State Senator William Owens of Massachusetts, a founder of the Black Political Assembly, filed a reparations bill with that state's legislature in 1989. Detroit city councilman Clyde Cleveland introduced a resolution to give reparations to Blacks by establishing an education fund of forty billion dollars; this resolution was passed unanimously by the Detroit City Council.[61] And with the support of another Detroit activist Ray Jenkins, U.S. Representative John Conyers has introduced a "reparations bill" in the U.S. House of Representatives.[62]

Black nationalism as a resource for political mobilization is also associated with the emergence of Black empowerment activism. The influence of Black nationalist labels and rhetoric can be witnessed at the national level. The presidential campaigns of Jesse Jackson in 1984 and 1988 indicated increasing political activism among the Black electorate. Although the campaigns reflected the outlooks of both integrationists and nationalists pursuing a common agenda in the electoral arena, much of the Black community's mobilization was based on nationalist appeals. The Nation of Islam's involvement in the presidential race of 1984 showed not only increased participation in general but also the participation of a nationalist sector in the Black community that basically rejected the saliency of pursuing goals and interests in the electoral arena. This involvement will probably continue if we can judge by Min. Louis Farrakhan's endorsement of Lavoy Zaki Reed as a candidate in Missouri's recent Democratic party gubernatorial primary.[63] The Nation of Islam also provided important support for the reelection of Congressman Gus Savage in Chicago in March 1990, and several representatives of the Nation of Islam ran for electoral offices in Washington, D.C., in this same year, including seats for the city council, school committee, and congressional representative.[64]

Jesse Jackson did tap nationalist sentiment in the Black community in 1984. But, to produce political victories in the primary circuit, Jackson also had to mold and present issues is such a way that would dampen this very same nationalist sentiment. He had to be careful about pursuing this balancing act; it was necessary to keep the attention and loyalty of the activist sector that, although motivated by a sense of nationalism, could only remain mobilized on the basis of concrete issues. If they had perceived that Jackson watered down "Black issues," then they would not have supported him to the extent that they did in 1984. The focus on issues was carried into both campaigns. One survey of Black voters in Cleveland, a city Jesse Jackson won in the 1988 Democratic presidential primary campaign found "that Jackson's support has moved from simply supporting him because he is the 'Black' candidate to more closely examining the issues."[65] The description and analysis that posited an increase Black participation in recent years owing to an emotional response or the charisma of the candidate himself, therefore, is not accurate. Adolph H. Reed, for example, proposed that the success of the 1984 Jackson campaign had more to do with emotionalism and ritual in the Black community; there were many instances of this theme in the media's coverage of Jesse Jackson in 1984 and 1988.[66] But this suggestion presumes that the Black electorate is monolithic and static. Heretofore unregistered sectors of the Black electorate were motivated by tapping nationalist sentiment, which then had to be organized by emphasizing concrete issues that challenged politically corporate America.

The 1988 Jackson campaign's focus on the needs of workers and poor families is evident both during and after the campaign. According to activist William Fletcher, it reflects how class issues are emerging in the electoral arena:

> There are several different levels of raising class issues [within electoral politics]. Within the labor for Jackson work, the North Carolina concentration on a Workers Bill of Rights which was taken up by Black Workers for Justice is one level. Jackson had said the Southern primaries should be a refer-

endum on "right to work." Jackson maintained this as an agitational issue, but his campaign did not figure out how to organize around it. Now Jackson is beginning to work with the Amalgamated Clothing and Textile Workers Union to organize the South.[67]

According to Black activists interviewed for this study, this orientation will continue to win support in the Black community.

The challenge to corporate America and the focus on concrete issues, not Jesse Jackson's charisma or Black emotionalism, kept the Black electorate highly mobilized. It should be noted as partial evidence for this that Jackson was as charismatic in the 1970s as he was in the 1980s, but his personality did not elevate him to the position of leadership he now holds. Other evidence sustains my argument. Jesse Jackson's charisma failed to sway Black voters in several local elections where he asked them to vote a certain way but they did not. In the 1986 campaign for Peter Rodino's mostly Black congressional seat in New Jersey, for example, Jesse Jackson asked Black voters to reject incumbent Rodino in favor of Black challenger Donald Payne. Black voters ignored this call and continued to support Rodino, who won 58 percent of the vote.[68] Similarly, in 1986 in Queens, New York, Jesse Jackson endorsed Black Assemblyman Alton K. Walden, the choice of the Democratic party, over Black challenger Reverend Floyd Flake who actually won that congressional seat in 1986.[69] In two instances Jesse Jackson could not use his charisma to influence the preferences of Black voters at the local level, but my point here is more general: Factors other than charisma are at play in explaining the political success of Jesse Jackson at the national level. The Black electorate today is not simply responding to either charisma or possible access; Black voters want much more than this as fruit for participating in the electoral arena.

Another instance in which Jesse Jackson could not motivate Black voters to pursue a particular political goal is evidenced in the failure to achieve a high Black voter turnout in Chicago's mayoral Democratic party primary in April 1989. Jesse Jackson was unable to convince enough Black voters to turn out and support Eugene Sawyer or Timothy Evans, who ran as an Independent after Richard Daley, Jr. defeated Eugene Sawyer in the primary. The charisma of Jesse Jackson was not useful in this episode; in fact, some activists in the Black community criticized his role. Writing a political commentary Abdul Wali Muhammed claimed that Eugene Sawyer had indeed substantial support from many Black aldermen until "a transoceanic phone call from Rev. Jackson in Kuwait, and upon his return to Chicago, things started to change. We needn't go back over those events; suffice it to say that deception and mass hysteria were actually used as tools to drum support for the Evans candidacy."[70] This illustrates that in terms of influencing Black political behavior at the local level the charisma of Jesse Jackson is limited, unless he responds to the kinds of issues and policy positions that Blacks feel are in their best interests.

This continues to suggest the possibility of a changing Black political consciousness at the national level. There is further evidence of this claim. For example, one report after the 1984 presidential election stated:

> For Blacks, the next few years could become a period of rethinking and re-direction of effort. Black politics appear to have reached a strategic dead end at the national level. As is often noted, one party takes Blacks for granted and the other writes them off. Altering the situation will require putting the fear of God back into the Democratic party. Thus, we may see a period of experimentation, marked by a more independent stance vis-à-vis the Democratic party, a renewed emphasis on grass-roots lobbying, and increased dialogue with the Republicans.[71]

Many activists are suggesting that Blacks are in a period of political experimentation.

Elaine Dillahunt describes some of this experimentation:

> "Black Workers for Justice" conducted a "Black Primary Ballot." This was a twenty-seven question worker's rights survey done throughout North Carolina. It was used during the Jackson campaign to determine the issues on the mind of the Black community. The goal was to come up with a worker's platform . . . to be used for education, agitation and organizing. . . . By having a mass organization before entering an electoral campaign the mass organizing can be strengthened. . . . Our goal is empowerment of all working people and Black people controlling their communities, not just putting one person in office.[72]

The Alabama New South Coalition also reflects Black political experimentation within the electoral arena. According to Gwen Patton, this organization has been successful in screening and endorsing candidates favorable to issues important to poor and Black people in Alabama:

> The Alabama New South Coalition is a multipartisan, multi-racial group formed in 1986. It has 3,200 members. It endorses candidates via an endorsement convention. [We look at the candidate's] accountability, platform, history, intangibles like affinity and track record. A committee ranks the candidates, and a plenary votes on them. Key issues this year were loans for family farms, disclosure of campaign contributions prior to elections, appointments of positive thinking people to boards like the Parole and Pardon Board.[73]

These efforts parallel a growing receptivity to independent political strategies and mobilization in the Black community today.

Ronald Walters claims that possible independent political action has been an underlying theme in the current period:

> There has been a persistent attempt by some Black leaders to appeal to their colleagues not to give away the bargaining leverage of the collective Black community by making individual commitments to the major party candidates in advance of the candidate's public commitment to specific Black issues. In the past this appeal has fallen on deaf ears, largely because of the attractiveness of private incentive and the vulnerability of elected officials to the power of a potential president.[74]

Walters continues to argue, however, that a more "independent-leverage" is gaining wider acceptance among Black leaders and activists. To illustrate this development he examines the Jackson campaign and points to the numerous calls by some Black leaders not to quickly endorse white major party candidates in 1984 and 1988 because it would have diluted Black bargaining leverage.

Lucius J. Barker made a similar claim, based on his analysis of the 1984 Jackson candidacy:

> The strength of Jackson's candidacy, in combination with other factors such as the party's attempt to develop a more centrist image, might well spur blacks and other disadvantaged minorities to take much more aggressive stances within the Democratic party and to embrace a more independent style of politics that could well go beyond that party. . . . These factors could well provide the incentives for blacks and others to take more aggressive stances within the Democratic party and even move toward a more independent "movement" style of politics that could go beyond the party.[75]

The observations of both Walters and Barker are reflected in the statements of Blacks activists around the country, as well as in various opinion polls. And support for the outlook grows. Roger Green, activist and state assemblyman in Brooklyn, New York, has called for "another political formation to hold both parties [Democrats and Republicans] accountable."[76] Another Brooklyn-based activist, William Banks, repeated this theme: "In New York State, you have the Democrats, Republicans, Conservatives, and Right to Life Parties. . . . There needs to be a party that speaks for Blacks and Latinos."[77]

Surveys also show some support for Black independent party strategies. The National Black Election Study found that of Black respondents surveyed in the early 1980s 29 percent favored a Black political party. The Joint Center for Political Studies found that 18 percent of Blacks polled in

1986 would support Jesse Jackson as an independent in the 1988 presidential election.[78] It seems that more and more Black activists are attempting to at least explore or consider an independent political strategy in relation to the Democratic party or white power structures. Although it has been difficult to build and sustain national third party alternatives to the Democratic and Republican parties, many local efforts have met with some success. Gwen Patton described one instance: "In Alabama we have the proclivity to run as independents. Most Black elected officials in Alabama began first as independents. We started first with the Black Panther Party. Its name was changed to the Eagle Party [to distinguish it from the BPP of Huey Newton]. The Eagle Party is currently gathering signatures in certain counties to keep the institutional listing of the Party."[79]

In Philadelphia, Shafik Abu-Pahir describes his involvement in a third party: "I'm part of a third party called the Consumer Party. We run candidates on a people's platform developed out of neighborhood concerns. Our candidates got 133,000 votes for City Council in 1987. I feel strongly that we must move toward independent parties in order to gain empowerment."[80] Chicago activist Conrad Worrill feels that since "there were 428,000 people who voted against the Democratic nominee Daley . . . there is a basis for an alternative party" if it is built on a grass-roots level, from the "bottom up," not "top down."[81] Jitu Weusi describes an effort at independent electoral mobilization in New York State: "There is a New York statewide convention planned for May 1990 to set up statewide apparatus for an [electoral] party. We will run a candidate for each of the four major offices-governor, lt. governor, controller, and att. general. The candidates will include Blacks, Hispanics, and whites. This effort has Black leadership, but everyone is invited. We're willing to coalesce with others . . . but on our independent terms."[82]

In the early 1980s several national meetings of Black activists were held to establish a national Black Independent party. About 2,000 Black activists met in Philadelphia in November 1980 to develop plans for a Black independent party, and 700 delegates met in August 1981 to ratify a charter for the National Black Independent party. The constitution of this party illustrates how Black activists were beginning to move toward electoral activism with a progressive and radical agenda intact. It established an "Electoral Politics Committee" as a standing committee; but more important, it called for participation in the electoral arena on the basis of "mass-based strategies." As stated in the constitution, "Our actions will be guided by three basic mass-based strategies . . . Community Organization and Mobilization, . . . Institutional and Community Development, . . . Public Policy and Electoral Politics."[83]

Even before the 1972 National Political Convention in Gary, Indiana, grass-roots activists like Imamu Amiri Baraka were calling for a progressive electoral activism; as he stated, local Black organizations interested in social change "must not only conduct voter registration, actually voter education-drives, but also run candidates in all elections. . . . We must get beyond idle neophyte militancy to effective political organizing and build allegiance from our people by coopting all so-called or seemingly legitimate political processes in the black communities."[84] The proposal here was to use the electoral arena—on an independent basis—as another forum by which to effect social change.

I should point out now that many organizers of these earlier meetings and advocates for an independent Black politics actually worked in both of Jesse Jackson's presidential campaigns; some even held positions of leadership in these efforts. The call for Black independent political activism has increased among Black leaders and rank-and-file voters. This new alliance not only reflects the disillusionment of Blacks who heretofore have been loyal to the Democratic party, but it also recognizes new Black actors participating in the electoral arena and the growth of nationalism among Blacks.

Other examples of renewed and perhaps more radical Black local activism include the Organization for Black Struggle in St. Louis, Missouri. This organization is described by activist and journalist Jamala Rogers, the cochair along with fellow activist Al Lumpkins, "as a grass-roots mass organization whose primary focus is on community empowerment."[85] The political and social agenda of this group illustrates in part the movement away from public policy positions that could be described loosely as "liberal." This organization has mobilized the Blacks to protest police brutality, inadequate housing, and growing presence of drugs in the Black community. But they have sought to use the electoral arena to support candidates and officials who challenge the corporate progrowth agenda for St. Louis.

In December 1987 another instance of reemerging protest manifested itself within a context of Black empowerment; several activists planned a major political and economic campaign against the business community in New York City for its alleged insensitivity toward and contributions to the poor living conditions of Blacks in that city. The Committee for Economic Sanctions Against Racism in New York targeted the giant Macy's department store for picketing and boycotting until the executives of this store agreed to contribute funds for nonprofit, cooperative housing for low-income families. One organizer of the sanctions campaign proclaimed: "We must let the captains of industry of New York know that there will be no more business as usual."[86] In Chicago, the

Citizens United for Better Parks protested for resources in the low-income areas of the city. This group protested not only the inequitable level of funds targeted for Black and low-income areas but also the lack of citizen input into decisions that have an impact on the management of local parks and recreational facilities.[87] In both these local instances supporters of Black empowerment activism challenged the distribution of wealth and the institutional arrangements, including the private sector, that maintain such distribution rather than seeking either access or integration into these arrangements. The rules of the game were challenged by these two political efforts. They also reflected independent political action taking place outside the normative channels of political participation. And both efforts, based on statements of its leadership, used nationalist and separatist rhetoric to mobilize the Black community.

Civil Rights activist Benjamin F. Chavis, Jr., has also pointed to an emergence of activism based on the idea of empowerment as described in this study. He describes the campaign of Blacks in Keysville, Georgia, who organized to hold an election, "the first in 55 years and the first in which African Americans—80 percent of the population—voted. . . . Administration of Keysville had been turned over to the county during the Depression. African Americans want it back."[88] This electoral event was made possible as a result of new Black voters in the Keysville electoral arena. Blacks were mobilized in part by an appeal to self-determination and the possibility that Black political power could be translated into economic gains for the Black community.

Both the election of Harold Washington as Mayor of Chicago and the policies of his administration reflect a politics of Black empowerment. Abdul Alkalimat points out that "Washington summed up his reform package as having three points of attack: the structure of government, development of the city, and the general mood and direction of government."[89] Mayor Washington's victory was based in the introduction of new Black and Latino voters into Chicago's electoral arena. The appeal to many of these voters was contingent on raising the group consciousness of Blacks and convincing them that a mayor like Harold Washington would pursue a progressive economic and social agenda for the city of Chicago. One Latina activist, Maria Cerda, stated that mobilization of new Black and Latino voters would not have been possible without developing a political and economic program different from the typical program for Black and minority inclusion into the status quo. Many of the new Black and Latino voters and supporters represented sectors that had been spurned or ignored by both the Democratic party machine and the periodic reform opposition.[90]

Mayor Washington also began to introduce public and governmental policies that would bolster neighborhood groups, and the Black community in particular, whereas previous Chicago administrations undermined neighborhood priorities. Gregory D. Squires and his colleagues point out that Washington's approach was especially evident in the area of urban development:

> Viewed in the context of past city administrations' attitudes toward urban redevelopment, the Washington administration's 1984 Chicago development plan represents a substantial shift in course. Principal among its objectives are job creation as the central criterion for assessing the worth of particular projects, the balancing of downtown and neighborhood development, and the mobilization of activities.[91]

These three major features of the political agenda and activism represented by Mayor Washington were not part of the traditional liberal or conservative political programs for urban America.

In each of these local instances Black grass-roots activists and organizations attempted to build a different political agenda than that put forth by interest groups aligned within the liberal foundation of power or its economic development program—the "growth ideology" and "austerity state" in urban America. In some places these efforts are beginning to generate political victories and successful coalitions. For example, Black political insurgents and activists in Brooklyn, New York—such as state assembly representatives Al Vann, Roger Green, and now Congressman Major Owens—were able to challenge successfully the drawing of city council district lines that discriminated against Black and Latino residents; they also have been able to defeat machine candidates in several elections. Through building coalitions and mass organizing these Black elected officials also helped reject a $500 million prison bond issue; they argued instead for better training programs and prisoner rehabilitation services. They were also effective in restoring $50 million in services for family planning and child care in the state budget. The influence of these activists is independent, tied to neither the Democratic party nor the mayor's political network. These Black officials have been able to stay in office by developing a political agenda supported by Black citizens, many of whom have been alienated from traditional political and party structures.[92] This kind of activism and political agenda reflects Dolbeare's economic democracy rather than the traditional liberal-conservative public policy alternatives that have been part of urban America since the New Deal.

In the last several years a broad range of Black activists in several cities have been seeking to develop certain public policy agendas as alternatives to the liberal and conservative approaches to socioeconomic conditions in their communities. Local calls for the development of Black agendas have emerged in major cities—New York, Chicago, Milwaukee, Rochester, Philadelphia, Detroit. This activism focuses on making Black politics more responsive and effective regarding depressed conditions in the Black community and developing a political strategy that would force local government to advocate more strongly to the private sector on behalf of the quality of life in the Black community. In Boston Black activists and elected officials representing more than sixty community organizations and churches developed a process by which to generate such an agenda. In an interview, Lloyd King, president of a ten-year-old political grass-roots organization, stated that such an agenda would be a first step in allowing Black leadership to challenge the role of the private sector in Boston, particularly its political behavior and practices in the Black community.[93]

A brief review of some principles and values underlying the Black Agenda Project in Boston suggests a political orientation that differs from those guiding public policy in urban America. One principle, adopted by both a major convention of Black activists in this city and the Massachusetts Black Legislative Caucus at its annual meeting in April 1989, stated: "Political power is inseparable from economic progress."[94] This principle opposes those public policies that emphasize efforts at economic mobility in ways that do not encourage Black political mobilization at the same time. Liberal, but also neoconservative, public policy generally has overlooked the necessity of Black political mobilization in attempts to improve economically the status of the Black community. The separation of these concepts is increasingly being rejected by Black activists.

Another principle differs from a generally expressed one in the writings of liberal and neoconservative students of urban public policy: "Economic progress is measured by the improvement of all sectors in the community, and not necessarily of the basis of individual mobility, or progress for a select kind of families." The concept of community progress, rather than individual or family progress, has not been addressed by liberal or neoconservative public policy. As reported in the *Chicago Crusader*, this effort was similar to the "Black Survival Agenda" held in Chicago in 1987 where sixty resolutions and principles were adopted.[95] As is illustrated by the Boston Black Agenda Convention, other Black agenda-building efforts around the country, and the national African-American Summit in New Orleans in 1989, more and more Black activists are attempting to build political networks and agendas that redefine the concept of economic progress for the Black community. The political activism associated with these kinds of efforts involves different actors and leadership than that activism associated with the pursuit of liberal public policy.

Much of this new activism, as stated earlier, involves the idea of controlling land in Black urban communities. This immediately distinguishes it from traditional white ethnic political activism. Although white ethnic politics was based on territory and neighborhood turf in the initial stages of ethnic mobilization, it eventually moved away from the question of land control as a result of economic and cultural integration in the social structure of American society. As sociologist Donald Warren has pointed out, "White ethnic groups are different not only in the likelihood that many become indistinguishable members of the anonymous majority 'community,' but also that in structural terms territory no longer needs a basis of organization and power."[96] This integration happens because at some historical juncture, "ethnics became whites," as activist William Fletcher noted.[97] Thus, in many instances a racial hierarchy allowed European ethnic groups to assimilate into American economic and social structures on the basis of race, not land.

Black empowerment activism, however, focuses on control of land. Indeed, the question of land control is major under a politics of empowerment. It surpasses affirmative action, job discrimination, or school integration as priorities; many Black activists I interviewed felt that control over land or urban space was much more important than other issues. Under the political umbrella of empowerment the issues that are supported focus on institutionally strengthening the Black community. Empowerment activism does not advocate strongly for public policies whose effects primarily benefit Black individuals or enhance the possibility of individual Black mobility within the American economic system. In the latter case, control of land by a "group" is not as important as individual characteristics such as education or available opportunities for entering economic and occupational structures.

The focus on control of land as a basis of Black political power is not a new idea—it has a long history. Prior to the 1970s there were basically "two positions on the Land Question. . . . One of these positions presupposes the existence of what is termed a New African Nation with its homeland being the 'Black Belt' south, U.S. The other position presupposes Africa as the national homeland of black people."[98] But a third position regarding the politics of land and race emerged in the last two decades; this position posits that Blacks should control economically and politically the land occupied in the American city. In the early 1980s this was one of the major platforms of the National Black Independent Political party. The control of land by Blacks and Latinos was also a major theme in the Community Control Movement in New York City in the late 1960s and early 1970s.

This argument for economic and political control of land is supported by political economist Lloyd Hogan; he argued that both rural and urban control of land was critical for the physical and social survival of Blacks in this country. He suggested, furthermore, that the control of land represented a major evolving conflict between Blacks and whites and between dominant and subdominant groups.[99] Conrad Worrill, national chairman of the National Black United Front, also suggested this:

> The expanding African-American population in the United States' inner cities has been a major concern of white decision makers since the passage of the 1949 Urban Renewal legislation. Since that time, strategies have been attempted to hold down the pattern of African-Americans becoming the majority, or close to the majority population in cities like Chicago, Philadelphia, Pittsburgh, St. Louis, Washington, D.C., New York, Detroit, Cleveland, Kansas City, etc. . . . The question for the African-American community in Chicago and other inner cities of the United States where this trend exists, is why should we again be maneuvered from the land we occupy? Our history in America has been one of forced and manipulated migration. Its obvious that we need a massive organizing strategy to reverse this trend of Black removal.[100]

Chicago offered a good example of underlying racial and class conflict shrouded by a controversy about the control and utilization of land and urban space. A few years ago, a group of white homeowners in that city introduced a "Home Equity" proposal for the purpose of maintaining "racial integration" in some of the city's neighborhoods. But in fact, as pointed out by John H. Stroger, a Cook County commissioner, "The very notion of the city's home equity ordinance goes against the fundamentals of property ownership rights and is prescribed to control the movement of Blacks and Hispanics."[101] Several Black aldermen criticized this program as nothing more than a way to keep Blacks from moving into certain white areas of Chicago.[102]

Other examples of land use by whites and powerful interests to control, not just the movement of Blacks, but their politics and degree of economic freedom can be witnessed in Dearborn, Michigan, and Dallas. To prevent Blacks from using parks in Dearborn, a city where only a small number of Blacks reside, a referendum was passed in 1985 denying park access to nonresidents. One observer pointed out that "sensitized by events in South Africa and disturbed by any manifestations of 'apartheid' in public law, Detroit black leaders were outraged by the Dearborn action."[103] Dallas has also historically restricted land use for Blacks and their physical mobility. During the 1940s, 1950s, and 1960s certain interests violently prevented Blacks from moving into certain sections of the city or owning homes in such sections. Although the local government in Dallas was not directly involved in a series of systematic bombings over many years, local governmental leaders simply did not respond seriously to this, according to journalist Jim Schutze. Because of nonresponse to an established pattern of bombings Schutze gives the impressions that the violence was condoned by the city's oligarchy and governmental leadership.[104] Blacks were prevented from exercising any control over land, despite the economic means to do so.

In Newark, New Jersey, long-time community activist Amiri Baraka described that city's struggle over control of land:

> By now it is no secret that low income housing is being leveled and eliminated. For the last eight years, the local politicians and the housing authority let 300 million dollars intended for the upgrading of existing public housing sit unused. Why? So finally they could carry out the heinous scam they intended in the late '60s—wipe out the central ward, drive the residents out, and gentrify the area, put up high cost efficiency apartments and coops and condos and attract the yuppies and buppies. Rutgers, NJIT, . . . Seton Hall, St. Benedict's could all serve to remove old housing and residents and turn the central ward into a largely white middle-class area, transforming the politics of the area as well.[105]

Maria Borrero, an activist in Hartford, Connecticut, stated that she thought for a long time that voter registration was "a waste of time" until she realized its implications for land control. She argues that land control—that is, being able to decide that "housing is built on a lot, rather than a Burger King"—is a way of effectively organizing Latinos and Blacks in poor communities.[106]

In East St. Louis there is an ongoing political struggle to control the riverfront in that city. A newsletter for the Organization for Black Struggle reported, for instance, that the "white power structure . . . wants the riverfront in East St. Louis, but Black mayor Carl Officer won't cooperate. In the case of the license collector, Billie Boykins, they'd like to get their grubby hands on those patronage jobs and the millions of dollars in fees and taxes collected by that office."[107]

Chuck Turner, a long-time Boston community activist, phrased the issue of land control in Black communities more dramatically: "We are in the midst of a fierce fight over land in Boston. While there are a number of aspects to this struggle, the one that concerns us most is the one between the relatively low income population in most of Boston's neighborhoods and higher income people who desire to move in. . . . There is also the issue of institutional expansion, the competition between industrial and commercial uses of land."[108] Another Boston activist, Miren Uriarte, also describes the political history of Blacks and Latinos here on the "basis of struggle for land and space."[109] Joyce Brooks of Philadelphia's Money for Neighborhoods Coalition has been fighting the privileged status of developers for many years; she sums up this struggle succinctly: "The developers want what we have, and that is land. Our land is valuable."[110] In Atlantic City, where the casino industry and local government made promises of economic development and jobs, residents are finding out that the Casino Reinvestment Development Authority is about to clear people from the "Inlet" area in order to rebuild. In this case threatened with removal are not only many elderly people but also people who for years have provided the casino industry with cheap labor.[111]

St. Louis activist and State Representative Charles "Quincy" Troupe described the role that the ownership and management of land has for the political empowerment of the Black community:

> When I look at the mayoral races in St. Louis, one thing that clearly surfaced was that there is no plan to empower the African American community. What I mean by a plan to empower African Americans is that you just can't have a plan to run for office. It's got to be a total plan and the plan is, in order to empower us, we have to own and control the land. Until Black politicians decide that we need a land use plan that will determine how many taverns we'll have on every corner, how many liquor stores, how many hardware stores, how many churches, cleaners, grocery stores. . . . Then we can never develop an economic base. . . . The basic economic plan is a land use plan. . . . I just see this as being critical in 1990.[112]

And in a study of politics in Washington, D.C., one researcher commented on the control of land and space as a basic urban conflict; he points to the "existence of a fundamental process of competition for space in the nation's capital."[113] The political activism associated with Black empowerment reflects a focus on land control and racial and physical consolidation of a community rather than integration or dispersal.

In summary, the goals, style, actors, and leadership characteristic of Black empowerment activism differ from those associated with traditional politics at the local and national levels. It is important to note that I use the term Black empowerment specifically, unlike some other studies. For example, Lawrence J. Hanks uses this terms somewhat loosely when he describes a Black political empowerment process as having three measures: "(1) blacks holding offices in proportion to their numbers in the population; (2) the enactment of public policies favorable to the black community; and (3) the rise in socio-economic status of the black community."[114] These characteristics may reflect successful attempts at Black political participation, but they overlook the systemic and perhaps even ideological challenges to government arising in cities like Boston, Milwaukee, Detroit, and New York.

Conceptually, in this study I approach Black empowerment as a collective orientation for social change and political dislodgment of those interests perceived as either having power or controlling wealth. In other words, I study Black empowerment as a "social movement" because the kinds of issues identified with it seek "to bring about fundamental changes in the social order,"[115] and they lead "to changes in thought, behavior and social relationships";[116] the issues also "promote a change or resist a change in the society of which . . . they are . . . a part."[117] Furthermore, Black empowerment politics emphasizes the cultural contributions that Blacks as a group can make for the entire society; as a matter of fact, mobilizing Black empowerment and building political organizations are partially based on cultural or nationalist foundations, as well as a different economic vision.

Except for its reference to violence, the conceptualization of social movements by Daniel A. Foss and Ralph Larkin is appropriate and relevant: "A social movement is the developing collective action of a significant portion of the members of a major social category, involving at some point the use of physical force or violence against members of other social categories, their possessions, or their institutionalities, and interfering at least temporarily—whether by design or by unintended consequence—with the political and cultural reproduction of society."[118] Robert H. Salisbury's essay on the two major characteristics of social movements is useful here. The social movement indicators that he discusses, such as attempts to alter status relationships by changing the social structure, identifiable organizational components that act as "carriers" and "mobilizers" for the movement, and a mass support base, are generally reflected in much recent Black political activism at the national level.[119]

Social historians Michael Omi and Howard Winant also justify approaching certain kinds of Black political activism as a social movement.

Social movements create collective identity, collective subjectivity, by offering their adherents a different view of themselves and their world; different, that is, from the characteristic worldviews and self-concepts of the social order which the movements are challenging. Based upon that newly forged collective identity, they address the state politically, demanding change. This is particularly true of contemporary racial movements. In fact these movements largely established the parameters within which popular and radical democratic movements (so-called "new social movements") operate in the US.[120]

These various definitions of, and approaches for understanding the nature of social movement, allow one to describe Black empowerment activism as different from traditional Black electoral activism.

Lawrence J. Hanks argues that very few studies of Black political participation have been conducted outside the confines of "model" theories. But "the socioeconomic model, the structuralist arguments, and the fear model individually explain little about black political empowerment. . . . There is nothing in the political behavior literature which explains the process of organization building although it is a crucial factor in facilitating black political participation."[121] Hanks further refines his ideas: "The literature on black empowerment comprises models primarily, without any detailed studies of the efforts to gain this power. Even if a quantitative model explained all of the variance, one could only surmise about the dynamic process of empowerment. In order to understand the process of empowerment, one would have to study black political empowerment efforts as if they were social movements."[122] Studying Black empowerment as an incipient social movement rather than a temporary political aberration on the part of isolated Black militants also allows one to understand how and why new leadership, organization, and issues are emerging today in the Black community and delineates the relationship of such developments to broader social issues.

As this new kind of Black political activism becomes more prominent in the nation's larger cities it could begin to challenge not only local government but also the social and economic values and arrangements that provide a foundation for the larger and more powerful corporations in American cities. Related to this, Martin Shefter has proposed several imperatives of urban politics today: "Urban politicians have compelling incentives to pursue policies that will (a) generate votes, (b) maintain the health of the local economy, (c) preserve the city's credit, and (d) regulate and contain conflicts among the city's residents."[123] Although these imperatives are critical for urban government, they can be challenged by Black leaders and activists not considered cooperative by the leadership of private and powerful institutions. Both local government and corporate-based leadership will logically attempt to limit and generally diffuse the potential political effectiveness of Black activism and leadership that seeks empowerment rather than access or who may reject the liberal public policy preferences traditionally associated with mainstream Black political leadership and electoral participation.

This kind of Black political activism is, in effect, posing racial and economic challenges to the social status quo; increasingly, it elicits greater attention from both local government and corporate-based leadership as its political credibility and electoral viability increases. Although the cooptation of Black leaders is possible, and still an effective way to mute Black protest, it will become more difficult as the development of a progressive social and economic agenda for Blacks becomes crystalized. As long as Black political activism was an integral part of the liberal agenda and coalition it did not pose serious political or economic systemic or symbolic threats. Accordingly, it was ignored by the leadership of corporate America. The rhetoric of Black activists within the liberal framework may have alarmed some political conservatives, but it did not question the economic foundation of power; in other words, the relationship between wealth and corresponding power was not questioned. Thus, institutional arrangements that supported the ownership, accumulation, and management of wealth could be considered safe by interests benefiting from these particular institutional arrangements. This may change, however, as mobilization associated with a more radicalized Black political activism moves into the electoral arena or wins an increasing number of adherents; this possibility, however, becomes a matter of serious political concern for those with wealth and influence in the private sector.

CHAPTER THREE

The Changing Black Political Agenda

Why can't Mel King be like Andrew Young?

Mayor Kevin White, Boston (1967–1983)

Why can't Jesse Jackson be like Tom Bradley?

George Will, Columnist

Ron Daniels, 1984 national campaign adviser to Jesse Jackson, argues that the goals and activism emerging in the Black community reflect social change rather than accommodation to an existing order. Daniels proposes that today Black activism and electoral politics, as an extension of the civil rights movement, are beginning to reflect a broad process of social change focusing on human rights and an equitable distribution of economic benefits in the United States.[1]

The 1984 presidential campaign of Jesse Jackson exhibited aspects of social movement rather than simply an electoral attempt on behalf of the candidate for the Democratic party's presidential nomination. Political scientists Lucius J. Barker and Ronald W. Walters propose the following idea:

> The Jackson candidacy developed into more than just an ordinary campaign for a major-party presidential nomination. His drive for the nomination was just one phase of a much longer mobilization which, in many ways, revives and expands the civil rights movement of the 1950s and 1960s. . . . The central objectives of this campaign-movement encapsulate Jackson's overall goal to bring about the *full* inclusion of those who have been traditionally "locked out" of society.[2]

This goal is also reflected at the local level in some cities.

84

Brooklyn activist Jitu Weusi stated that the Black activism associated with the campaign victory of David Dinkins as the first Black mayor of New York City means high expectations for the Black community. He identified several policy issues associated with the heightened level of Black activism in that city. These policies include greater equity regarding city contracts to the African-American community, massive amounts of low- and lower middle-income housing, neighborhood-based veto power over developers of luxury apartments, expansion of squatter's rights and urban homesteading, massive aid for health care facilities and operations controlled by community groups, and expansion of educational opportunities for all children.[3]

If this accurately describes some of the demands associated with the progressive face of Black political activism, then these new goals will likely be resisted fiercely by interests who benefit from the current arrangements of wealth and power in this society. Even racial accommodationist goals that have not seriously threatened the current arrangements for economic development at the city level or the wealth status quo have been resisted continually in America. As pointed out in one study, "Black demands, even when initially raised in modest form, proved threatening to a wide array to whites: to neighborhood residents who faced racial integration and its expected consequences; to politicians who feared the loss of traditional constituents as a result of population change; to school officials who sought to preserve time-worn patterns of organizations, definitions or school issues, and personal political ties."[4] This was the case although the immediate goal of Black demands within this context was inclusion in and reform of the political system so that it might be more open, fair, and accessible.

Toward New Racial and Political Goals

In spite of resistance to Blacks' political attempts to accommodate themselves into the political and economic status quo some evidence indicates that Black grass-roots activists in major cities are using the electoral arena as not only a response to depressed socioeconomic conditions in the Black community but also a way to directly challenge those private leaders who continue to support public policy frameworks that have not substantively changed racial and economic hierarchies in urban America. Two major issues or questions are raised here: the first considers the utility, effectiveness, or consequence of the electoral arena for social change; the other focuses on the nature of the Black agenda in urban America. In the latter case that agenda can focus on either rendering accessible given socioeconomic and political structures and institutions or challenging those very same institutional arrangements. The electoral arena relies primarily on convincing—legally, politically, or morally—those who control dominant power structures that a certain degree of openness for new groups should be allowed, but the Black agenda really focuses on rearranging, eliminating, and creating new competitive structures that change the hierarchy of wealth in society.

Samuel Huntington has written that a modern society is partially defined by the presence of a heightened level of political openness and participation.[5] Thus, the guarantee of access provided in the civil rights legislative packages of the 1950s and 1960s was an important step in moving America toward a more modern and open society, but it was only one step. Indeed, basic economic contradictions in America were slightly transformed rather than confronted. The victories around the "politics of rights"—to use Charles V. Hamilton's term—were not enough to respond to depressed economic conditions of Blacks.[6]

Black Power theorist and activist James Boggs also discussed the limitations of access and argued for a politics that would move "from a struggle for rights to a struggle for power."[7] And much later this sentiment was again expressed by one who, to satisfy the needs associated with civil rights, called for greater Black political challenges against the corporate sector:

> It is becoming increasingly evident that racial and ethnic inequalities cannot be separated out from those inequalities which characterize American society in general. . . . For civil rights activists to effectively alter the objective conditions of minorities in the United States, they must begin to address these fundamental inequities. Challenging corporate power in general is not a substitute for effective civil rights enforcement and affirmative action. But it represents a dimension to the civil rights struggle which must be addressed if the civil rights challenges of the 1980s are to be met.[8]

In fact, victory in the realm of civil rights only forced Black leaders to take "the road from right to reality" as the president of the Ford Foundation, McGeorge Bundy, explained to the 1966 Annual Meeting of the National Urban League.[9] Some disputed this as they pointed to the successes of individuals as evidence of both an economic system that was indeed becoming more efficacious for Blacks in this country and gains that contributed to political access.

To be sure, victories of access in the educational, economic, and political arenas did allow a relatively small group of Blacks to achieve elite status. But aside from its challenge to segregation, this achievement reflected the limited goals of the civil rights movement. Social historians Michael Omi and Howard Winant summarize this position:

The modern civil rights movement was initially organized within the dominant paradigm of ethnicity. The ethnicity perspective provided an analytic framework by which to assess the situation of blacks, and correspondingly shaped the movement's political agenda. The early movement leaders were racial moderates who sought to end "race-thinking" and assure "equality" to each individual. The movement initially focused its energies on the South, where the ethnicity paradigm remained a challenging ideology to the racist logic of segregation.[10]

Political and economic success for a relatively small sector of the Black community, however, does not prove that the status quo works for most Blacks. The kinds of political victories that reflect access cannot alter social relations between Blacks and whites; moreover, they have not alleviated depressed conditions of life in Black communities.

The victories in the area of political rights during the civil rights movement, while necessary for the continual democratization of the nation, were merely reforms that quelled tensions arising from economic, racial, and social division in American society. Economic tensions and the potential for conflict arising from the different systemic interests that the poor and working-class Blacks pose to powerful groups continue to characterize social relations in America; this is occurring, moreover, within a racial and economic hierarchy that is becoming more, rather than less, rigid. As Fred Harris and Roger Wilkens point out, the development of two societies—one Black (and now also Latino) and the other white, as described in the report of the 1968 Kerner Commission more than twenty years ago—is a significant characteristic of American racial relations today.[11]

Even before the Kerner Commission's study, Black activists suggested that ideals of equality and social stability could only be realized by resolving structural contradictions between the quality of life for masses of Blacks and the practices and needs of current economic infrastructure. Paul Robeson addressed this matter in his autobiography: "The granting of our demand for first-class citizenship, on par with all others, would not itself put us [Blacks] in a position of equality. Oppression has kept us on the bottom rungs of the ladder and even with the removal of all barriers we will still have a long way to climb in order to catch up with the general standard of living."[12]

After the 1964 Civil Rights Act passed, President Lyndon Johnson declared that the mere appearance of equality in America was not enough. In his 1965 commencement address to Howard University he stated: "It is not enough just to open the gates of opportunity. All our citizens must have the ability to walk through those gates. . . . This is the next and the more profound stage of the battle for civil rights. We seek not just legal equity but human ability, not just equality as a fact, but equality as a result."[13] In their documentary legal history, *Civil Rights and the Black American,* Albert P. Blaustein and Robert L. Zangrando reiterated this idea. In the late 1960s they reported:

> In the past quarter century the Negro has achieved his legal rights, but he has yet to win a full role in the social and economic life of the nation. A vicious circle of residential segregation, job discrimination, inferior educational opportunities, limited mobility, and, in many cases, a crippled self-image are affixing upon a new generation of Negroes, the kind of economic and psychic damage that no executive order, court decision, or piece of federal legislation can readily correct.[14]

Thus, as long as access is separated from results the potential for social and economic tensions between Blacks and whites in the United States will continue to characterize the national polity.

Access to goals that emphasize and reflect political and economic participatory rights as well as attempts to change white attitudes toward Blacks can provide opportunities for individual mobility in the Black community. Clearly the right to vote and the right to pursue one's economic interests are significant. There has been considerable progress in racial relations, and the improved economic status of some Blacks is a result of access victories. But this is only half the picture. Nicholas L. Danigelis explains this fact in another way; he has suggested that psychological and sociocultural factors related to race relations should be treated and studied differently than structural factors. Those who advocate for a politics of power prefer to target structural factors; they believe that the psychological and sociocultural factors Danigelis refers to, in fact, reflect structural relations between Blacks and whites. Danigelis suggests that these factors are equally significant:

> The present debate between optimists and pessimists on the matter of continued full Black electoral participation seems to support the optimists. If this optimism is warranted, then the effects of potentially hostile structural factors (e.g., the potential political power represented by increased numbers of Blacks in large cities) might be less important than if sociocultural and psychological factors were absent or conducive toward an intolerant climate.[15]

However, those Blacks who are poor, working-class, and living in the inner city will not, ipso facto, have their socioeconomic conditions improved as a result of greater psychological or sociocultural acceptance of

Blacks by whites. Danigelis's proposition may be relevant and valid for the upwardly mobile, individual Black, but perhaps not for masses of Blacks living in poverty or near poverty.

This argument implies that political activity is of little value to the social or economic success of minority groups. As one social analyst writes, "political activity and political success have been neither necessary nor sufficient for economic advancement";[16] in addition, "politics has special disadvantages for ethnic minority groups, however much it may benefit individual ethnic leaders."[17] This contention is naive in part because Thomas Sowell uses political activity in a conceptually narrow and simplistic way, that is, voting. It is clear that voting, however, is not a panacea for the social alienation and economic depression found in Black urban communities across the United States. Although his argument is based on a mistaken assessment of an apolitical history attributed to more "successful" ethnic groups, he does raise the question regarding the efficacy of political activism. He concludes that the successful economic experiences of white ethnic groups were achieved without significant political activism. He believes that Black economic progress, as well, is not determined by political action. Moreover, Sowell treats this subject ahistorically, despite his stylistic trappings of "historical" data. Sowell does not discuss adequately the role of power in determining economic differences among groups. Nor does Sowell bother to justify his claim. "Political activity" and "power" were not important to the success of some white ethnic groups. An increasing number of Black activists are asserting that politics and economic progress, in fact, are inseparable. But political activity must involve more than just access to those with power, as discussed earlier.

Before listing several grass-roots political events that reflect this, however, I should point out that such occurrences may today be perceived as disjointed; this perception is partially correct. Keith Jennings, a Black activist in Atlanta, agreed, commenting that "there is something going on but it isn't organized. It lacks any semblance of organization."[18] Black scholar and activist William E. Nelson echoes this sentiment: "My sense is that independent community organizing across the nation is discontinuous and relatively ineffective." He adds, furthermore, that the "emphasis on electoral politics has tended to mean that broadscale mobilization has tended to be periodic, issueless, and narrowly focused on the goal of placing specific individuals into specific offices."[19] Despite this warning, the frequency of certain kinds of political events in the Black community suggests the emergence of new political agendas.

Do certain community-level political happenings point toward a new kind of Black political activism? As mentioned earlier in this chapter C. V. Hamilton has proposed that Black activism is moving from a "politics of right" to a "politics of resources."[20] This may provide a useful framework for analyzing the frequency of community-based developments that suggest a groping for new kinds of political relationships between Blacks and white power structures. These new relationships respond to gaining power and influence over wealth, rather than achieving access to power or wealth. By definition, a politics of resources challenges both the racial and economic status quo. There are significant differences between politics organized in pursuit of access and accommodation and politics challenging racial and economic hierarchies in this society. And the reaction to each kind of politics elicits different responses from powerful groups.

As described earlier, proposals such as the Mandela referendum in Boston, the call for an independent Black school district in Milwaukee, the mobilization for self-government by Blacks in Keys County, Georgia, represent the cropping of a different kind of Black political activism today. The mobilization of a boycott against certain businesses in New York City or the Black boycott and protests of white businesses under the call, "we can't take it no more" in Winston County, Mississippi, may pose new developments; these boycotts are aimed at greater Black economic power, not solely desegregation of public facilities or job sites.[21]

Despite the fact that activists describing themselves as Black nationalists have not done very well in the electoral arena—even in places like New York City—this tendency may be changing, according to activist and political scientist Basil Wilson. The so-called Black nationalists have been unable to form effective coalitions and transform the "noise" they make into electoral gains, but the change in the structure of the New York City Council from thirty-six to fifty-one seats may open up local opportunities for electoral inroads. Also in New York City, Black nationalist-oriented activists met to discuss again the possibility of developing an independent political platform, perhaps even a party.[22] This may yet be another example of the kind of activism that is making inroads into the more traditional electoral activism in the Black community.

At least two other events intimate change in the overall direction of Black political behavior. First, Blacks decided to run Timothy Evans as a mayoral candidate under the Harold Washington party in Chicago, where Black activists rejected the symbolism represented by Eugene Sawyer, Chicago's Black acting mayor. Sawyer's elevation to power was perceived as a reflection of the white-controlled Democratic party machine once ruled by Mayor Richard Daley. According to Abdul Alkalimat, this development was owing to some progressive and grass-roots activists' decision to work with the Washington administration rather than focus on a mass mobilization of the community: "At the time he was elected, progressives joined his administration rather than build the mass movement in the communities. After the death of Harold, the Black middle class split, and this split layed the basis for the new machine to take over power."[23] Sawyer, despite the fact that he is Black, represented an agenda that the Black electorate rejected during the Democratic mayoral primary in February 1989. The Black community defeated the acting mayor because it opted to organize an independent campaign that rejected Sawyer's political and economic program.

Another issue that reflects political change in the Black community is some activists' disillusionment with Jesse Jackson's apparent movement from some of his 1984 positions, including his growing "detente" with the Democratic party, and also his overbearing personality in the management of the Rainbow Coalition. Several Black and white activists also felt that Jesse Jackson had softened his stand on both cuts in the military budget and the plight of the Palestinians.[24] An editorial in the Black newspaper *The City Sun* in Brooklyn, New York, pointed out Jackson's difficulty in establishing a politically viable wide base of support:

> The ideological maverick of 1984 has become a political hostage in 1988, trying to win white approval at the expense of the broadest Black imperatives that should have guided him—and us—all along. . . . We are to pretend that our problems are just as bad as everybody else's so that Jesse Jackson can "win" white America. In the true spirit of brotherhood, we are to fuel the fire so that it can warm everyone else—first.[25]

Besides concerns regarding Jesse Jackson's shift in certain policy position, others have expressed dissatisfaction with his role in the Rainbow Coalition's national and local organizations.

In early March 1989 at a national meeting in Chicago certain organizational changes were made in the formal structure of the National Rainbow Coalition; basically these changes give Jackson more power to appoint or remove state chairpersons and local coalition officials. According to an editorial in *The Guardian,* these kinds of changes are "bound to disappoint many activists, particularly those who believe one purpose of the Rainbow should be to help foster a progressive current independent of the Democratic Party."[26] Furthermore, Jackson has been criticized for not supporting several progressive electoral candidates running on independent lines, such as congressional candidate Bernie Sanders in Vermont in 1989. Although Black activist and scholar John Brown Childs claims that

"Jackson himself has played a major role in promoting the 'institutional-ization' effort that would remove some of the excessive emphasis on him personally," many other Black activists around the country feel that the reverend is attempting to personalize the Rainbow Coalition by building this organization top-down, rather than bottom-up.[27] These activists feel that Jackson, as an individual, should not be the focal point in institu-tionalizing the mobilization of Black political sentiment.

Although the Vermont Rainbow Coalition has bolted the national organization, in part owing to this problem, some Black activists around the country have muted their criticism of Jesse Jackson's personal role in the interest of political unity. Abdul Alkalimat cites a concern about this: "When the left gets involved in politics, they become economists. Our objective is to create workers and people's power. The experience of socialist societies will provide something to learn from. The way the Rainbow is run and the way Jackson's campaign was run is a negation of this. So what we need to build are new organizations that provide workers and people's power like SNCC did. We need grass-roots based democratic organizations." According to Alkalimat, "this would lay the basis for electoral politics" and guarantee that electoral activism not become coopted against the interests of working-class people.[28]

Labor activist William Fletcher reflected a broader concern:

> Jackson's building of the Rainbow around himself is a major setback, but all the cards aren't in. The theme that Jackson's time is gone is being re-ported. Jackson is now being given a polite but cool reception by the Demo-cratic party. Jackson's rationale for the Rainbow structure was to have a place in the Rainbow for all Black politicians who supported him—without analyzing the basis for their support of him. With their snubbing of him, he may be forced to go back to the left. We still need to institutionalize on a national level the gains won through the Jackson campaigns.[29]

Although many Black activists greatly respect and admire Jackson, they express the opinion that too much emphasis on him as a charismatic leader poses two problems. First, the emerging movement for social change may not respond to an agenda emphasizing power but rather to Jackson's individual political needs. Second, Jackson's charisma and his relationship with the Democratic party could muffle momentum for Black independent political strategies at the national level. For example, some of these activists who worry about Jackson's personal investment reflected great concern about the presidential candidacy of Lenora Fulani and the New Alliance party in 1988. They felt that, as long as Jesse Jackson continued to muffle the realization of a political movement not tied to any major party, organizations like the New Alliance party would continue seeking to exploit an undercurrent of support for independent activism in the Black community.

For instance, Min. Louis Farrakhan received Lenora Fulani at a rally in Atlanta on July 14, 1988, the day before the opening of the Democratic party's presidential convention. Farrakhan praised Fulani for her nationalism and called for independent political activism, despite major differences in the philosophical position of both organizations regarding economic development, left-wing ideologies, and gay rights. Several Black newspaper columnists, including Tony Brown, also referred to Fulani as promoter of independent political action that the Black community should consider supporting to punish the Democratic party for ignoring the loyal Black voter.

Much distrust and considerable suspicion surround the origins and practices of the New Alliance party in several local areas, but the party acknowledged that if Jackson moved away from a growing sentiment for autonomous political activism that this party supported then the party could exploit this to its organizational advantage. Others felt that another danger might be Black movement toward the Republican party, although not necessarily reflecting support for a conservative agenda. Editorials in several Black newspapers across the country, for example, called upon the Black electorate to teach the Democratic party a lesson by supporting the Republican party. Many Black activists interviewed expressed the opinion that Black sentiment for independent political strategies is growing. But Black leadership must mold this sentiment by directing it toward a social change that challenges the political and economic status quo, without accommodating to it.

Elected officials with a history of grass-roots activism are raising issues that reflect Black disillusionment with the political and economic status quo and a growing rejection for mere access to that status quo. For example, a community control movement is budding in Roxbury, Massachusetts, spearheaded with legislation sponsored by long-time activist and State Representative Gloria Fox. Her legislative strategy includes backing a minority development fund that would give residents of Roxbury control over major development decisions and funding. Although this bill has been defeated twice, in 1986 and 1988, several grass-roots organizations in the Black community support it. While Fox is focusing on the state legislative arena, two other Black elected officials are attempting to use the city's electoral arena to increase the influence and power of neighborhood residents over real estate speculators and developers. City Councillors Bruce Bolling and Charles Yancey are promoting neighborhood empowerment.[30]

These examples all show Black elected officials seeking more than mere access or opportunities to participate in the status quo; these instances point to increasing use of the electoral arena as a platform for developing an agenda of issues that emphasizes the objective of real power, not mere access.

Other recent examples show urban grass-roots activists using the electoral arena as a political tool to challenge racial and economic hierarchies in America's cities. Taken together these disjointed instances of community activism represent the beginning of a broader political movement that challenges the goal of access and integration into the economic status quo as a response to worsening living conditions for the majority of Blacks in America. One might describe this developing political and social process by using Boston activist Mel King's typology of Black political development. He states that Black politics in the urban arena has moved and is continuing to proceed through three stages: service, organizational, and finally institution building.

The service stage reflects a politics based on the individual acceptance of Blacks by those in power; as Mel King writes regarding the Black community in Boston: "We fought to have access to the services available to others in the society, pressing to be allowed to vote, to eat and drive where we wanted, to be able to use public facilities, hotels, motels, parks and other resources which had been denied to people of color for generations."[31] From the service stage, a Black community—as was the case with Boston—can move to an organizing stage. This usually occurs as a consequence of unmet economic and social needs in the Black community under the service stage.

> In this organizing stage, we have an understanding that not only are we *deserving* of services in our own right as members of this society, but we are also capable of serving ourselves on our own terms. We were essentially powerless during the service stage, but as we moved into the organizing stage we began to assume some power in the process of working together to make institutions more responsive. Our collective voice began to be heard more clearly than our timid individual pleas for entry, and the political implications of working together began to be obvious.[32]

This stage led to the institution-building period in Boston's Black political history. But this stage never flowered completely. According to King, the final stage was stopped by the "Nixon administration's policies in housing and education, and the oil and energy crisis, inflation and a general recession, many of these fledgling institutions perished for lack of resources; others retreated to our isolated course of self-preservation which has prevented much interaction with other kindred efforts."[33] Although this framework captures much of the transformation of the Black political agenda from a liberal to a more progressive orientation, it still falls short of suggesting that emerging Black political activism may break with the liberal goals of access traditionally associated with Black politics.

I should point out that Black political activism organized around challenging the prevailing economic arrangements rather than gaining access to such arrangements has always been at least one component of Black protest in this country; it, however, only episodically commanded the allegiance of significant numbers of Blacks. An example of this was Marcus Garvey's Back to Africa Movement and his United Negro Improvement Association. The Black Power Movement in the 1960s provides yet another example. Given the demographic and social developments in the last couple of decades, Black political activism that could be described as populist and nationalist oriented will continue to grow and challenge the traditional liberal agenda. These challenges imply massive redistribution of wealth from those sectors higher on the economic ladder to those lower, and restructuring of the hierarchy of wealth in America.

White Populism and Black Activism

Two activists affiliated with the Northshore Rainbow Coalition in Massachusetts have described 1988 as "the year of Black-led populism."[34] Whites, of course, have also raised populist public policy themes and agendas. In fact, indications demonstrate that populism is "once again alive in the land and doing battle for the hearts and minds and, most especially, the guts of the Democratic party. As an emerging political force, populism has already been credited with helping the Democrats win several Senate races in 1986, thus returning the party to power."[35] White-based populism, however, is not as economically or socially threatening as populism that includes the strong support of the Black community.

Several differences emerge between a Black mass movement supporting populist public policies and white-led populist movements. First, the more efficacious challenges to the social and political status quo have emanated from the Black community, perhaps best exemplified by the civil rights movement. A white-led populist agenda is more easily controlled and coopted by interests protecting the economic and social status quo than a populist-oriented Black movement toward control of local government. The limitation of white populism was suggested in V. O. Key's classic *Southern Politics*, where he illustrated how a southern bourbon class was able to control, dilute, and direct potential populist sentiment among whites by using the specter of race and racism.[36] Decades before this classic work in political science W. E. B. Du Bois portrayed how the white working class in Europe and the United States was recruited and coopted by capitalist interests with a promise in sharing the goods and benefits resulting from "worldwide freebooting."[37]

The weakening of economic and social impact, as a consequence of racially chauvinistic populism, is functional for major economic interests in American society, as explained by political economist Larry Sawers: "The reality of capitalist life continuously generates and reproduces a fragmentation of this [working-class] unity. . . . Capitalists thus find it natural to segregate jobs by sex, discrimination against blacks in housing, or hire strikebreakers of a different race or ethnic group than that of the strikers in order to stir up racial and ethnic hatreds."[38] The existence of an ideology of white racism inhibits the economic effectiveness and impact of populism. White populists have not been spared from behaving in racist ways in dealing with Blacks.

Moreover, as political scientist Minion K. C. Morrison reminds us, "Many of the most demagogic race-baiters in southern political history were populists, who saw themselves as protectors of the poor little man who was unable to negotiate benefits from the powerful and wealthy. Nevertheless the latter did not prevent these anti-big government leaders from exhibiting great antipathy for the black poor."[39] Although a significant string in American politics, populism was weakened by racism at various points in its development, as labor historian James Green argues.[40] Racism has effectively weakened populist or reform movements in the United States.

Two other factors discourage some white interests from reforming society's racial power imbalance. Whites benefit economically in many ways from an American racial hierarchy. This includes white workers who have sought to keep Blacks out of their unions, neighborhoods, and schools. At a grass-roots level significant numbers of working-class whites seem very concerned about the job and housing competition that Black access to certain institutions may generate. Second, corporate interests co-opt potential white labor resistance; corporate leaders are less threatened by white-led populist movements than by Black-led. Big cities lack a large, alienated white underclass to the extent that it exists in many larger Black urban communities. A numerical base of alienated youth may make it easier for Black populism to develop into a form of Black radicalism that would be much more threatening to corporate and government interests.

Due to racism and ethnic chauvinism, even white-led reform movements with major potential for challenging the structure of American power and wealth have not effectively actualized this potential. In his history of white reform movements in American society Robert Allen concludes:

> It is apparent that virtually all of these movements (with certain limited exceptions) have either advocated, capitulated before, or otherwise failed to oppose racism at one or more critical junctures in their history. These predominantly white reform movements thereby aligned themselves with the racial thinking of the dominant society, even when the reforms they sought to institute appeared to demand forthright opposition to racism. Instead of opposition, the reformers all too often developed paternalistic attitudes that merely confirmed, rather than challenged, the prevailing racial ideology of white society.[41]

Thus, maintaining class relations may not have been particularly difficult in a society where its white working class has exchanged perhaps a historical and ideological role for social change in return for leisure, material possessions, and the social status deriving from racial political and economic superiority over their fellow Black citizens.

Populist literature has sometimes overlooked the impact of race and racism on the weakening of populism in the United States. Carl Boggs points out that in the current period, "the very social basis of new populism—grounded in the new middle strata of professionals, white-collar workers, intellectuals, and students—may impose limitations upon its capacity to advance counterhegemonic struggles."[42] Boggs elaborates:

> New populism, like the old left it set out to transcend, fails to articulate a concretely transformative politics, for its own social setting. . . . The reality is hard to decry: new-populist strategic preoccupation with the bourgeois public sphere forces assimilation of bourgeois forms and practices. The new populism, following the old, embellishes both an interest-group politics and a bureaucratic modus operandi beneath its rhetoric of democratization. The difficult historical task of overturning the multiple forms of domination, so essential to reclaiming the democratic heritage for the left, is replaced by a more "realistic" agenda oriented toward the "control" regulation, and rationalization of these same forms.[43]

Although the role of racism is a major factor in producing these weaknesses in white working-class populism and middle-class reform, Boggs barely mentions or discusses it. Yet this factor is crucial in understanding how these movements succumb so quickly to the forces they are attempting to overcome and control.

In Werner Sombert's earlier, and now classic, lengthy essay, "Why Socialism Has Failed In The United States," one finds the same weakness: a failure to even acknowledge the existence of racial dynamics and hierarchy in American society and its significance.[44] Here, the author laments the failure of socialism to become a strong force in this country, but he neglects to discuss at all racism's role in thwarting the class consciousness of white workers. The inability of white reform and populist movements historically to confront and help resolve racial hierarchy in America meant that these same movements could not challenge effectively those groups with major economic and political power in the country.

Some social change movements focused on gaining access to the prevailing economic and political system rather than fundamentally changing that system. Thus, the reforms that white populists pushed should have generated some coalitions with Blacks based on common agendas. Again, this did not occur because white populists and reformers failed to challenge the nation's persistent racial hierarchy. But despite Blacks' disillusionment regarding the moral weaknesses of white populists and reformers, the goals and subsequent legislation adopted via the civil rights movement still focused on access and equal protection of the laws for Blacks, rather than a restructuring of society.

What has been referred to as the civil rights movement emerged, generally speaking, during the early 1940s.[45] It was dominated by a series of events characterized by the legal battles of the NAACP and a focus on desegregation in education and public facilities, especially after the two *Brown* v. *Board of Education* decisions. This movement was also marked by its particular leadership's southern orientation, a multiracial front, and, of course, passage of the first civil rights legislation since the 1870s.

After World War II the civil rights movement also considerably internationalized the struggle for equality in America. Following earlier efforts by Marcus Garvey, W. E. B. Du Bois, George Padmore, and Paul Robeson, many Blacks began to approach and organize support for the civil rights struggle in America within a worldwide context. In fact, more than twenty years before Malcolm X advocated using the United Nations in the Black struggle for equality in America, a petition on this matter was presented to this same body in 1941.[46] The international view of America's struggle for Black equality and political rights gained momentum under the leadership of thinkers like Kwame Nkrumah, Frantz Fanon, Ella Baker, Malcolm X, Martin Luther King, Jr., Angela Davis, and others. The goal of integration ultimately gave way to the notion of power during this period. This shift was evident in the positions of not only some integrationists, but also some nationalists. As Paulette Pierce writes, "The need for black power led Malcolm during 1964 and 1965 to significantly alter the traditional meaning of black nationalism and subsequently led King during his final years to radicalize his vision of the civil rights movement. Both understood that questions of power and effective use of the ballot would have to become the focus of agitation and organization."[47]

By the mid-1960s frustration regarding lack of progress for Black social and economic aspirations resulted in hundreds of racial riots. Anthony Downs reported that between 1964 and 1968 local enforcement agencies required outside assistance in 239 major racial riots.[48] The riots occurred concomitantly with the radicalization of certain elements within the civil rights movement. Although underlying causes of the riots were similar in many cities, in general the eruptions were organizationally disjointed. But this should not lead one to underestimate the social significance of the urban eruptions. Thus, Ira Katznelson and Mark Kesselman argue: "The racial violence in New York in 1964, Watts in 1965, Newark and Detroit in 1967, and in hundreds of other cities during the decade, was profoundly political. The targets of attack by blacks, including the police and white-owned property, were visible symbols of public order and a capitalist social structure."[49] The riots did point to patterns in the continuing problems of racism in housing, employment, education, and police services. As these authors suggest, the riots in effect questioned the legitimacy of American political and economic institutions by a range of sectors in the Black community.

Generally occurring after passage of major civil rights legislation these uprisings exemplified the alienation and disillusionment in Black and Latino communities still unaddressed by legislation. As is pointed out poignantly by one historian, "On 6 August [1965] Congress passed and the President signed the Voting Rights Act, and on 11 August the terrible riot in Watts initiated four summers of violent racial explosions all over the country." C. Vann Woodward continues, "Thus within one week a historic movement reached a peak of achievement and optimism and immediately confronted the beginning of a period of challenge and reaction that called in question some of the greatest hopes and most important assumptions."[50] The stage referred to as Black power was both a logical extension and an inevitable counter-reaction to the established leadership of the civil rights movement and its integrationist orientation.

The Beginning of New Politics and Goals

According to Ronald Walters, the emergence of Black Power included two major facets by the early 1970s:

> The first was the Black Nationalist/Pan Africanist Movement which had all but taken the place of the former Civil Rights Movement by the end of the 1960s, and which emphasized pro-Black, politically independent strategies in various arenas of action. . . . At the same time, in the early 1970s, there

arose a body of Black elected officials, (BEOs) largely as a result of the increased use of the vote in the Black community, made possible both by the
Voting Rights Act of 1965 and the ambitions of northern Black politicians
who understood the mass mobilization potential of the new Black-oriented
movement.[51]

This development not only raised different concepts than civil rights, but
it also generated major differences among those calling for Black power.
As one observer has written,

> The call for Black Power is creating—had to create—splits within the move-
> ment. These splits are of two main kinds. The first is between the Black
> Power advocates and the civil rights advocates. The civil rights advocates,
> sponsored, supported, and dependent upon the white power structure, are
> committed to integrate blacks into the white structure without any serious
> changes in that structure. In essence, they are simply asking to be given the
> same rights which whites have had and blacks have been denied. By equal-
> ity they mean just that and no more: being equal to white Americans.[52]

Among Black power advocates James Boggs described "idealists" or
"romanticists." These individuals and the organizations they represented
did not present strategies in the pursuit of political power; instead, they
concentrated on separation or a "militant" strand of integrationist goals
and programs. The latter, in fact, were at times merely dissimilar in style
to advocates in the civil rights movement. Many integrationists moved
toward this strand of Black power by the late 1960s and early 1970s.
Some Black power advocates rejected not only the traditional civil rights
agenda but also a romanticized and quite commercialized Black power,
which, according to Robert Allen, merely involved African cultural trappings becoming "a badge to be worn rather than an experience to be
shared. African robes, dashikis, dresses, and sandals have become standard equipment not only for the well-dressed black militant, but even for
middle-class hipsters who have gone Afro."[53] But leaders like Malcolm X
and Stokely Carmichael, Bobby Seal and Angela Davis argued during this
period that civil rights legislation without an anticapitalist version of
Black power could not adequately respond to the immediate and long-
range socioeconomic needs of the majority of Blacks and Latinos living in
America's urban ghettos.

The civil rights movement failed to challenge effectively an economic
hierarchy that helped spur a resurgence of Black nationalism on the local
urban level in the mid- and late 1960s. Growing Black nationalist sentiment forced local government and the corporate sector to acknowledge
existence of a community with latent interests different than those of

groups with power and wealth and at the same time not so easily accommodating with the status quo. Ira Katznelson has written:

> The holistic world view of black nationalism produced demands that in two respects were radically different from the usual articulation of urban issues. First, it did not respect traditional boundaries between issues. School, welfare, police and housing issues were treated together, as aspects of a total condition. As a result, authorities had to manage conflict that was much more intense and less susceptible to piecemeal solutions than they had been accustomed to. Second, these policy areas were the objects of demands for a radical redistribution of resources and opportunities. At issue, was not simply a set of divisible benefits of patronage and services; rather, such questions, which had been at the core of modern urban politics since the antebellum period, were joined to questions of governance, and together they were connected to a larger analysis of black-white relations that demanded a fundamental transformation of the social structure.[54]

The Black challenge to the legitimacy of American institutions was also described by Jewell Bellush and Stephen David in their analysis of political conflict in New York City in the late 1960s:

> The black community, in growing numbers, is turning inward and rejecting the legitimacy of institutions and norms associated with the white world. Increasingly, we are becoming aware that we are confronted with a crisis of authority. Increasingly, institutions associated with the white world are finding it difficult to obtain the allegiance of black Americans through consent, and are, more and more often, being forced to resort to coercion in order to rule.[55]

The establishment partially responded to this kind of challenge by incorporating some Black leaders and activists in the antipoverty structures supported by new federal programs and monies.

Peter Bachrach and Morton S. Baratz studied Black urban activism in Baltimore. They reported:

> Federal programs and funds have been the main means directly and indirectly, by which the black power [advocates] have gained a foothold in Baltimore's political system. The programs and money have helped directly by enforcing the administrative guidelines on citizen participation in planning and distributing services. They have helped indirectly in that the poor are increasingly being enlisted to support different local welfare agencies in their competition for a larger share of the citizen's available funds. . . .
> Federal grants for programs have helped to raise the expectations of a larger and growing percentage of the poverty population, thereby causing them to develop a set of interests, and to make use of the political system in furthering their interests.[56]

Although Black activists may have been allowed to "further their interests," such action was only possible within a framework of access to—not changing—political and economic institutions. The antipoverty programs were functional for quelling the rise in anger and threats to the legitimacy of institutional arrangements. These structures provided not only resources that Blacks could use for electoral mobilization, but they also supplied a base upon which Blacks could pursue electoral aspirations. But the agenda of these aspirants usually did not go beyond the call to substitute white elected officials with Black ones.

Continuing Racial Hierarchy

Antipoverty programs coupled with the participatory victories of the civil rights movement helped generate major electoral victories for Blacks. Consequently for the first time in American history Black mayors were elected in major cities—Detroit, Gary, and Newark. Blacks were also elected to the Congress and to various state legislatures. When compared to the lack of Black representation in the 1940s and 1950s, these victories did seem like a "revolution" of sorts, at least as far as numbers are concerned. I should point out, however, that this kind of "revolution" is not as sanguine after closer examination, even if one focuses only on numbers. And other than numbers, the fundamental social and economic relations between Blacks and powerful interest groups have not changed.

A study by Lawrence J. Hanks reported that twenty-one of eighty-seven counties with a majority Black population in the South do not have Blacks on their governing body. In fifty-one of these counties there are no Black law enforcement officials, and in thirty-eight there are no Blacks on the school board.[57] According to the Joint Center for Political Studies in Washington, D.C., of 276 Black mayors in 1985 only 27 were in cities of 50,000 or more persons, and 158 were mayors of cities of cities with less than 2,500 persons.[58] It was also reported that in no state in this country does the proportion of Black elected officials even come near the proportion of voting-age Blacks in the total voting-age statewide population. In 1985 10 percent of all elected officials in Louisiana were Black; this state had the highest proportion of Black elected officials of any state. But even here, this was far lower than the 26 percent of the voting-age population that is Black. The states with the next highest proportion of Black elected officials were South Carolina (9.6 percent), Alabama (9.0 percent), and Mississippi (8.4 percent). But the proportion of Blacks out of the entire voting-age population for these same states are, respectively, 27.7 percent, 23.0 percent, and 31.3 percent. Hanks reported that the gap is smallest in Virginia, where Blacks made up 18.9 percent of the total population in 1980 and the Black proportion of total officials was 4.1 percent.[59]

Aside from the issue of numbers, a review of Black political history shows that while social, economic, and political conditions for Blacks may change temporarily from period to period, the power and social relationships between whites and Blacks are much more difficult to alter; the former are continually the dominant and the latter, the subdominant. The essential status of neither the former nor latter has been transformed significantly. Black individuals with requisite educational and social skills, however, may periodically overcome the economic and racial barriers. America's racial hierarchy has proven effective and enduring in maintaining dominant and subdominant social relations between organized white interests and masses of Black people.

Legal scholar Derrick Bell and political economist Manning Marable suggest that an ideological hegemony of racism exists in America; although certain features of race relations may change, the fundamental nature of a racial hierarchy remains intact.[60] Political scientist Reginald Gilliam states that this feature of racism is reflected in Black residential patterns and how they are molded and constrained. Residential patterns of Blacks are basically uniform across the urban landscape and consistent over time.[61]

An important characteristic of Black politics—and one that reflects a tenet of pluralist analysis—is that the struggle for equal political and economic participation and social acceptance has historically concentrated on gaining access to white-dominated institutions, via a sort of "piece of the pie" approach; merely winning election or appointment to governmental office has taken precedence over challenging the ownership and organization of wealth and power as it influences the quality of life for masses of Blacks. Harold Cruse argues that this explains the failure of Black political victories—despite the excitement of Black and white liberals over such victories—to be transformed into social and economic gains for Blacks.

> In the game of electoral politics, black leadership has no issues of political leverage, only numerical voting strength. However, this voting strength has never been predicated in a political power based grounded in tangible economic administrative, cultural, or social policy issues with the viability of forcefully influencing public policy. Hence, merely winning public office became the one and only tangible good for black political leaders. . . . With

rare exceptions, they brought nothing with them into political office that bore the least resemblance to a black economic, political, and cultural program that meant much to anybody, friend or foe, black or white, beyond the politically mundane business as usual stance of the liberal consensus.[62]

Wilbur C. Rich presented this in a slightly different way. He believes that too often Blacks have allowed the development of a legitimate "Black agenda" to be superseded by the agendas of powerful white liberal interest groups. William E. Nelson suggests that as a result of patronage and cooptation this kind of development led in recent years to the political emasculation of the Black independent "21st District Democratic Caucus" in Cleveland.[63] The incentives for discouraging activism directed at the development of an independent Black agenda usually include promise of access, trickle-down benefits for Blacks, and threats of financial nonsupport or defunding by white public and private interests.

Successful Black forays into the electoral arena have concentrated on the goal of winning and replacing white politicians; Black politicians have simply disregarded the need to develop a base of power that could challenge powerful and wealthy interest groups and structural arrangements that sustain the influence of such groups. The development of a Black power base, coupled with a collective Black public policy agenda, would allow Black elected officials to offer and pursue more effective public policies formulated in response to the group needs of Black communities.

Unlike experiences of white ethnic groups, Blacks have had to respond to a racial and economic hierarchy in which they were on the bottom with little group movement in terms of improved economic status; furthermore, unlike white ethnics, Blacks have continually had to resist efforts at reducing even mere access into white-dominated social and economic institutions. Both the ballot and education have proven consistently effective for white ethnics, but that is not necessarily true for Blacks. Arguments suggesting that Blacks and European ethnic groups could be analyzed by ignoring the existence of racial hierarchy are dismissed by Stanley Lieberson with his term, "Great Non-Sequitur."[64] Lieberson contends that the economic and social conditions faced by early European immigrant groups may have seemed similar to those conditions faced by Blacks but it does not follow that the two groups can be compared with the same approach or model. Blacks faced certain kinds of conditions that immigrant groups did not experience at all. Earlier immigrant groups were able to obtain the ballot without major controversy, relatively speaking, and then use it effectively in some areas; this is not the case for Blacks. In fact, the controversial history of Black political enfranchisement and the apparent ineffectiveness of the ballot in some areas has led to an important debate in the Black community regarding the usefulness of the ballot and the associated costs necessary of obtaining and using it.

Tim Black, an activist in Chicago, for instance, believes that even Harold Washington was falling into the trap of responding to an electoral/organization agenda, rather than pursuing a political agenda of Black empowerment after his first term. Tim Black suggests that some Black support for Harold Washington eroded as the mayor attempted to extend his base outside the Black community. This activist felt that Washington's movement reflected, not any Machiavellian intent on his part, but rather an idiosyncracy of electoral activism.[65]

Similarly, some activists have argued that, despite recent victories, electoral activism within the current political and economic structural context of American cities is ineffective in responding to the needs of Blacks, unlike the case with white ethnic groups. One long-time Chicago activist wrote about the political lessons to be noted at time of Mayor Washington's death: "The main illusion fostered by electoral politics is to identify election to political office, or connections with elected officials, with social or political power. For the left this illusion is deadly, since our political aims can be achieved only by masses mobilized around a determination to make fundamental changes."[66] This observation is repeated by Abdul Alkalimat:

> The critical question in Black Chicago politics is whether there is a likelihood of more militant and radical political leadership. It is a critical question because with this leadership can come ideology, organization, and a coherent political line designed to deal with the main problems people face in the city. There are many radicals in the city today who are having second thoughts about how much commitment they made to electoral politics. They, too, face the challenge of developing a new leadership with a new game plan.[67]

At a Roundtable Meeting of the National Conference of Black Political Scientists focusing on the 1988 Jackson presidential campaign, William E. Nelson underscored the need not only to coordinate Black electoral efforts with political mobilization in other areas but also to include protest supportive of goals that would politically and culturally strengthen the Black community.[68] This joint effort is important to withstand the lure of electoral activism to defuse other kinds of mobilization. Cornel West, a Black theological scholar and activist, reiterated the obstacle that electoral activism under the influence of liberalism—that is, the Democratic party—may pose to mass Black mobilization and protest. He argues that electoral mobilization under the framework of the Democratic party apparatus produces "paralysis and powerlessness among black voters."[69]

This point is handled differently from a liberal and conservative perspective by William Julius Wilson in his *The Truly Disadvantaged* and Abigail M. Thernstrom in her *Whose Votes Count?: Affirmative Action and Minority Voting Rights*. Arguing that a broad-based liberal coalition is necessary for the well-being of Blacks, Wilson thus acknowledges the importance of politics, but he also discourages Black attempts to use the electoral arena or protest to influence the public agenda in terms of race-specific items. He calls for a political coalition to overcome the resources and influence amassed by the neoconservatives and suggests nevertheless that Blacks should maintain themselves in a sort of junior partner status within this coalition so as not to alienate potentially supportive whites. In fact, he actually hopes that Blacks will not present demands in ways that alienate the larger public—presumably those white, liberal interest groups that he believes are fundamental to adopting public policy favorable to Blacks. Wilson does point out that considerable gains have been realized in the area of political participation; his evidence includes increased voter registration rates and the wave of Black mayors and elected officials in the last twenty years. But all in all, he is proposing that Blacks minimize electoral activism that is not in the interest of broader, white-controlled liberal coalitions.

Thernstrom, however, is even disturbed by Blacks insisting and mobilizing for guaranteed footholds in the electoral system. She argues instead that diluted Black political representation, in coalition with whites, would provide far more Black political influence; "pressure for such interracial inter-ethnic coalitions lessens with the existence of single-member districts drawn to maximize minority officeholding."[70] It is clear that both liberals and conservatives resist and discourage the pursuit of independent Black power and the call for policies and a politics that might be defined as too "Black-oriented" by white interests.

In many instances the white American left has generally shied away from electoral activism as a potential tool of social change.[71] Recognizing the dialectic relationship between electoral activism and protest, Frances F. Piven and Richard Cloward nevertheless describe how the former can inhibit the latter:

> The very availability of the vote, and of the social ritual of the periodic election, is like a magnet attracting and channeling popular political impulses. Other forms of collective action, and especially defiant collective action, are discredited precisely because voting and electioneering presumably are available as the normative ways to act on political discontents. . . . The electoral system tends to limit the goals of popular politics. . . . Involve-

ment in electoral politics exposes people to the fragmenting influences associated with electioneering, and can thus weaken the solidarities that
undergird political movements. . . . Electoral political institutions generate
seductions that distract people from any kind of oppositional politics.[72]

Electoral activism is thus seductive; it diverts attention and energy away
from social change that would improve working conditions for poor
people, the working class, and Blacks.

Clearly Black political participation, electoral gains, and the disparate
economic benefits gained over the last couple of decades represent a
significant development for racial relations in the United States. But the
social situation for Blacks is not as sanguine as Ronnie Moore and Marvin
Rich suggest: "The evidence indicates that Black officials can bring about
real change that improves the lives of their constituents in such important
areas as jobs, housing, food, health care, day-care centers, education and
job-training."[73] One major study reported that Black elected officials make
a difference because they "influence the number of black appointments to
government positions, and the level of those appointments."[74] Despite
these gains, greater levels of Black political participation have not slowed
the growth of a young, impoverished, and relatively large sector of persons
in the Black community.[75] Black political participation, including significant accomplishments such as capturing elected or appointed positions,
has occurred at the same time that masses of Black citizens are experiencing
an increasing economic and social deterioration in this nation's major
cities. This deterioration can be documented in the areas of poverty,
unemployment, housing, health, and education. Thus, Robert Smith's
query regarding the incorporation of some Black interests into American
pluralist arrangements must be answered in the negative. As he noted,
"The question then, is, can the black lobby—representing the gradual
incorporation of blacks at the middle—level of power—fundamentally
alter the terrible conditions of the black underclass?"[76]

The very rules and arrangements of the urban political game may not
allow Blacks, even if they control the electoral levers of power, to respond
effectively to the socioeconomic needs of large Black communities. At
least four theoretical weaknesses with the urban political game inhibit
liberal policy makers from effectively answering the deterioration of
Black life conditions.

Economist Charles E. Lindbloom has pointed to a serious weakness
of the American political economy: attempts to solve problems by public
policy are "excessively fragmented."[77] From a technical point of view this
is both a strength and a weakness. Strength derives from such fragmentation, a way of equalizing the influence of different interests. But the weakness develops because it is relatively difficult to develop coherent public

policies aimed at systemwide socioeconomic or educational problems owing to uncoordinated multilayers of government and bureaucracy.

Lindbloom describes another major weakness: the "problem posed by the privileges that businessmen need as a condition of their performance."[78] Simply, much public policy is based on making the city conducive to business investments. Developing a socioeconomic and cultural environment that business finds comfortable, however, may contribute to other serious racial and economic problems. Attempts to attract downtown developers, at the expense of quality at local schools and neighborhoods, clearly exemplify the problem. Local government may be generally reluctant to demand what business considers to be too many fiscal concessions. Local politicians fear that an overly aggressive populist-oriented government and high taxes may drive businesses to other cities and regions of the country. Lindbloom reminds us that this is a "continuing, inescapable problem in public policy-making from which no market-oriented system can escape for a year, month, day, or hour."[79]

According to Lindbloom a third problem is associated with the macropolitical arrangements of major cities: the inability of resulting public policy to solve growing problems of unemployment, crime, housing, and education in Black and some white communities. In some parts of every major city these problems are becoming worse and seemingly less affected by whatever kind of public policies emerge from local government. In addition to Lindbloom's three aspects is a fourth problem: the inability of decision makers to develop comprehensive public policy as contrasted with "specialized" or "technocratic" public policy. For the most part public policy in one area, such as public education, is developed and pursued in such a narrow and specialized way that productive linkages with public policy in other arenas, such as housing or health, are overlooked. But creative linkages across policy areas may produce more efficient and effective public policy than "specialized" public policy. Comprehensive and effective public policy, however, bumps into entrenched bureaucracy, lethargic government, and often recalcitrant business leaders.

The continuing presence of a large and growing Black impoverished sector is urban America's most significant development. John R. Howard points out:

> If the formal political system proves to be an ineffective instrument for meliorating Black ills, then existing racial tensions will become more intense. As the resentment and aggression of the urban Black underclass grows, the fear and hostility of whites, perceiving threats to their physical well-being and to the established social order, will mount. The capacity of

the system in its present form to survive such tensions is doubtful. . . . The stakes, then, in urban Black politics are fairly high, and the policy and program outcomes of Black leadership at the municipal level are still in doubt.[80]

Sidney M. Wilhelm has raised an important, related question: "The socioeconomic disparities between Black and White coexist with tremendous opportunity for equal rights. The impediments of segregation that haunted Blacks for over a century have, especially since the fifties, tumbled. . . . [But how] "is it possible for Blacks, on the one hand, to be granted rights and privileges once the sole prerogative of White people and, on the other hand, to find their living standards substantially lower than whites?"[81] C. Vann Woodward, among others, has also pointed to the juxtaposition of political progress and economic stagnation or retrogression in the Black community:

> Political gains speak somewhat more directly than economic gains to the question of integration. Here there should be no question about the direct responsibility of old civil rights movements for most of the accumulated gains. The Voting Rights Act of 1965, the government measures taken to enforce it, and the hard work of organizations and individuals account for the massive registration of Negro voters that made a breakthrough possible.

He qualifies his attribution of success to the old civil rights movement by adding,

> All these gains, of course, still left blacks as a whole far behind economic parity with whites and left millions of blacks in poverty. There were, moreover, signs that the gains of the 1960s were eroding in the 1970s. While the ratio of black to white unemployment had improved briefly, it had returned to the two-to-one level by 1973, and the number of blacks below the poverty line had risen to 33 percent as compared with 9 percent of whites.[82]

It is both fact and paradox that at the same time Blacks are realizing political gains social and economic life conditions have generally worsened for this group of American citizens. During the 1980s Black citizens suffered setbacks of some of the political and economic gains realized in the late 1960s and early 1970s. By the 1980s segregation in housing and public schools in major American cities had intensified, and unemployment in Black communities had reached its highest level in forty years. Poverty among Blacks increased during this period; the worsening socioeconomic conditions of Blacks in America reflects a development yet to be arrested by significant Black political victories.

As a result of this urban scenario more than one social observer has asked whether the very survival of Blacks in America is now at stake as a result of continuing and intensifying conditions of poverty and alienation. Wilhelm asked: "'What is to be done with 'our' Black minority'? has been the question haunting White America for three and one-half centuries. The question is even more compelling now that increasing numbers of Blacks become economically dispensable."[83] Another scholar observes: "As American society, representing a national entity of just over two hundred years, approaches the year 2000, the social and economic conditions of American blacks as a group reflect disturbing indications that they might become, racially and ethnically, an endangered species. Black social, economic, political, and cultural survival is not guaranteed."[84] For many in Black communities across urban America social and economic trends portend yet worsening living conditions.

Neoconservatives contend that a liberal-oriented politics has failed Blacks in urban America. But are the reasons for this the cultural or group attributes of Blacks or government's incapacity and inability to solve social pathology? Or is the failure owing to an ineffective political activism based on access to the status quo rather than on power to change significantly the status quo? The neoconservative indictment is useful insofar as the weaknesses of a political activism based on the goals and framework of liberal public policy and its accompanying politics are highlighted. As long as Black politics is organized and pursued within the traditional liberal agenda, the social and economic needs of the Black community cannot be satisfied, regardless of how successful and effective this politics might be for individuals in this community. This realization is motivating many Blacks in the 1990s to explore a different agenda and an alternative politics.

CHAPTER FOUR

Race and the Failure of Political Managerialism

And so we shall have to do more than register and more than vote; we shall have to create leaders who embody virtues we can respect, who have moral and ethical principles we can applaud. . . . We will have to demand high standards and give consistent, loyal support to those who merit it. We will have to be a reliable constituency for those who prove themselves to be committed political warriors in our behalf. When our movement has partisan political personalities whose unity with their people is unshakable and whose independence is genuine, they will be treated in white political councils with the respect those who embody such power deserve.

Martin Luther King, Jr., *Where Do We Go From Here: Chaos or Community?* (1968)

Blacks represent a significant portion of the population whose social, economic, and cultural conditions uniformly reflect a subdominant group status. This was the conclusion of two major studies focusing on the status of Blacks in American society.[1] Given this historical and continuing subdominant status, we can speak generally of the state of "social relations" between Blacks and whites in America. Social relations not only has objective components—such as the socioeconomic characteristics of a group—but also subjective elements.[2] When Blacks and poor people assert behavior that threatens existing social relations, liberal policy advocates call for improvement in the objective living conditions of the rebellious sectors. Conservative policy

111

advocates usually seek to punish or physically limit behavior considered antisocial, that is, threatening to contemporary social relations between Blacks and the poor and powerful white-dominated interests.

The subjective components of social relations between Blacks and powerful whites, however, are not changed qualitatively within either the liberal or the conservative policy paradigms. The racial and economic hierarchies of society are basically maintained under both broad approaches. Change in social relations between the masses of Blacks and whites controlling and representing dominant interests requires rearranging the hierarchy of power and wealth in American society. Very few Black political victories or events, electoral or otherwise, have substantially changed social relations between Blacks and whites.

Protest and activism in the 1950s and 1960s produced significant gains in voting as well as increased election of Blacks to public office; this includes, of course, the mayorships of the nation's biggest cities. Despite the fact that electoral gains of Blacks are still relatively small given the proportion of Blacks in the total population and in some local jurisdictions, the particular electoral breakthroughs have been significant. By the mid-1960s Blacks started a trend of controlling the electoral structures in some major American cities. This trend continued in 1990, and, despite setbacks, it seems that it will continue.

Increases in the Black population made it possible for this group to take over urban political structures. Furthermore, a review of voter registration and turnout data show that whites no longer have the numerical advantage that they enjoyed over Blacks just a few years ago. In the 1984 presidential election, for example, the percentages of reported voter registration and turnout for whites and Blacks were very close: whites were registered at 68.3 percent, and Blacks at 66.3 percent; the turnout rates were 61.4 percent for whites, and 55.8 percent for Blacks, a gap of only 5.6 percentage points.[3] These trends were also evident in midterm elections during the 1980s.

Unlike the case for white voters the percentage of Black voters increased at the national level. Registration and turnout rates of white voters have scarcely changed singe the mid-1970s, while Black voter registration and turnout has increased significantly. According to one report,

> The registration and turnout rates among whites in 1980 were almost exactly what they were in 1976. And in 1984 they were almost exactly what they were in 1980. Among Blacks, however, registration and turnout were dramatically higher in 1984, even more so in the North than in the South. Registration rose ten percentage points among Northern blacks in 1984, and nine percentage points among Southern blacks. Turnout increased eight

percentage points among Northern blacks, six percentage points among Southern blacks.[4]

Thus, the potential role and impact of the Black vote has increased significantly in national elections.

The kinds of gains described here are expected to continue nationally for the next decade. The U.S. Bureau of the Census projected the total Black population of voting age at 20.4 million by November 1988. The growth of the potential Black electorate is considerable in some states: for example, in Mississippi Blacks comprise 31 percent of the total electorate, in Alabama 23 percent, and in North Carolina 20 percent.[5] These gains have led some to argue that Blacks can now compete for status and rewards as have other groups, confirming the elastic but stable nature of America's pluralist arrangements. Sociologist Thomas F. Pettigrew argued sometime ago that the year 1967 "witnessed the beginning of a new era in American politics, the beginning of significant black entry into the political decision-making of urban America."[6] Similarly, political scientist John R. Howard writes:

> The enfranchisement of blacks, dramatically accelerated as a result of the civil rights movement of the 1960's, and the passage of the Voting Rights Act is seen as adding blacks to those groups which compete electorally for status and rewards within American society. And just as other groups, farmers, labor, business groups, Jews, and consumer groups, are seen as getting something, although never all that they want, so blacks, within the framework of pluralist theory, should realize certain of their objectives and not others. Just as the system is seen to 'work' for other groups, from a pluralist perspective, it should also 'work' for blacks.[7]

This kind of enfranchisement resulted in the election of Black mayors, congressional representatives, and a host of state and local officials.

In many ways such electoral victories have proven important. Black elected officials, according to one study, do make a difference. Black elected officials "influence the formulation and implementation of policies, . . . sensitize their white associates not only by overt proposals but simply by their presence, . . . provide a link between government and the black citizenry, . . . [and] establish a sense of legitimacy and normalcy about blacks holding office."[8] At the national level the growing influence of the Black vote was witnessed in the defeat of Ronald Reagan's nomination of Robert Bork to the U.S. Supreme Court. Burt Neuborne, former legal director of the American Civil Liberties Union, commented:

> Sixteen of the 17 white Democratic Senators from the states of the old Confederacy voted against Bork. . . . The negative votes reflected a mastery of

basic mathematics. In the years following the enactment of the Voting Rights Act, black participation in the voting process in the South underwent a virtual revolution. Today, no Democratic candidate can hope to win state-wide office in most of the Southern states without the enthusiastic support of black voters. In other words, a vote for Bork would have been political suicide for a southern Democratic Senator.[9]

Despite this kind of political breakthrough, however, the capability of addressing Black social and economic needs through urban electoral processes today is not as optimistic as these statements might suggest. Hopeful but perhaps a bit more realistic, is Lucius J. Barker, who bases his analysis on participation in the 1984 presidential campaign; he writes that "the nature of electoral politics suggests the need to form coalitions that can win popular majority support. Although these coalitions are difficult to achieve when a candidate is attempting to bring about fundamental, and therefore controversial, policy change, it does not mean that such efforts should not be attempted. What it does suggest is the difficulty of achieving them through electoral politics."[10] By quickly reviewing worsening urban problems for vast sectors of the Black community, enthusiasm and expectations for even the Black mayors elected in major cities must be tempered. Many Black mayors have decided to meet the needs of poor and working-class Blacks and whites by creating and giving priority to establishing favorable climates for corporate America; they thus reflect the progrowth strategy discussed in earlier chapters. Political scientist William E. Nelson describes this kind of mayoral orientation:

> Upon ascending to the mayorship of Philadelphia, Wilson Goode announced that his top priority was not jobs, health care, and education for Blacks, but persuading the Eagles not to move the franchise from the city. Much of the forward movement achieved by Washington in Chicago has been undermined by the reactionary policies of the Sawyer administration. Andrew Young has championed a policy of transforming Atlanta into an international city while neglecting the human needs of his local Black constituents. Sidney Bathelemy in New Orleans has moved away from the confrontation politics of the Morial administration and attempted to assuage the anxieties of whites by de-emphasizing programming directed toward the Black poor in New Orleans. Thomas Barnes, Hatcher's successor in Gary, has followed a similar course. He now openly boasts about his warm and friendly relations with the Lake County Machine. In Cleveland the impact of the progressive face of Black politics has been muted by the emergence of a Black machine concerned exclusively with the extension of material benefits to politically active middle-class Blacks.[11]

This progrowth orientation dominates many big city mayors, regardless of the official's race or ethnicity.

In Philadelphia, as is suggested Thaddeus P. Mathis, a political scientist and national official of the National Black Independent Political party in 1981, a general disillusionment and loss of electoral efficacy has followed Mayor Goode's inability to produce a higher quality of living standards for all citizens. Mathis writes,

> A number of political objectives have been achieved and a new Black leadership elite has been created. In spite of these successes, however, many argue that little progress has been made in improving the quality of life for the masses of Black Philadelphians. This lack of social and economic progress has caused some to question the efficacy of Black political leadership in this period and the mode of political participation which brought them to power.[12]

This disillusionment also characterizes a retrospection of Newark's more than twenty-year rule under two Black mayors. Kirk E. Harris observes,

> Newark's economic development to date ostensibly supports corporate interests, the interests of middle class suburbanites, and offers some entrepreneurial and government employment possibilities for a select segment of African-American middle class community. However, few if any economic benefits "trickle down" to the economically disadvantaged African-American community residing in the central city. Thus, it appears that the corporate model of economic development . . . has offered little promise for change, and in this case it operates to further exacerbate the economic difficulties of a large segment of Newark's African-American community.[13]

The first Black mayor of New York City also faces a dilemma that could diminish enthusiasm for his leadership. Despite the critical role of Black grass-roots support in his election, Mayor Dinkins has been pressured to pursue economic development in ways that would not disrupt the business community. Journalist Sam Roberts reports: "with the city facing projected deficits and what analysts say is a cooling economy, some members of the business community have expressed concern that Mr. Dinkins, by temperament and ideology, may deviate from the fiscal conservatism that generally marked the Koch administration's successful efforts to restore the city's credit in the securities markets."[14] Mayor Dinkins has given some early indications that he does not intend to challenge aggressively the interests of the business community in New York City. Journalist Barbara Day reports that many activists worked for Dinkins as "the candidate who would alter the city's skewed priorities and promote economic justice for the working class poor. But after six months, a growing number of African-Americans find Dinkins' priorities little different than those of his predecessor."[15]

Despite significant electoral victories for Blacks, these victories have not yet been translated into improvements in living conditions for the poorer and working-class sectors of this community. Poverty data from the U.S. Bureau of the Census between 1970 and 1980 for the fifty largest central cities in America shows social and economic conditions improving for whites, while they deteriorate for Blacks. For example, as reported in one major newspaper, during the 1980s the Black poor, as a percentage of the total population, increased from 6.7 percent to 8.3 percent; and the Black poor as a percentage of the total poverty population increased from 44.3 percent to 46.8 percent in 1980. The number of Black poor living in poverty areas increased from 2,138,470 in 1970 to 2,621,058 in 1980, an increase of more than 22.6 percent.[16]

Interestingly, most Black mayors' victories demonstrate overwhelmingly Black voter support, but mayoral responses to economic development favoring the middle-class and corporate sectors have taken precedence over the interests of this community. Nelson reasons that this may reflect the poitical socialization of the Black mayors. He writes that some mayors of the 1980s and 1990s were neither steeped nor trained in the civil rights battlefields; the mayors came to power more as managers rather than tacticians skilled in mass mobilization.[17] Activist Gwen Patton touches upon this point when she notes that the 1980s' wave of Black elected officials differs from the first wave of officials: "In the South, the first round of elected officials came from the ranks of Blacks involved in the NAACP and other civil rights organizations. We didn't see the Black middle class taking over electoral politics. They vote, but they don't run for office—they look for managerial positions."[18]

In a different way, C. Ashford Baker points to the backgrounds of Black mayors as a factor in governing. Baker writes that it is precisely because "the recognized leaders of the Black community are so steeped in the civil right politics of the fifties and sixties that they have been unable to move beyond its confines into the power politics of the eighties."[19] Thus, she sees a civil rights background as a disadvantage in terms of explaining the failures of Black electoral politics. Mathis believes the mayoral leadership styles and patterns are very telling; they reflect systemic factors leading to the emergence of elected Black mayors. Mathis writes:

> Confronted by the intensity of the mass struggle during the 1960s, the State was forced to concede, if only to limited extent, to the demands of Black people for democratic representation. However, the forces of capital, working through the established political party system, primarily the Democratic Party, set the terms for this concession. . . . The masses of Black people, in

spite of the intensity of their movement, did not have the political apparatus, resources, or expertise to take full advantage of these concessions.
Therefore, they were only able to support for election those individuals in
the Black community who had the ambition, resources, and/or expertise to
make the most of these new political opportunities; or to support those persons selected by the established parties to "represent" the Black community.
In either case, the Black community itself played little more than a minimal,
though necessary, role in the actual determination of the composition of
Black electoral leadership.[20]

Reflecting broad systemic forces, therefore, the election of Black mayors
did not necessarily result in a strata of individuals who would raise issues
generally directed to the empowerment of Blacks vis-à-vis private wealth
and power.

Political participation engenders some responsiveness to a group's
political and economic needs, but this relationship is not clear as far as
Black political participation and electoral gains are concerned. This question is not new. About two decades ago on August 9, 1972, at a union
gathering in Florida activist Jesse Jackson first challenged civil rights and
labor organizations.

To use the power we have to put economic rights the number one point on
the human rights agenda of the nation. We have the right to go to almost
any school in America, but we can't pay the tuition. We have the right to
move into almost any neighborhood in America, but we can't pay the house
note. . . . So now we find ourselves in an era where we have the right to win
in a pool where there is no water. . . . The struggle for economic well-
being, for the general working population, is the highest priority for this
decade.[21]

For most Blacks, despite the election and presence of Black governmental
officials, today the challenge remains the same.

Because electoral victories have failed to translate into change in the
status of Black poor and working-class sectors, and because urban demography points to growth, Black political activism, reflecting the needs
of these sectors, is beginning to challenge long-held systemic values and
institutional arrangements. The joining of social protest and electoral
activism in the Black community, the introduction of new Black actors
into the electoral arena, as well as deteriorating social, economic, and
educational life conditions for the vast majority of Blacks in this country, offer new fuel to Black political activism. These developments can
become the basis for a renewed "crisis of legitimacy" in major cities in
America. Such a crisis would pit Black activists who win electoral platforms from which to launch political agendas against the public policies

that reflect the interests of the dominant groups in the urban pluralist arena.

Another potential development is the crystallization of an ideological split within the Black community; this would allow two faces of Black activism to emerge.[22] The philosophical underpinning of the traditional face of Black activism is access to the status quo, but the progressive face of Black activism focuses on "community control." The former relies on the electoral arena for access, and the latter merges protest, mass mobilization, and electoral activism. Access calls for some sharing in the benefits accruing from the particular distribution of wealth; Black activism that can be described as progressive proposes a more radical redistribution of wealth and challenges those processes that characterize its accumulation and management. Although the traditional face of Black activism emphasizes coalition, the progressive face further acknowledges that such coalitions do not reflect the interests of the poor and working class if the empowerment of grass-roots sectors is absent or weak. Liberal whites form the critical reference group for Blacks seeking access into the status quo, but poor and working-class sectors in the Black community are given priority under the progressive face of activism. Ultimately, then, political incorporation into an economic order reflects the traditional face of Black activism, while progressive Black activism seeks to structurally rearrange that economic order.

The campaigns of Andrew Young for mayor of Atlanta, Tom Bradley for mayor of Los Angeles, and L. Douglas Wilder for governor of Virginia reflect traditional black politics. All these campaigns were built upon seeking access into the political and economic status quo, making the corporate sector understand that it must move over or pull up extra chairs in the boardroom. But other Black political campaigns demonstrate a different kind of activism. The local campaigns of Harold Washington in Chicago and Mel King in Boston reflect a Black politics that challenged the status quo of power and wealth rather than merely seeking access to that power, whether public or private. Both presidential campaigns of Jesse Jackson challenge basic values and outlooks underpinning American power and wealth. In these four particular campaigns we also note the participation of new Black electoral actors. Their presence was illustrated powerfully in one instance: Min. Louis Farrakhan's call to the Nation of Islam for Blacks to register in 1984 to vote for Jackson. This plea was especially noteworthy because during its more than fifty-year history the Nation of Islam has argued for Black noninvolvement in the electoral arena. New actors also included Chicago street gangs who participated in the mayoral campaign activities of Harold Washington. This was not the first time that Chicago gangs participated actively in this city's politics; gangs joined Martin Luther King, Jr., in some civil rights demonstrations and planned collaborative activities with the Black Panthers. But gang members in the 1980s participated in voter registration activities during the first Washington campaign.[23]

Black political activism, fueled by demographic changes and greater political participation from alienated sectors in the Black community, has the capacity today, to present systemic challenges to groups with power and money. In the 1980s the presence of new Black actors and voters in the electoral arena partially allows for this possibility; many new Black voters have a heightened sense of group consciousness, largely developed while alienated from the electoral arena. The participation of voters in this sector is significant "because they represent the groups that in previous times were the least likely to register to vote: the young, the poor, women, and the elderly. Today they are beginning to believe, like many of their middle-class brethren, that they can make a difference. This is especially true when the choices presented seem to attack their ethnic pride or group identity or when opposing forces are seen as hostile to black interests."[24] This sector has the potential to present the system with a crisis of legitimacy, even as it is mobilized within the electoral arena.

Sheila Collins states that such a crisis arises during a period "when the institutions through which the public is socialized to accept a given socioeconomic order no longer work to ensure mass loyalty to the system."[25] If the political behavior of large numbers of people exhibits this kind of challenge, then it threatens corporate leadership because it undermines the legitimacy of the political and social framework that guides the accumulation, management, and distribution of wealth.

Dominant political and social arrangements in urban America have been challenged previously. The civil rights movement basically represented a "reformist" challenge from the Black middle-class sectors, but poor and working-class Blacks in American cities sustained the urban riots that followed, and the Black consciousness movement in the mid-1960s more systemically confronted the establishment. Black consciousness questioned the values and policy parameters underpinning Robert Salisbury's "ruling executive coalition" of urban America.[26] As Ira Katznelson writes, the urban crisis and turmoil of the 1960s challenged the legitimacy of the urban polity:

> What kind of crisis was the urban crisis of the 1960s and early 1970s? Systematic academic work has conceptualized the "crisis" in many ways: as a crisis of confidence, a crisis of service delivery, and a fiscal crisis (among the more conventional ideas). These approaches all capture partial truths, but

they miss the larger point that the most unsettling, and promising, feature of the unruly urban scene was the extent to which the traditional American urban class system was challenged. As such, the urban crisis was a crisis of social control and, more powerfully, a crisis of American class and group relations.[27]

Thus systemic, rather than reformist, challenges that may be reemerging in the 1980s and 1990s first materialized during the urban crisis of the 1960s.

One study described how Detroit's dominant liberal coalition in the 1960s kept Black activism reformist and confined it politically:

> As important as the liberal coalition had been and would still be to the election of blacks to political office in Detroit, the growth, expansion, and increasing politicalization of the black community were rapidly becoming the dominant factors in the black community's political development. Liberal coalition politics of necessity placed ideological constraints on independent black political development. Not unlike other ethnic and nationality groups in Detroit and other cities, blacks in Detroit and elsewhere were straining at the political leash for their turn to lead big city politics. It would only be a matter of time before liberal coalition politics would collide with the movement for increased black political independence.[28]

The Black community's systemic challenges, reemerging more powerfully in the electoral arena twenty years later, indicate the continuing ineffectiveness of governmental responses to economic and political problems facing Blacks in urban America. The liberal coalition and agenda has not effectively integrated, either economically or socially, the majority of Blacks into white America.

Traditional Black electoral activism has functioned to manage social tensions arising from the different structural interests between masses of poor Blacks and powerful white groups. During the civil rights movement the federal government attempted to substitute voter registration with direct action and protest as a way to control "the tactical direction of the civil rights movement." One writer reports that "many recognized the advantages of voter registration activities, but others saw voter registration as an attempt by the Kennedy Administration to divert the energy of the civil rights movement from direct action."[29] The key social functions and goals of allowing the capture of electoral or appointive positions, therefore, may not only cushion the impact of depressed economic conditions in the Black community, but also supply a means by which to manage social conflict and prevent latent tensions between Blacks and powerful groups. Keeping these tensions from erupting is important for maintaining the social relations that support the economic status quo.

Whereas in the past this potential structural confrontation has been managed effectively, relatively speaking, in the 1990s urban demography and continuing economic depression for the majority of Blacks portend continuing, and perhaps increasing, tensions between Blacks and powerful white interests.

Political Managerialism and Activism

Historically, a major function of America's big city mayors was to provide "political managerialism" beneficial to local and powerful economic interests. With the assistance of their political organizations—and Black liaisons—big city mayors of earlier periods had to perform these duties in order to stay in office. They had to create and maintain a healthy environment for the interests of economically influential groups; but this is a far more difficult task today. The office of mayor had to not only manage the demands of labor upon industry, including the demands of highly organized public-sector workers, but also maintain the allegiance of politically volatile, white working-class groups, using either City Hall patronage or sometimes the subtle threat of Black and Latino "invasions" during electoral campaigns. Increasingly, since the 1960s, mayors of major cities must now politically contain increasing numbers of Blacks and Latinos whose social and economic interests seem unaffected favorably by traditional economic frameworks. A social function of political leadership of big cities was, and continues to be, maintaining a socially stable environment in which banking, real estate, and the academic, commercial, and media conglomerates can realize political and economic goals.

If local government, for whatever reasons, cannot maintain stable political and social environments, then corporate leadership seeks to take over the public setting of a city's agenda and direction. For example, the establishment of the "New Detroit Committee," formed after the racial riots of July 1967, testified to the local government's inability either to manage Blacks, potential dissent on the part of or to respond effectively to the crisis of legitimation generated by Black activism. As Dan Georgakas and Marvin Surkin pointed out, "When Detroit burned in July 1967 in the most widespread and costly of hundreds of urban rebellions throughout the United States, the men who rule America knew they had to take immediate action to end the general crisis. In Detroit, they formed a self-appointed blue ribbon New Detroit Committee."[30] This committee sought to respond to the city's political crisis by replacing "inner city squalor with the sleek new architecture of modern office buildings, banks, condominiums, hotels, convention attractions, and a host of related enterprises. The program was designed to stimulate economic development, create jobs, and provide social stability and confidence for a troubled city."[31] The committee, however, failed to control Black political activism, hence its ineffectiveness was guaranteed.

More than twenty years later, in places like Detroit and other major cities, it is still difficult for local government to respond effectively to the socioeconomic needs of Blacks. This gives credibility to Black activists who raise fundamental, rather than reformist, issues regarding the city's economic order. Thus, while the fiscal failures of local government give rise to technocractic questions about how best to govern in the Black community, they also reopen ideological discussions about governmental authority and legitimacy, the status and future of race in America. A study by Eric Lichten points out that fiscal crisis includes more than just technocratic considerations; it also raises systemic issues:

> For some, fiscal crisis is merely an aggravated case of fiscal 'strain,' in which the main problem is resource management. According to this view, predominant in mainstream political science policy analysis, fiscal strain results from declining resources, which bring about an increase in interest group politics. In a sense, the interest groups scurry after the meagre morsels of revenues. The task of a city administration is to reassert its formal authority . . . perhaps by centralizing the decision-making process and thereby gaining the ability to manage retrenchment. Here, the budgetary process seems to be a technical one, requiring technocratic solutions. . . . The managerial perspective that is dominant in the private sector is brought to bear on the public sector and on public policy.[32]

Barbara Ferman's comparative study of San Francisco and Boston reminds the reader that fiscal crisis is linked very closely to questions of ideology and authority:

> The dilemma of gaining and maintaining political authority has worsened because of structural and political changes at the local and national levels. The decline—in many cases, elimination—of local political parties has removed an important source of mayoral campaign support, patronage, insulation, and conflict management. . . . But other structural reforms have weakened the mayor's ability to deliver. Civil service reforms removed still another source of patronage and, more important, curtailed the mayor's control.[33]

Although this analysis is basically correct, it is not complete. In evaluating why cities are working or not working race must be approached as a major factor; furthermore, the reaction of the Black community to fiscal crisis and governmental response is a critical issue for understanding the direction of urban government in the late twentieth century. To understand why cities are becoming ungovernable and less politically effective in the brokerage of divergent social interests it is necessary to explain the potential impact and effects of Black activism. As the Black agenda moves from one that focuses on access to another involving shared power, highly politicized cities with sizable Black populations become less governable and manageable. As far as political managerialism of the American city is concerned, this is a new development.

Available economic resources made it easier for white ethnic bosses to play effectively the role of "political managers" in the nineteenth and early twentieth centuries. The machine in the pre-World II period provided a political and social nexus that joined lower-, middle-, and upper-class interests. Political scientist Lyle W. Dorsett states: "It is often assumed that the bosses had only ethnic minority and working class support. They handed out jobs, food, and clothing to the underprivileged, and in return received loyal support on election day. But this is only part of the picture. To be sure, every successful city boss had support from the lower economic class, but he had to have support from part of the business community and from middle and upper class groups as well."[34] Thus, in earlier periods the boss could manage conflict arising from the city's competitive social and economic interests for two main reasons. First, formal or informal segregation reduced the competitiveness of Blacks as another group seeking benefits from the system; second, that expandable system could accommodate the conflicting interests of both poor, working-class whites and the business community. As C. V. Hamilton explains, however, the system had more elasticity in previous periods, and therefore political managerialism within a given political and economic framework was relatively effective.[35]

The major social and political function of the urban machine was to integrate poor and working-class ethnics into the prevailing economic hierarchy of the big city. Similarly, this was the major function of the sanctioned Black submachines that arose in cities like Chicago, New York, Philadelphia, and Memphis. As Edward Greer states, "Just as the machine institutionalizes the subordination of the working class to the hegemonic political forces of the society, the Black sub-machine institutionalizes the subordination of the Black community to the dominant political power."[36] Prior to the World War II, urban machine politics largely neutralized and passified potential Black political clout. According to Martin Kilson, "In the years 1900–1940 the goal of white-dominated city machines toward Negroes was to neutralize and thus minimize the political clout of the Negro urban community and not infrequently even to distort that community's social and political modernization."[37] This

Black "depowerization" could be attributed in part to the federal government and its New Deal policies.

In effect, the Roosevelt administration made available to Blacks various benefits in return for accepting token status within the Democratic party and the emerging liberal power arrangements. Black leadership joined this new coalition without infusing it with an economic and political base. Harold Cruse explains this phenomenon: "By virtue of its proxy federal roles in the public sector, the New Deal scattered its limited social reform benefits moving blacks in such fashion that the nascent leadership was transformed into a new class of spokesmen and spokeswomen whose function was to beseech the administrators of white power establishments in the public sector for fair treatment in behalf of their black constituents."[38] Thus, some Black leaders sought access—a piece of the Democratic party pie—rather than real political and economic power. Although Blacks received some jobs, this limited access lacked the power to overthrow the segregationist social order of the 1930s and 1940s. Such an overthrow required group power that Blacks did not yet have, despite the access of a few individual Blacks who served in the New Deal.

Toward Structural and Institutional Changes

The relationship described by Cruse was revitalized and repeated in the 1960s. Many Blacks became increasingly dissatisfied with the limited social reform benefits of the New Deal. In the period between the advent of the New Deal and the apex of the civil rights movement American cities witnessed explosive growth in both the Black population and social and economic problems that the local economy could not accommodate without strong federal intervention.

Both Black power and community control movements signaled a politically aggressive posture for Blacks, something city-based political machines were forced to accommodate given the number and incidence of Black insurgency. Urban governments' failure to neutralize this insurgency represented a major political and social threat to the nation's stability and social order.[39] Black insurgency could be neither controlled nor managed by local government or political bosses without assistance from the corporate sectors and major foundations. One study reported: "Since 1967, hundreds of millions of dollars have been invested by foundations, corporations, and government in 'community development corporations' which have as one of their objectives the development of leadership in minority communities. . . . From these programs came models of responsible leadership, who demonstrate that the system works. . . . This is also part of the story of the transformation of 'Black power' into Black capital-ism."[40] Corporate America, then, was much involved in determining the direction of Black activism in the 1960s.

The insurgency of the 1960s led to decisive Black electoral victories. A "Blackening" of city machines and governmental structures forced some change in the traditional political relationship between the Black community and the corporate sector. The white business sector was, and continues to be, resistant to Black political takeover of major cities. But once the local electoral takeover by Blacks is complete, the powerful sector of the business community generally seeks collaboration (consider Detroit, Los Angeles, Philadelphia, and especially Atlanta). At least two factors are important in understanding collaboration between these two arenas.

First, despite Black electoral control, the business community retains control of many kinds of fiscal resources that it uses to maintain a favor-able business environment, regardless of the political rhetoric from city hall. The business sector can also influence the implementation of public policy and ensure that business interests determine the general orienta-tion and direction of governmental decisions. Clarence Stone illustrated such business involvement in his case study of making and implementing public policy in Atlanta. He showed how community groups could win political battles regarding the adoption of favorable urban renewal public policy or even vetoing unfavorable policies. But ultimately, the process of implementation reflected the interests of the big business community. Stone confirmed the fears of those skeptical of the electoral activism's potential to produce long-term change beneficial to the powerless in that city. Although neighborhood groups could win concessions at the policy-making stage, via electoral victories, they could also lose their gains during the stage of policy implementation; at that point the rules of the game, as well as the natural workings of bureaucracy tend to favor busi-ness interests. Thus, the system has a natural bias in favor of business interests that, despite the result of elections by the public, "is not easily altered."[41]

Second, after initial periods of social and racial tension both the business community and white ethnics become more comfortable with Black political rule because they find that their interests and social posi-tions are not threatened. Political scientist Peter Eisinger found this typi-cal in urban and ethnic political transitions.[42] This was also a finding of sociologist Floyd Hunter in his revisit of Atlanta's power structure after the election of a Black administration.[43] Thus, if the structure of wealth and power remains intact and fundamentally unthreatened, then Black political victories of access, even if resisted initially, are generally tolerated and accommodated.

Despite this collaboration and accommodation, however, major political problems remain. Because the latent interests of Blacks are still structurally and even culturally juxtaposed with prevailing economic and social arrangements, the particular political development of Blacks must still somehow be controlled or managed by those benefiting from these arrangements. This concern is critical to those with power and wealth because the tensions in urban America, born of competing social and economic interests, are greater and much more complex in the 1990s than earlier in the century. As evidence of how little conditions have actually improved, more than two decades ago one radical activist group made several observations about Blacks' potential for systemic challenges; these thoughts remain valid and timely: "Blacks . . . are the ones who have been least integrated into the American way of life. They have benefited least from its material progress and been corrupted least by its abundance. They are therefore in the best position to question its mode of operation and reject its fundamental values."[44] The economic disparities between the middle class and the poor are much greater today, especially in cities experiencing a renaissance of corporate development. A *Boston Globe* special report, "America's Cities: Revival and Despair," noted:

> The revival of American cities over the past two decades has created thousands of new jobs, new opportunities and new neighborhoods. But it has also opened up class cleavages among blacks and whites that few predicted in the late 1960s. Cities have prospered. But the poverty rate in them has increased. More and more blacks are moving up into the middle class and into college and the professions. But more and more have also become trapped in a vice of violence and diminished opportunity.[45]

Racial and economic tensions can no longer be managed as effectively as in earlier periods. Another writer argues in a similar vein:

> During the twentieth century, capitalism in the United States has demonstrated a significant capacity for adaptation and reform, with numerous serious abuses successfully curbed or eliminated altogether. . . . The democratic upsurge of the 1960s and 1970s, although bringing some improvement in the treatment of the sick and aged, and in other areas, has not been graciously accepted or conducive to social harmony; it has aroused further conflict over the excessive largess to the underserving poor, the unreasonable tax burdens on the productive classes, and over-regulation of business.[46]

Given national economic constraints, it is difficult for the American city of the 1990s to serve its Black and poor citizens in meeting basic social and educational needs.

Political managerialism as a governing approach that accepts the prevailing economic arrangements and seeks to assuage the systemic tensions arising from this status quo is no longer adequate either to meet certain needs of population groups or to maintain political and racial stability. The political and social framework under which local government operates limits its effectiveness. One might suggest raiding the domain of the private economy in order to enhance the capacity of local government, but this is especially difficult. In the 1970s local government could turn readily to Washington, D.C. for federal assistance, but that is no longer the case. The federal government, retreating from the local arena, has forced the curtailment of local services. This situation is exacerbated by local anti-tax revolts as is reflected in public referenda, such as Proposition 2 1/2 in Massachusetts and Proposition 13 in California; white middle-class citizens have eagerly supported fewer local services as a way to maintain low taxes. Local government has responded to the federal government's reduced presence and tax revolts by cutting or eliminating social, health, and educational services that benefit primarily the working class and the poor. Because urban economies can no longer absorb the poor and the working-class to the extent possible when manufacturing opportunities were more prevalent, the tensions between rich and poor, Black and white, have heightened with tax revolts and reductions in federal social expenditures.

Political managerialism maintains social and racial stability by managing access into the economic status quo. But some Black activists reject this approach. At the local level they argue that the struggle for equality and full political participation must now begin to focus on structural change, not mere access or patronage. The activists who espouse change in the structural and social relations of Blacks and powerful interest groups are also spending more time in the electoral arena. Before this development the electoral arena was dominated by Blacks who sought access into corporate America, not those who had concluded that corporate policies represented a major part of the problem. The synthesis between social activism and electoral participation emerged as a partial response to (1) the failures of both approaches when operating independent of each other and (2) the successful example of Ronald Reagan who used the electoral arena for a specific social, albeit reactionary, agenda.

Sheila Collins summarizes one political effect of Reagan's success:

The election of Ronald Reagan in 1980 shocked many left activists into discovering the dialectical relationship between social movements and electoral institutions. As leaders of social movements saw their demonstrations ignored by an increasingly conservative Congress, and as blacks discovered that the black mayors they had elected were unable to advance their interests, discussions of the need for a new wedding between movement-building and electoral politics assumed a fresh urgency.[47]

This possibility has led many left and nationalist Black activists, who previously spurned electoral activism, to begin experimenting with electoral processes for challenging the fundamental social and economic relations between Blacks and whites. Many Black activists not only perceived the electoral arena as inherently biased against those interests without wealth or power, they also realized that, in general, elected officials—whether Black or white—reflected these biases.[48]

Despite continual suspicion of electoral politics, many citizens interested in social change are turning to the electoral arena for mobilization. This newly emerging Black political consciousness, which is not simply more registered voters or higher turnout levels, is having a profound impact on the electoral arena as far as issues and Black mobilization are concerned. The change involves much more than the "new breeders" described by Joyce Gelb in an earlier study of Black politics in New York City. She reported that the "difference between the 'new breeder' and the 'old timer' is a function of age, background and involvement with the community."[49] And more recently another observer, finding evidence of a "new breed" of Black politicians, reported this group to be "young, highly educated, and politically pragmatic." Stuart Rothenberg has stated that the "new breed" Black politician "believes that his constituents ultimately will be better served by growth in the private sector, not by government social welfare programs."[50] The author suggests a generational change in the attitudes of Black politicians; once bent on more favorable governmental programs, they now prefer to focus on the private sector's trickle-down benefits. These assessments may be true, but it does not explain the emergence of yet another "new breed" of Black politicians and activists who focus on neither trickle-down private-sector benefits nor governmental social welfare; rather they seek independent power molded partially through electoral activism. This last group of new breeders representing what was described earlier as the progressive face of Black activism increases the logistical difficulties and capacity of political managerialism.

The Traditional Face of Black Politics

As already mentioned, one face of Black politics can be described as traditional; it maintains economic arrangements and social power that have characterized major cities since World War II. During the succeeding four decades the significant actors in American local politics were private-interest groups, the federal government, and mayors and their machines. In the late 1950s the public service unions were added to this urban ruling "executive coalition."

During the 1960s the Black thrust for political participation in the big cities was reflected partially in the community control movement and the call for Black power. Although the post-World War II urban executive coalition acceded some concessions to Blacks—and other citizens' groups inspired by the Black community—an institutionalization of membership into the executive coalition did not occur. In fact, according to Clarence Stone, the foundation of this coalition rested as much on a passive lower-class constituency as it did on the decline of traditional politics. Therefore, a "political vacuum that could easily be filled by executive leadership" evolved.[51] Neither local government nor the more powerful members of the ruling coalition enabled Blacks or the poor to join in partnership with the powerful; instead temporary political arrangements and reforms were instituted to appease Blacks both politically and socially.

Until the urban ruling executive coalitions, tied to powerful interest groups in the private sector, are successfully challenged politically, the socioeconomic needs of the Black community will not be satisfactorily resolved. Grass-roots activists in the Black community continue to explore the possibilities of electoral activism as a tactic for political power—not merely influence, or access. What is sought is a change in power relationships between Blacks and some members of the executive coalition—that is, a change in the junior status of Blacks—that will allow Black leaders to offer public policy alternatives that may more effectively change social relations between Blacks and whites. Public policies that reflect a shift in urban social and economic priorities, policies more favorable to Black interests, will be necessary for Black leadership to maintain a relatively high level of political mobilization among grass-roots sectors. To meet the social needs of neighborhoods, Black leaders must either increase governmental revenues or force the corporate sector to share in the social costs of investing in and managing a major city. This kind of shift can only take place if a strong and independent mayor can win election and then reelection—a scenario that indeed requires a high level of political mobilization from the electorate that has not benefited from traditional liberal or conservative urban policies.

Some examples of the kinds of public policies needed to respond substantively to the needs of the Black community include linkage, plant-closing legislation, fiscal support for public schooling, limits on real estate speculation, and investment in the infrastructure needs of neighbor-hoods. These public policies cannot be successfully pursued without some degree of political and economic restructuring in the American city.

The Progressive Face

The emerging progressive face of Black politics focuses on different approaches to politics and public policies in ways that challenge existing arrangements of power and its subsequent social relations between Blacks and whites. Specific electoral activities under the two faces of Black poli-tics may be similar in some cases. Both, for example, symbolically call for mass political participation, the use of the franchise as a means of holding government accountable, and the mobilization of voter support for candi-dates of choice. Although the thrust of traditional political activism is to secure benefits from those holding wealth and power in this country, the alternative is to challenge political and economic relationships that keep Blacks as a group in subdominant status.

The two faces of Black politics emerge vividly in a city like Atlanta. This city, touted as a mecca for the black middle-class, has been under Black electoral control since the mayoralty of Maynard Jackson in 1973. Atlanta is known for its many prominent Black-owned businesses. But at the same time, census data shows this city to be one of the poorest in America. Like other cities, the growing poverty of Atlanta starkly con-trasts with the new high risers in the downtown section.[52] As one Atlanta columnist wrote, "Tucked away behind gleaming skyscrapers and great universities, there is the 'other Atlanta.' . . . It is an Atlanta where thou-sands of children are starving. . . . It is an Atlanta of the homeless and the poorly housed . . . where 50,000 families live in public housing."[53] At-lanta and many other cities share two realities, one for whites and a handful of upwardly mobile Blacks, and the other for the majority of Blacks, poor, and the working class.

Black activists can choose one of two general responses to this social situation. On the one hand, they can accept the traditional economic development paradigms of liberal policy or "Yankee capitalism" (to use once again Kenneth Dolbeare's term). Another variant is "cowboy capitalism" as explained earlier. Both variants raise a central question: What is required to enhance economic opportunities for major busi-nesses? Presumably beneficial tax and economic policies for downtown businesses result in expanding jobs and attracting more businesses to the city. On the other hand, Black activists can focus on direct services for the poor, the working class, and the neighborhoods; thereby they enhance the economic productivity of those on the bottom. Part of this rationalization involves a bottom-up, rather than a trickle-down, dynamic. That is, greater economic security for Blacks and people at a neighborhood level produce two social benefits. First, urban society is strengthened because more citizens are productive; second, high social and health costs associated with depressed living conditions are reduced. Moreover, as more jobs at decent wages are made available to Black and Latino youth, problems related to crime and drugs might become more manageable.

These two approaches faced Mayor Andrew Young in Atlanta on at least one occasion; he chose minority and female business enterprise as a greater priority over residential relocation after displacement. On January 4, 1988, this mayor, with the support of several city council representatives, vetoed a resolution that would have reserved $700,000 for the relocation of eighty-four households near Hartsfield International Airport. Mayor Young's explained his veto: minority business enterprise was more significant for economic growth than the concerns of poor and working-class displaced families. But the elected representatives of the displaced households charged that only middle-and upper-income Blacks benefit from this kind of economic growth, and at the expense of a "class [of people] that has been subjected to chronic displacement for the convenience of the rest of us."54 Mayor Young has consistently chosen the interests of the wealthy and upper middle-class over the poor and working-class sectors. In his first few months in office he supported a sales tax to reduce property taxes although the former is more harmful to the pocketbooks of the poor and the working class. He has sided with business interests over neighborhood interests. To illustrate the choice that this mayor, a former leading activist in the civil rights movement, has made one need only repeat his proclamation: "I've made my peace with capitalism. . . . There's nothing better for coping with sin. It rewards people for working hard."55

Philadelphia activist Joyce Brooks gives another example of the two faces of Black politics. She describes the response of her city's Black city council representatives to adopt "linkage" legislation:

> The focus in 1986 was to establish linkage legislation to get a fee to go into a trust fund controlled by the grassroots—money for commercial strip development, housing, job development and childcare. This got to the point of linkage legislation being introduced. . . . It never got out of committee because the city council is totally big business oriented—including its Black members. There [were] 7 Black city councilors out of 17; thirteen democrats

and 4 republicans. The linkage bill was introduced by a Puerto Rican coun-
cilor and received no support from Black councilors. The Black community
was shocked at the stand of the Black councilors.[56]

In Chicago, activist Abdul Alkalimat argues that the two faces of
Black political activism involve class interests, as has been suggested
above. But he adds that the politics of the Black middle class are becoming more oppressive toward the social well-being of the Black poor and
working class:

> During Harold Washington's tenure in office his Chief of Police and the
> head of the Housing Authority came up with a plan for social control
> which was developed further under Sawyer and now implemented under
> Daley. The general view was that the housing projects are full of degene-
> rates. So under this plan cops make raids without search warrants on entire
> buildings and look for drugs, guns, unproperly supervised children, etc.
> They block off the building and give I.D.'s to all the people who enter or
> leave—a "pass system" as in South Africa. Initially they even had rules that
> residents in these projects could not have a spontaneous overnight guest—
> but that rule was dropped because of the outcry against it. The Black mid-
> dle class sees this treatment as a good thing.[57]

Alkalimat's observation offers credence to the idea that Blacks who have
established themselves politically and professionally are unwilling to
jeopardize their newly acquired power by supporting the interests of the
Black poor and working-class.

Philosophical and political conflict between the two faces of Black
political activism is also evident at the national level. Mayor Andrew
Young's response to the presidential candidacy of Jesse Jackson exemplifies this conflict. The *Atlanta Voice* severely criticized Mayor Young
for not supporting Jesse Jackson in 1988. In a leading story after "Super
Tuesday" the editors implied that elected officials, such as the mayor, are
very much "out of touch with constituents" and "should be prepared to
meet strong opposition in the next elections."[58] But the more important
point to note here is the stark difference between the approaches, reflected
in the Jackson campaign and the negative response of Andrew Young, as
well as other prominent Black politicians like Detroit Mayor Coleman
Young. The critical issues were neither the personal jealousies nor the
generational rivalries as suggested by some in the media; rather the situation represented a clash of two political orientations in the Black community.

These issues lead to several important questions: Can Black community activism be organized as a tool to change the nature of social
relations between Blacks and whites in the United States? And if social

change is possible, and some Black leaders can be effective in presenting alternative public policies, then how will powerful interests in the private sector react to Black demands for a share in power, rather than the traditional call for access? How will the traditional face of Black political activism interact with corporate leadership in urban America and the more progressive face representing poor and working-class interests? To obtain an understanding of some of these queries, the role of corporate America in the urban political arena, and its posture toward Black activism must be examined.

CHAPTER FIVE

Black Empowerment and the Corporate Sector

> In dealing with blacks, the typical New York white power group . . . frequently circumvents the politically tested and viable sectors of the black community and its leadership, and instead deals with a marginal leadership sector. . . . The power structure thereby creates within the black community a faction beholden to it.
>
> Martin Kilson, *Dissent* (Fall 1987)

Most cities mentioned in this study feature a strong corporate presence accompanied by involvement in local politics. According to social analyst Fiona Williams, participation with local politics is generally linked to three broad functions related to long-range business health: (1) accumulation, or "maintaining conditions favourable for the accumulation of capital"; (2) reproduction, or "ensuring a healthy, educated and housed workforce, but at the same time disciplining and controlling through that provision"; and (3) legitimation, or "maintaining political stability, social harmony and social control."[1] How these three functions are pursued in the United States and the effectiveness of strategies aimed at pursuing these functions or goals are questions directly related to political and social relationships between the corporate sector and Black urban communities.

Several cities where the Black population is significant and growing also serve as headquarters for many major corporations. Roger Friedland claims that local headquarters reflect corporate influence:

The presence of such headquarters indicates the local presence of corporate elites—many of whom are resident in the central city—the presence of local plant investment within the city, and the presence of a major corporate office complex, whose continued presence and growth is of vital importance to the central city economy. Thus, the presence of national corporate headquarters indicated the organizational basis of both corporate participational and systemic power.[2]

It is interesting that many cities with evidence of Black empowerment activism have also experienced a revitalization of corporate activity and growth in the last couple of decades. Although a few path-breaking studies have examined the relationship between urban-based corporate leadership and emerging Black leaders and organizations that may challenge long-standing political arrangements, for the most part corporate activity in molding Black activism in urban America has not been studied extensively.

But note the observation of G. William Domhoff:

Most sectors of the American economy are dominated by a relative handful of large corporations. These corporations, in turn, are linked in a variety of ways to create a corporate community. At an economic level, the ties within the corporate community are manifested in ownership of common stock . . . as well as in joint ventures . . . and in the common sources of bank loans that most corporations share. At a more sociological level, the corporate community is joined together by the use of the same legal, accounting and consulting firms. . . . Then, too, the large corporations come together as a business community because they share the same values and goals in particular, the profit motive. Finally, and not least, the common goals of the corporations lead them to have common enemies in the labor movement and middle-class reformers, which gives them a further sense of a shared identity.[3]

It is noteworthy that the author identifies only the labor movement and middle-class reformers as "common enemies." In a case study of urban politics and the conflict between the citizenry and the corporate sector in Boston and San Francisco, another author similarly ignores the impact or role of Black political activism during the 1960s and 1970s.[4]

Several other scholars likewise ignore or overlook the impact of Black activism on the political and economic responses of the American city's corporate sector. Another writer describes how the corporate sector, particularly the transnationals, have been able to pursue strategies that hurt the economic interests of the poor and working class because of the mobility of capital; he then asks, "Can the transnationals continue to move capital destructively from high- to low-wage places with impunity? What counterstrategy options are open to the working class and its allies for saving their jobs, cities and homes?"[5] But alas, the possibility and significance of Black-led challenges to corporate leadership is also overlooked here. This oversight may attest to either a perceived powerlessness attributed to Blacks or perhaps even a notion that as Black political influence materializes and grows it is quickly funnelled into support and legitimization for the corporate community's agenda. The possibilities of Black-oriented and Black-led political and economic counterstrategies to corporate leadership have not been fully considered in the germane literature.

Norman I. Fainstein and Susan S. Fainstein do acknowledge the political role Blacks have played in challenging corporate leadership, but they adopt a chauvinistic position about this issue: "Race is an essentially divisive base on which to build a political movement. The identification of the movement for community control with black power delegitimized that movement among white people . . . rather than providing a common bond for equally powerless black and white communities."[6] Harold Baron's study, however, overcomes this kind of racial defensiveness and suggests instead that as Blacks assert themselves politically and electorally in some major cities there may emerge a "Second Atlanta Compromise" where a political truce is declared between Black political power and white private and corporate economic power.[7] This statement, although incomplete in its mention of but one possible philosophical and ideological possibility akin to Booker T. Washington's "Atlanta Compromise," at least implies that Black political activism can have a major impact on the American city and its relationship to corporate power.

The writings and observations of some political observers suggest or propose that Black-led and Black-defined political mobilization directed against the interests of corporate leadership remain insignificant owing to the inability of poor and working-class whites to overcome their own racial fears and insecurities. These authors, consequently, neither explore fully the possibilities or the conceptual parameters of Black political insurgency against the corporate sector today nor do they consider the range of possible political responses from this sector. The likelihood of eruption of systemic conflict between exclusively white or white-dominated corporate leadership in the American city and Black political insurgency is not discussed in many studies. But given the Black insurgency of the 1960s and political developments in the Black community of the 1990s, this neglect is unjustified.

Although there are significant populations of color in the larger cities of some European nations the American experience is unlike that of urban social movements in other Western countries. According to Katznelson, Gille, and Weir, this is a major point in understanding the significance of race in providing a basis for social change in the United States:

> The urban social movements which have been an important element of political conflict throughout the West in the past quarter century has been based on various group characteristics. Most have had class as the main, or as a leading element. Even where urban movements have been wholly divorced from the concerns of workers as labor, they have articulated demands in a rhetoric of class, typically as members of a working-class community, and in so doing, have broadened the meaning of class and class struggle. Not so in the U.S., where race, not class, had defined the most important insurgent movements.[8]

An example of the impact of Black political revolt is the legitimation crisis during the 1960s. As one study points out,

> Continued efforts at clearing even larger amounts of land were brought to a standstill during the middle sixties and early seventies, when urban riots and political movements attached the hegemony of the city officials and downtown business interests who comprised the "pro-growth" coalition. Urban minorities thus limited the economic potential and threatened the political control of core locations; urban areas became the site of a legitimation crisis.[9]

White populism, as pointed out in an earlier chapter, does not have the potential to generate a legitimation crisis to the extent that is possible with Black revolt. The possibility of major or key challenges to the social, cultural, and economic order, in other words, will come from Blacks—if at all—rather than whites.[10]

Several campaigns and issues in cities such as Chicago, Boston, and Milwaukee have focused on gaining power for the Black community rather than mere access to decision makers. Concomitantly, some of these cities have been used by corporate America to establish major management operations. Reflections of political activism aimed toward empowering the Black community rather than seeking access to decision makers include the Harold Washington campaigns and administration in Chicago. In Milwaukee the call for an autonomous Black school district could also be characterized as a "power" rather than an "access" issue. Peter Murrell, a community activist who helped lead this campaign, described this issue: "We felt that our best chance for success was to take this issue to the state level for a legislatively mandated special school district which would not be under the control of the local school board, but rather would be a model for community involvement and control."[11]

This campaign was aimed at increasing the control that Blacks at a grass-roots level have over public schooling; they did not demand access into an integrated school setting. In Boston, the Mandela proposal sought to empower Blacks by incorporating the predominantly Black community of Roxbury. Mel King's 1979 and 1983 mayoral campaigns were also based on changing the city power structure favorably for Blacks by challenging downtown business interests to defer to neighborhood concerns and needs. This is different than the direction chosen by Black mayors such as Atlanta's Andrew Young, Los Angeles's Tom Bradley, and Philadelphia's Wilson Goode—all of whom have opted for public policy and political activism that reflected alliance with the economic status quo endorsed by the corporate sector.

The political relationship between Black communities and the corporate sector provides a critical focus for understanding the behavior of corporate leadership in urban America today. The corporate sector has played a significant role in the overall development of cities.

> The private sector is an important arena in city politics. Many resources are found within the private arena. Chief among them are taxes; the larger the tax base, the greater the mayor's budgetary resources. We have already seen the importance of campaign contributions by business. The private arena also holds the resources of jobs, expertise, and prestige: attracting major corporations to the city can enhance a mayor's prestige and the informal influence of the office. As federal programs at the local level are eliminated and local budgets shrink because of decreasing federal aid and tax-cutting measures . . . the resources of the private sector will become even more important to the mayor and to the city as a whole. The mayor who has more control in this arena will be in a stronger position.[12]

Although it is clear that the corporate arena has resources useful in governing large American cities, it is not as clear that a strong mayor can easily control this arena. Certainly this was not the case in New York City during the mid-1970s fiscal crisis when corporate leadership stepped in and took control of the city's finances and its politics.

New York is not atypical. Corporate leadership has been a major actor in urban politics. During certain periods in some cities, such as Philadelphia, this leadership has exhibited relatively uniform political behavior; in other cities, such as New York, the leadership is characterized by what David Rogers describes as pluralism run wild.[13] One study points out that "business dominates the political system. It finances candidates in both major political parties. It acts as a powerful interest group affecting elections and referenda. It controls the mass media. And the business class fills most top state administrative positions and elective offices."[14] Regardless of the cohesion of corporate leadership, or lack thereof, corporations have been major, albeit at times quiet, actors and movers in urban political arenas. In many ways the corporate sector dominates the direction of state and government.

Despite relatively minor differences from city to city, or region to region, corporate leadership basically advocates two kinds of overlapping and complementary frameworks for managing urban social and economic crisis. One approach is reflected in the powerful growth ideology underpinning much public policy in urban America. According to political scientist Todd Swanstrom, "Growth politics can be defined, simply, as the effort by governments to enhance the economic attractiveness of their locality, to increase the intensity of land use by enticing mobile wealth to enter their boundaries."[15] The other corporate strategy is what Eric Lichten refers to as the "austerity state."[16] Both these complementary management and philosophical frameworks contain certain "rules of thumb" inimical to the interests of most members of Black communities.

Fainstein and Fainstein have argued that the economic objectives of capital in the American city are tied together by several "interlocking efforts." These efforts lower the priorities of the Black community in the hierarchy of needs within the American city. According to these social scientists, directives include: "bring back the white middle class"; "remove lower-income and minority households"; "maintain and reestablish racial and class territorial segregation"; and "encapsulate the lower classes in peripheral locations."[17] A key question for Black local activists today, therefore, is how to mobilize community and neighborhood interests to challenge effectively the urban agenda of corporate leadership. This question emerges more clearly as Black activists become more successful and effective in organizing and mobilizing a numerically significant constituency.

The terms "growth ideology" and "austerity state" capture the essence of the corporate program for urban America. Lichten clearly describes the austerity state:

> If fiscal crisis is now a predominant concern for politicians across the country, austerity is now their solution. Austerity has become the policy of the 1980s, and no mainstream American politician has mounted a campaign against it. Instead, conventional political wisdom now asserts the historical inevitability and absolute necessity of an austere public sector. Austerity, with its underlying ideology of scarcity and Social Darwinism, goes unchallenged, and in the process the social welfare apparatus, for which so many have struggled during the past fifty years, is now endangered. . . .
> Both austerity and austerity-minded politicians have become central features

of political life and discourse in the 1980s, as a consequence of the same basic social process: the crisis of capitalism and capital's struggle against labor. Austerity is now the dominant strategy, asserting the domination of labor by capital—within the state and at the workplace.[18]

Austerity is the key word for understanding the corporate agenda for the public sector, but growth ideology is the term for what should be occurring simultaneously in the private sector.

A group of researchers used Chicago as a reference point to describe "growth ideology":

> The essence of the growth ideology can be stated succinctly: none of the nation's urban social problems can be resolved until greater economic growth occurs, and the way to stimulate that growth is by providing financial incentives to private investors. Other legitimate concerns must simply take a back seat, according to this perspective, which has been advocated by public officials at all levels of government and by prominent private citizens throughout the nation.[19]

Growth ideology, paired with Reagonomics at the national level, has exacerbated social problems and urban blight by using the city's resources primarily to benefit the corporate sector. Corporate interests rationalized preoccupation with growth by guaranteeing a healthy environment for profits and investment opportunities—cutting taxes, or at least maintaining current taxes, and allowing greater business freedoms—that in theory gives cities the opportunity to help its poorer and working-class residents.

This kind of economic and social strategy may be somewhat effective in attracting white, middle-class citizens back to the central cities. Washington, D.C., may be typical; those areas targeted for "revitalization," while not completely halting the white middle-class exodus from that city, nevertheless have "contributed more to stemming that loss than has any other condition in the city."[20] In a similar vein it was reported that in Washington, D.C., the "gentrification experience has served to prevent the rather substantial loss of white households it would otherwise have suffered."[21] But based on years of experimenting with this local "supply-side" economic strategy in many cities, it is clear that this kind of process does not substantively help either the inner city or predominantly Black areas of major cities.

In fact, the record of growth ideology is not sanguine in terms of improved living conditions in the Black community. For example, the District of Columbia reveals serious problems for Blacks:

It is in Washington, of all major American metropolitan areas, that blacks have achieved among the highest collective living standards. Even with these accomplishments, nevertheless, blacks still lag considerably behind whites in socioeconomic circumstances. If this is the case in the Washington metropolitan area, it does not bode well for blacks in many other urban areas, where opportunities are likely to be less in evidence.[22]

For its success, the growth ideology, therefore, requires political acquiescence on the part of neighborhoods, working-class citizens, and especially Blacks and Latinos who would not immediately benefit from this kind of urban design.

Political acquiescence, if not passivity, is necessary because a growth ideology in this country precipitated greater social and economic separation between those interests with capital and those without. In a study of Chicago Gregory D. Squires and his colleagues have found that the growth ideology has generated

> . . . two communities moving in divergent directions in this urban area. On the one hand are the city's central business district, the gentrified city neighborhoods such as Lincoln Park, old affluent neighborhoods such as the Gold Coast, and the more prosperous suburbs such as those on the North Shore. On the other hand are the low-income black and Hispanic communities like the West Side and Logan Square, struggling white ethnic neighborhoods like Chicago Lawn, and the older suburban industrial communities like East Chicago and Hammond, Indiana. Propelled by the Chicago growth machine, one group is accelerating while the other is running on empty.[23]

In Chicago, as in several big American cities, a typical political reaction emerges; it reflects the growth ideology and the interests this represents.

> An emerging community of political, labor, neighborhood, and consumer organizations and activists is exploring other approaches to the city's problems. They envision a different future than do the industrial leaders, developers, and machine politicians. They have recognized that the growth ideology—though they may not use that term—carries with it enormous inequities for individuals and communities in the entire metropolitan area.[24]

This growing politicization has forced the corporate sector to take a greater interest in issues related to the quality of life in Black urban communities.

Corporate attention to Black communities is motivated primarily by self-interest; business needs healthy and stable social and economic environments. The Conference Board, a business information news service supported by more than three thousand corporations, banks, and utilities, conducted a survey showing that major corporations are especially concerned about the loyalties of workers in the twenty-first century. The author of this survey pointed out, however, that various kinds of community affairs programs "are being driven by bottom-line, profit or loss concerns, not altruism."[25] But an additional concern is the influence that Black political activists, operating under a framework of empowerment rather than access, could have on social and economic operations in the public arena. Corporate America is threatened by an emerging, progressive-oriented Black activism that challenges the political influence of major public and private institutions in urban settings. The control or management of both the economic and political local contexts is significant for the corporation's continual profitability and dominance.

In cities with sizeable Black populations, several kinds of activities may afford Black and neighborhood activists the ability to control or counter the private sector's power and influence. According to activist and scholar Georgia Persons in Atlanta, activists must control the zoning procedures that require businesses' adherence in order to invest in development or capital infrastructure. She believes that the control of zoning policies and procedures is directly related not only to land use and its accompanying benefits, but also to land valuation.[26] In Boston a neighborhood-based housing and development organization in the Black community—the Dudley Street Neighborhood Initiative—has developed a broad strategy by which to begin controlling zoning regulations for the benefit of neighborhood concerns: (1) monitoring the process for decision making; (2) pressuring local and city hall officials responsible for decision making; and (3) advocating for alternative mechanisms and procedures that would give residential representatives more power over development decisions in their neighborhoods.

In cities like Boston and San Francisco neighborhood activists have successfully advocated for plant-closing legislation, rollback of corporate tax abatements, and linkage programs that require corporations and businesses to share in the social costs generated by corporate activity. Some Black ministers also used economic boycotts when they sought money from white-controlled banks for housing in Atlanta. In other cities across the country instituting taxation fairness and ending corporate tax giveaways are important ways by which to control corporate behavior in favor of neighborhood interests. A concrete example of this was a tax abatement bill that was repealed in Philadelphia in 1988. Activist Joyce Brooks states that in this city "developers have gotten a tax abatement since 1978. About $63 million per year has been lost in real estate taxes—both commercial and luxury residential. A new 1988 tax abatement bill was to effect one building—but this . . . has been used by [many] big developers. . . . The newspapers exposed this. The outcry was tremendous and this 1988 [law] was repealed.[27]

One prominent activist believes that the rising movement to develop Black agendas with political and economic goals and strategies represents an important way in which corporate behavior can be held accountable by local Black activists. In New York City, Boston, Milwaukee, Newark, and Chicago, activists have sought to develop communitywide forums for building policy agendas that can guide the political mobilization of Blacks. Activist Gus Newport proposes that the absence of a clear and philosophically straightforward Black political and economic agenda in the 1980s allowed corporate leadership to define, in terms of its own interests, the needs of the Black community.[28]

To counter the capacity of corporations simply to move away from a city considered politically uncooperative, some have suggested investing in other ventures closely tied to the political economy and social well-being of a particular city. Richard Child Hill suggests, for instance, that, to limit the city's reliance on heavy metal industries and counter the continual threat of corporate flight, Detroit's local government should consider investing in light manufacturing. The venture capital for such investments could come from public and private pension funds rather than sources controlled by the corporate sector.[29] Many groups also advocate national plant closing legislation as a means to dampen the influence of corporations deriving from their ability to simply "close shop" when politics does not proceed according to their agendas.

A growing number of Black activists are pursuing strategies that challenge the distribution of power. This may interfere with corporations' need to manage work and social relations, either directly or indirectly tied to its production or service-producing activities. As Harry Braverman writes, the need to challenge the distribution of power arises from the historical requirement that corporations "had to extract from their employees that [required] daily conduct which would best serve their interests, to impose their will upon their workers while operating a labor process on a voluntary contractural basis."[30] But as corporations grope for more efficient and effective management as a response to increasing social and economic dislocation, activism reflecting Black empowerment will emerge with increasing frequency in major American cities. The primary reason for this, as suggested earlier, is that the corporate agenda cannot respond effectively to the needs of the Black community.

Urban America is witnessing an incipient social movement unfolding in the electoral arena; a political reaction on the part of corporate is logical and should be expected.

> Under attack, capital does not, however, sit back passively; it mobilized its own very considerable institutionalized power to threaten the fiscal solvency of the state, determine its economic environment, and influence public perceptions. Business interest groups spent untold millions on influencing electoral decisions with regard to municipal rent control, development bond referenda . . . the Superdome in New Orleans, and similar issues associated with accumulation. When antagonized by local regimes which tilted towards working-class interests, business organized to throw the dangerous elements out of office. . . . During both the Depression and the urban fiscal crises of 1975, capital went one step further and insisted upon reforms in state structure which would guarantee direct business authority over the program choices of urban regimes.[31]

The corporate sector can witness these and other actions as responses to growing Black political insurgency.

In seeking to uncover the influence of business over urban policy several kinds of evidence may illustrate such domination. Actual political participation may supply one kind of evidence, but this is not the most important corporate tool for influence. Much more important may be shaping issues and determining "the parameters within which political conflicts will take place."[32] Actual expenditures of public policies that clearly benefit the corporate sector could also indicate business influence over urban policy: "The political power of business is not inferred from participation in decision making, nor from their contribution to community mobilization, but from their ability to secure a continuous stream of public goods necessary to the profitability of the urban location."[33] Yet a third kind of evidence may be the corporate sector's specific responses to Black activists who raise issues and mobilize people to challenge the parameters of public policy. Corporate leaders may actively attempt to discredit such Black leadership or use other Blacks to accomplish this.

Emerging relationships between the corporate sector and Black urban communities and the nature of the political leadership within these communities represent key issues for urban politics during the next several decades. When approaching this issue one should not assume that the political and social interests and activities of corporations or a "corporate community" is simply determined by the technical requirements for greater levels of profits. Urban politics and conflict are not, as contended by some on the left, simply a "struggle . . . between profits and wages"; therefore, it does not necessarily follow that "in analyzing any urban problem . . . class relations are paramount."[34] At times, these ideas have led to the proposition that generating profits is the paramount concern of the corporate sector; certainly this is very important. But, as Michael Useem points out, this is not the total picture:

> Most corporate business decisions are viewed, correctly, as a product of the internal logic of the firm. Yet when decisions are made on the allocation of company monies to political candidates, the direction of its philanthropic activities and other forms of political outreach, an external logic is important as well. This is the logic of classwide benefits, involving considerations that lead to company decisions beneficial to all large companies.[35]

Economist John Kenneth Galbraith argues that the corporate sector is as political and as interested in pursuing power as are more obviously political actors. He proposes that a mythology has arisen regarding corporate leadership's lack of interests in the pursuit of political power.

> The agreed economics as it emerged after Keynes rendered another service. It elided or, more accurately, it continued to elide the economists' most troublesome, even intractable, problem. That is how to deal with the presence of power and the pursuit of power, the great black hole of economics. No one doubts that in politics people seek power—seek the esteem, applause, self-realization, and other satisfactions that come from having other people at their command. Because power is wanted for its own sake, hundreds of millions of dollars are expended in every American election to win it and thus to enjoy its rewards. . . . Economics as it is taught and studied has no way of assessing or measuring power and the will to power. . . . The solution to the problem of power and its pursuit has been to hold that power does not, indeed cannot, exist. . . . If all corporate and executive action is subordinate to the pursuit of profits, and all such pursuit is subordinate, in turn, to the rule of the market and to the ultimate sovereignty of the consumer, the problem of power does not arise. There cannot be any. The firm and those within it are the powerless automatons of their controlling motivation, which, in turn, is wholly subordinate to market forces. . . . All is subordinate in the context of the market to the pursuit of profit.[36]

Despite the importance of pursuing profits, the corporate sector is thus also an actor in the strictly political arena. This role becomes clearer as its ideological or structural foundations are threatened by other actors in that arena.

Corporate leadership's pursuit and maintenance of power reflects certain collective interests. Useem writes,

> The consensus among investigators is that although bankers and industrialists stand in opposition on some business and state policies, their corporate and class networks prevent deep cleavage. The networks produce something

akin to the "stabilizing effects of overlapping memberships" between interest groups so often identified by pluralists as the cement of American democracy.[37]

A continuing concern of the corporate sector is maintaining political and policy processes conducive for an environment that favors the interests of business. According to Harry Boyte, the leadership of the corporate community achieved a realization since the 1960s:

> The corporate agenda required more than a change in rhetoric. The fundamental obstacle to its implementation was political. From the business leaders' viewpoint, the sixties social movements had changed people's self-conceptions and sense of possibility and in so doing had added millions of new black voters, a grassroots poverty network, a women's lobby, and consumer and environmental forces to traditional reform groups.[38]

There does exist a corporate community that reflects the economic as well as cultural and political goals of a network of interests and arrangements in urban America. Domhoff points out that corporations

> . . . are linked in a variety of ways to create a corporate community. At an economic level, the ties within the corporate community are manifested in ownership of common stock on the part of both families and other corporations, as well as in joint ventures among corporations and in the common sources of bank loans that most corporations share. At a more sociological level, the corporate community is joined together by the use of the same legal, accounting, and consulting firms and by the similar experience of executives working in the bureaucratic structure of a large organization. Then too, the large corporations come together as a business community because they share the same values and goals—in particular the profit motive. Finally, and not least, the common goals of the corporation lead them to have common enemies in the labor movement and middle-class reformers, which gives them a further sense of a shared identity.[39]

Again, according to Boyte, the corporate community's involvement in major public policy issues has become stronger and more overt in recent times:

> The full corporate program was developed after Watergate. In a series of business forums, conferences, and meetings, corporate leaders developed an action agenda that in the coming years would reappear again and again in the rhetoric of corporate-connected politicians and ideologues. The central feature of the corporate crusade was an attack on the size of government itself. . . . Corporate executives sought tax changes to increase depreciation allowances and tax credits, lessen corporate income taxes, and encourage investment in the stock market. They zealously targeted environmental, consumer, and health regulations. . . . Behind the scenes corporate pressure

proved an important factor in the anti-Equal Rights Amendment campaign, corporations also initiated an effort to dismantle affirmative action enforcement procedures.[40]

Thus, if Black political activism is now perceived as a threat to the economic and political arrangements that prop the corporate sector, then corporate leadership responds definitively to protect its own interests.

To maintain a desirable business environment the corporation must remain cognizant of Black political growth. Such growth could present what Michael Useem describes as "critical challenges" to the corporate community. And owing to the "social and economic interdependencies among large corporations," these critical challenges to the power and position of business have added new elements of classwide unity."[41] A general pattern of corporate response to critical political challenges is driven by two important concerns: "How to control effectively the externalities of work place and total environment, which have grown enormously in importance with economic growth and the industrial/scientific revolution"; and "how to cope with the serious social costs of rapid technological change and the effects of great business size and mobility on the nature, quality, and security of work and problems of workforce adaptability and unemployment."[42]

In partial response to critical political challenges from the Black community, social and business leaders have attempted, electorally or otherwise, to divert Black activism, from its threatening ideological orientations. The responses of some corporate leaders to the civil rights movement may illustrate this. Some business leaders supported and even encouraged Black demands for integration and access as a way of preserving the well-being of the corporate community. In support of this argument Frances F. Piven and Richard Cloward state that during the 1960s "northern capital had no reason to oppose political modernization in the South. With the plantation economy in decline, the links between northern businessmen and the plantation system were dissolving. Meanwhile, northern capital was financing the industrialization of the South, and looked benignly on the prospect of managing the control and allocation of labor through market relations rather than caste relations."[43] Adolph Reed, Jr., provides insight for the business community's support of some traditional civil rights demands; he argues that it was socially and economically costly for corporate leadership to support a "racial order which demanded for its maintenance constant terror" whenever racial rebellion became possible.[44] This idea is also illustrated by Jack M. Bloom who analyzed class and race during the civil rights movement. He argued that the business community generally supported Black demands for access because they found it easier to maintain social order—even in the face of white resistance to integration-than to continue resisting Black demands that could escalate for goals beyond access. He writes that in New Orleans, Atlanta, Columbia, Dallas, and Augusta, for examples, the leadership of the business community actively supported political leaders who argued for the peaceful acceptance of desegregation. Bloom writes further that "even in Jackson, Mississippi, . . . business opinion generally came to believe that the state's economic development would be hurt by racial disorder. When they reached this conclusion, the weight of their influence moved toward easing the conflict through compliance with the federal law."[45] Business acceptance of some racial reforms is also argued by Manning Marable: "Domestically, racial unrest was costly to the private sector. Eastern U.S. capital and the multinational corporations had no direct commitments to the maintenance of rigid caste divisions within the American working class. They viewed the mild reforms proposed by Wilkins, Young and Randolph with no great anxiety."[46] The relationship between Black political activism and the corporate sector is a concern because of growing disaffection among Black citizens. Social disaffection may be reflected in various economic indicators of worsening living conditions in Black communities, as well as continuing social gaps between whites and Blacks in America. Major urban problems—crime, gang-related violence, drugs, poverty, and unemployment—may all point to the persistence of a potentially politically disruptive Black state.

Writing about New York City, Martin Shefter points out that such disaffection could threaten political and social stability. As he states,

> The disaffection of black and, to a lesser extent, Hispanic voters also poses a potentially serious threat to the stability of the city's current regime. Thus far this threat has been contained by low levels of electoral mobilization and isolation that has characterized the political situation of nonwhites in city politics since 1975. These conditions, however, have been undergoing change.[47]

The author suggests that the mayoral elections of Harold Washington and Wilson Goode and the 1984 Jesse Jackson presidential campaign provide examples of Black disaffection that was channeled into political mobilization.

But political mobilization reflecting disaffection could result in strategies and goals neither conducive nor easily satisfied by the responses that both local government and the corporate sector have traditionally used to assuage Black social demands. An emerging Black political agenda has been moving away from the integrationist demands of the civil rights movement and toward demands that require economic restructuring in America. As Martin Luther King, Jr., stated, it did not "cost America one penny to desegregate lunch counters"; now, however, programs of social justice will require billions of dollars. The cost of a diverse society reflecting only one society, rather than two, raises questions about the ownership, management, and distribution of wealth, and the role of the corporate sector in relation to this wealth. Renewed and intensifying activism is moving Blacks toward claims for power sharing with the corporate sector, instead of accepting mere access to this sector. The possibility of a radicalized agenda increases as Black urban communities continue to grow and expand numerically and a large sector of this community wallows in poverty.

Corporate America's concern about how Black activism may reflect growing social disaffection enhances the significance of the electoral arena. Electoral activism can be a tool for Black mobilization that either challenges corporate social and economic agendas or merely allows positions for individuals to acquire access into corporate structures. Beginning in the late 1960s Blacks found themselves able to exercise control over the electoral levers of several big city governments. In a study of Gary, Indiana, where the first Black mayor of a big city in America was elected in 1967, Alex Poinsett argued:

> If the 1960s was the decade of direct action and street rebelling against white racism, the 1970s can be the decade of massive black political empowerment. For the organizing and efficient use of the electoral process by the Black community is on the upsurge. It is quieter and less dramatic than the protest politics of the 1960s. It is not, however, a less potent weapon on the drive toward black liberation.[48]

He argued thus on the basis of demography, or Black growth tipping the racial scales, a trend that began in several big cities of America. During the 1970s the Black population of many larger cities increased significantly. Due to demography that continued to "blacken" many American cities, the trend toward electoral takeover continues.[49]

In some of these cities large American corporations have established their headquarters; here corporations seek to expand not only their base of operations but also their political influence. Browning et al. have proposed that demography and political coalitions may allow Blacks to exercise power as a senior player in the urban arena, a player who has the ear of the corporate sector.[50] Given the combined effect of demography and political action, a question is posed to Black people by the Browning study: has it made a difference in producing "gains for minority people"?[51] As Blacks organize themselves into a power bloc to answer this challenge, various obstacles to their effectiveness emerge from both local government and the corporate sector. Obstacles to growing Black political influence become more apparent as Blacks debate public agendas not endorsed or supported by corporate-based leadership.

Traditionally Black political mobilization has been partially organized in ways that emphasized opportunities for individual advancement and traditional divisible benefits like jobs, contracts, and appointments to a few. Groups in power and white ethnics have resisted this pattern—although reflective of local American politics—especially in the initial stages of Black political growth in big cities. Black activists who advocate empowerment rather than access issues believe that white-dominated local government and corporate leadership have played critical roles in maintaining a socially and politically subservient status for Blacks. According to some activists, therefore, Black politics must directly challenge the values and practices of the corporate sector rather than merely seek "trickle-down" benefits or opportunities for individual participation in this business sector.

Although faced with the possibility of Black insurgency, local government has still generally failed to respond effectively to the social and economic needs of the community. Whether the issues involve responding to poverty or balancing the needs of downtown development and neighborhood stabilization, local government's capacity is weak. This weakness or failure is forcing local government to turn more aggressively to the private sector for help. The International City Management Association reports:

> Local government officials are increasingly turning to the private sector as a source of funds for infrastructure spending. They are doing so for a variety of reasons. Some hope that private sector businesses can tap into long-term financing unavailable at a lower cost than for local governments. Some officials see public-private approaches as one of the few capital finance options open when there are severe restrictions on traditional approaches. And many see private sector contributions to local infrastructure as necessary for equity, given the benefits and costs attributable to the activities of the private sector.[52]

But the policies and programs, developed by local government to respond to worsening social and economic conditions, require not only private-sector participation but also different priorities in the relationships between profits, power, and the needs of the local citizenry. Gregory D. Squires and his colleagues assert the importance of the private sector's enlightened assistance to the urban public.

> Since most of the nation's wealth resides in the private sector, creation of such a program cannot be restricted to public expenditures. While public services like education and transportation are important in preparing people for and getting them to work, they are of far less value if no jobs are available. Public assistance in the forms of unemployment compensation and welfare keep many families from starving, but they are at best insufficient efforts to mitigate the damage inflicted on communities after the fact of disinvestment. If participatory democratic structures are to be created in order to achieve "quality" as well as "quantity" objectives, those structures must encompass private investment decision-making as well as government policy-making.[53]

Despite local officials' growing interest to involve the private sector in meeting basic needs of citizens more aggressively than in the past, models of collaboration have been limited to leasing, "exactions" or developer financing, and privatization. These approaches do not seek the rearrangement of priorities that is needed to overcome the problems associated with poverty, racial hierarchy, and social disaffection in the American city. Other kinds of alternative models for eliciting concessions from the corporate sector—such as linkage, plant-closing legislation, aggressive taxation for purposes of funding social services—generally have not been pursued effectively by local government.[54]

Local government's hesitancy to substantively invade the private sector prevents adopting and implementing public policy decisions that may represent more effective responses to desired living conditions for poor and working-class citizenry. Local government's hesitancy exists for several reasons. As Friedland, Piven, and Alford explain, the electoral and structural fragmentation of local government prevents concerted action and mobilization directed at gaining concessions from the corporate sector; such fragmentation also encourages discontented citizens to pursue political strategies in disconnected ways. This means that conflict is "incrementalized":

> The tension which might otherwise take form in direct struggles between business, industry, and finance on the one hand, and workers and consumers on the other hand, takes form instead in escalating demands on municipal agencies—for jobs, services, contracts, tax concessions—with the result that municipal activities and budgets expand, while municipal revenues are reduced. As a consequence, periods of potential social and class conflict become instead periods of fiscal strain.[55]

There are other difficulties for local government seeking greater levels of benefits from the corporate sector.

Corporations can leave a city that may be considered inhospitable to its interests. As one writer points out, "The mobility of capital—the flow of investment—is not controlled by the state or by labor unions or by the working class. Clearly, this flow of capital in and out of a city—or in and out of a nation, for that matter—can generate crises internal to the state. And once a crisis has been generated, the crisis can be used. This ability gives finance capital, and individual financiers, an enormous power."[56] This potential power can be used anytime, and it is effective even as a mere threat to leave a city or region. And, in fact, corporations have used this threat to extract major concessions from local and state government, including the reducing business taxes, relaxing pollution controls and other business regulations, and improving services considered important to mid- and high-level corporate employees.[57]

Even though the obstacles local government faces in order to pursue benefits that can be extracted from the corporate sector are formidable, the presence of a significant and growing urban Black population with a standard of living generally lower than that of urban whites can serve as a political foundation for more radicalized models of extracting public benefits from the private sector. The electoral arena is critical, along with other arenas of mobilization, for developing a progressive political foundation. Electoral activism is a significant political and social process because it establishes a framework of values and operations for local government. And local government has the capacity—even if it does not practice it fully—to establish the parameters of private-sector activity in a city. Thus, as Blacks take over local governments, they acquire the potential ability to establish frameworks of acceptable or desired operations among the private sector. Corporate leadership must become concerned when Blacks take over the electoral levers, or are about to do so, therefore, because adopting a public policy agenda that is responsive to the needs of masses of Blacks, rather than merely offering access for individual Blacks, may threaten "business-as-usual" in the corporate sector.

For many reasons concern among the private sector heightens when Blacks gain political power. Both the history of Blacks in America and the current status of this group could serve to spark new social change in America. As Sheila D. Collins has pointed out,

> Given the essential role of chattel slavery in the initial accumulation of capital in the Western world, and the pivotal role played by the color line in keeping the American working class historically divided and politically im-

potent, any political insurgency among the black masses was likely, if carried to its logical conclusion, to call into question the fundamental premises of the American enterprise.[58]

The Black community has a unique history characterized by a thrust for social change and continues to have the capacity to question fundamentally the American polity and the role of corporate activity; given the economically depressed position of Blacks as a group they also have the potential of raising issues not necessarily confined by America's ideological structure and values.

Blacks have expressed attitudes on a range of government and economic issues that corporate leadership might perceive as threatening. For example, in a 1976 survey of the philosophical and political attitudes of Black and white elected officials, major racial differences were reported. When Black and elected officials were asked to agree or disagree with, "True democracy is limited in the United States because of the special privileges enjoyed by business and industry," an overwhelming majority of Black elected officials (70 percent) agreed with this statement, and while slightly more than one-quarter (26 percent) of the white elected officials concurred. Half (50 percent) of all white elected officials concurred with the statement, "The first responsibility of society is to protect property rights"; but only 37 percent of the Black elected officials agreed with this statement.[59] A more recent survey questioned the role of government, "The government ought to reduce the income differences between rich and poor." There was a significant difference in the proportion of Blacks and whites who agreed with this sentiment. For Blacks earning more than $15,000 per year, 62 percent agreed with this statement; for whites in the same category, only 39 percent agreed.[60] Such findings may reflect Blacks' greater willingness to support an activist government that challenges corporations' conduct and their business decisions, especially those with major implications for the economy and social life of the American city.

Several indicators support the idea that Blacks generally favor greater levels of governmental spending. When researchers asked groups of Blacks and whites to state their preferences for increases in government spending, major differences arose between these groups, as illustrated in the chart below.[61] The political attitudes of Blacks in fact differ from those of most whites, regarding not only specific public policies but also the responsibilities and nature of the American economic system. Evidence for Black social disaffection may include attitudinal surveys. But it could also include the growing popularity of someone like Louis Farrakhan or the increasing incidents of social protest in the Black

	Blacks (%)	Whites (%)
Education	78	55
Improving cities	67	47
Health	75	57
Environment	67	52
Welfare	58	17
Improving race relations	88	23

community, such as the spate of race riots in Nashville, Chattanooga, Miami, Virginia Beach in the late 1980s.[62]

As I described earlier, the Black political spectrum is neither synonymous nor parallel with the American ideological spectrum.[63] It may be easier, therefore, for local government controlled by Blacks to adopt populist agendas responsive to the social and economic needs of poor and working-class people but that the corporate sector may find threatening to its interests. The values and policy approaches toward public policy advocated by Blacks are of great concern to corporate America because Blacks have the potential of controlling electoral levers and attempting to implement measures unfriendly to the growth ideology.

As ineffective as local government may be in responding to certain social and economic problems, it still represents a critical process for corporate growth and development. In fact, the importance of local government for the well-being of corporate America has grown as society becomes increasingly technological. Jim Chapin comments:

> Public power is now clearly greater than private power, in a way not true in past crisis: J. P. Morgan could stop a stock market crisis by himself in 1903, but in 1929 his successor needed federal help; similarly, banks could dictate a solution to a city fiscal crisis in 1933, but by 1975 saving the city required the state and the pension funds. The banker's ability to distribute a solution to the city passed in a few months in 1975 and by 1977 their policy demands could be rebuffed.[64]

Corporate leadership must be concerned about who sits in the mayor's office, on the city commission, or on school governance bodies—especially in those cities with growing numbers of poverty-stricken and working-class Black communities. Here the issue of what is appropriate for public discussion and resolution may be resolved.

How does the corporate community respond to local governments that threaten its interests? The networks of corporations or "corporate communities" found in some major cities have usually formed what Michael Useem terms "inner circles" to respond to their collective interests more effectively. These inner circles of corporate leadership are "well-positioned to intervene in virtually every forum." And, they are "at the forefront of corporate outreach to government, political parties, non-profit institutions, and the media." The inner circles have several bases of influence, including multiple-company connections within the general corporate community, a certain degree of social cohesion based on the upper-class status of its members, and the leadership positions, with attendant resources, enjoyed by individual members of the inner circle.[65]

The threat of corporate flight and noncooperation regarding debt services are other strategies business uses to warn both Black- and white-controlled local government of the dangers of public policy not sanctioned by corporate leadership. Martin Shefter shows how this power was used by the corporate leaders of New York City during the mid-1970s. He points out that whenever the business community has been presented with the political demand of better, improved, and cheaper public transportation services, this sector unites and suggests a specific municipal program:

> (1) Stop financing current expenditures with borrowed funds; (2) balance its budget by slashing current expenditures rather than by raising taxes; (3) use its borrowing capacity to improve the city's transportation infrastructure rather than for other purposes (such as building new schools); and (4) cover, to the greatest extent possible, the debt service and operating costs of these facilities with user-charges . . . rather than with local tax revenues. . . .
> When it is resisted by City Hall, bankers and businessmen have concluded that the incumbent administration is fiscally irresponsible and is sacrificing the city's long-term interests for the sake of current political gains.[66]

These same tools can be used to respond to other kinds of political demands emanating from the Black community or a Black populist-controlled local government.

Intervention by corporate leadership can take various forms: advisory councils to local government, assistance in the governance of large civic organizations, financial support for political candidates, and appeals through the mass media to sway public opinion. In Boston, the Vault, an organization representing a group of powerful corporations, has contributed directly to candidates deemed cooperative and supportive of a "better" Boston.[67] In Chicago, big business was quite open regarding attempts to use money to influence favorably the electoral efforts of

Richard Daley, Jr., to become mayor of that city. Money given to the 1989 Daley mayoral campaign, for example—including five contributions of more than $100,000 each—reflects not only the usual political insurance payment or a crass bid for city business but also deeper economic interest. One developer gave Daley $30,000 on the assumption that he would end the Washington administration's "hard bargaining" stance over developers' responsibilities to the city.[68]

Roger Friedland assesses business motives in broader terms: "Corporations have three major sources of political power in the city: their participation in local politics; their ability to institutionalize their influence and interests in the governmental structure; and their control over the logic of the local economic system."[69] But in seeking to control not only what is raised for public discussion but also the support that such discussion may attract among Black and poor citizens, corporations could also seek to control the orientation and nature of Black political mobilization and leadership. This becomes an important fourth source of political power for corporations, especially in these cities where Blacks are beginning to take over the structures and processes of government. This kind of response is clear in Boston where the corporate sector has played a major role in selecting that city's first Black superintendent and has boldly attempted to legitimize as "leaders" Black activists and civic officials considered cooperative and nonconfrontational.[70]

St. Louis-based activist Clarene Royston gives an example of how money is used to control the philosophical and political direction of Black elected officials.

> It's hard for Blacks and the grassroots to obtain elected office without going to whites for financing. Those who get this financing owe favors. When the Black elected officials step out of line by proposing positive electoral reform or other changes to increase Black empowerment, they are pulled back in line with the threat of exposure of unethical financial relations. These financial deals are not illegal, but are unethical. They are often the same ones whites have been doing for years but unlike many whites, Black elected officials do not have enough political or economic clout to prevent these activities from becoming public knowledge.[71]

Until the 1960s corporate-based leadership could rely on local government to control Black political activism that the leaders considered threatening to their interests because Blacks were not numerous enough to control local government structures and processes. White political machines and local governmental officials actually represented the political or electoral partners and managers for the corporate sector and its interests. Consider, for example, the relationships between political bosses and business leaders in many American cities. In Chicago, for example, "[Mayor] Daley

regularly consulted with business leaders on more routine planning matters, municipal finance, and related topics. He also made a point of
sprinkling his nominations for the schools board and other municipal
commissions with business and civic notables as well as politicos."[72] This
scenario has been the norm for several decades in big city politics. Before
the mid-1980s, Black political activism was not a problem for the corporate sector because local government was controlled by whites ethnics who
were primarily concerned with maintaining racial hierarchy in their cities.
Controlling local governments have used various mechanisms to prevent
Blacks from actualizing their full potential for electoral influence; thus,
they buffered the demands upon the corporate sector. These mechanisms
included residential segregation and gerrymandering.

Indeed, the effectiveness of the "ideology of white racism," to use
Martin Kilson's phrase, cannot be deemphasized; it offered significant
limits to the growth of Black political influence in urban America. In a
concise history of white-controlled local government's resistance to the
growth and exercise of Black political influence, Kilson has described
various patterns of behavior and relationships that diluted Black political
strength; this was functional for big business during various periods in
American history. Examining patterns of racial relations in a historical
overview of big city politics between 1940 and 1970 Kilson described
how "parallel" or segregated political clubs emerged. As the Black community grew in cities like Chicago and Philadelphia, however, the pattern
of parallel clubs led to a "politics of appointments." The political machine in the big cities next responded to growing Black communities with
"clientage," not equal access or acceptance. From clientage, the racial-
political resistance to Blacks moves to "interest-group articulation."
These kinds of responses represent a pattern among local government
leadership and its white constituents who ideologically and racially resist
growing Black political influence. Although these responses were effective, the corporate sector could rely on local government to manage
periodic eruptions of Black social disaffection.

Once Blacks started to make inroads into local government the corporate sector became especially concerned about the specific agendas of
Blacks. This was illustrated in the 1960s with Richard Hatcher's election as
the first Black mayor of Gary, Indiana. Edward Greer described him as "an
insurgent black politician" whose experience with corporate power may
prove enlightening for urban political developments:

> Since a large number of major industrial cities will probably experience a
> transition to black mayors over the next decade, the experience in Gary
> foreshadows a kind of political conflict which is likely to repeat itself with

some frequency. . . . Thus it is important that we learn from the experience of Gary precisely what kinds of obstacles and limits face insurgent urban political movements which capture some formal governmental power. Insight into these roadblocks and their structural bases is prerequisite to an advance beyond them.[73]

Greer offers some relevant observations about Hatcher's tenure. He explains how a powerful corporation resisted the initiatives and overture of a Black-led, progressive government in its attempts to combat air pollution. The Gary Works of the U.S. Steel Corporation used several resources or mechanisms to dilute the political effectiveness of Mayor Hatcher's city administration. These included private lobbying efforts with elected officials, exchange of personnel between industry and government, patronage, and legal maneuvers. These actions reflect an actual corporate pattern; for example, this pattern also operated in Atlanta as its business community attempted to mold urban renewal public policy in ways that benefited corporate interests.[74]

Large corporations have "contextual" advantages that are significant in discouraging Black demands considered threatening to business interests; these include the vague nature of regulatory laws in various areas that influence the behavior and actions of corporations and the hegemonic nature of corporate policy initiatives and actions. City governments are more pluralist, democratic, and diffuse than the private sector. It is much more difficult to develop uniform political and economic strategies in the halls of city government than it is in the boardrooms of big corporations. An important resource for bolstering city government's progressive agendas may be grass-roots mobilization and activism; but intense level of mobilization is difficult and costly for political leaders. The corporation can merely hire or assign workers to a particular political or policy struggle. Government has a hard time motivating and mobilizing a broad range of constituents.

The establishment of the "New Detroit Committee" after the July 1967 racial riots in Detroit was both a harbinger of corporate efforts one-quarter of a century later and a specific example illustrating some of the advantages held by the corporate sector in the political arena. Through control of private foundation's resources and assistance to organizations dealing with minority leadership and social development the corporate sector can mold an urban Black agenda that is not threatening to dominant social and economic interests. The New Detroit Committee emerged partially in response to a progressive Black public agenda that emerged from the racial disruptions in that city. For example, Georgakas and Surkin reported:

> The New Detroit Committee was not operating in a social vacuum. Already
> embodied within the process of destructive violence . . . was a fresh surge
> of positive revolutionary energy. . . . Black-owned newspapers and organi-
> zations of black industrial workers began to present a series of programs
> and revolutionary visions in sharp contrast to the ideas put forward by the
> New Detroit Committee. . . . Even as the New Detroit Committee began to
> put its plans into action, black workers unleashed a social movement of
> their own which soon forced a series of organizational, ideological, cul-
> tural, political, and economic confrontations with established wealth and
> power.[75]

Although the New Detroit Committee was ostensibly founded to help
business assume a greater role in the social crisis facing citizens of Detroit,
this involvement was also functional in allowing the corporate sector to
become infused into Black politics. This introduction gives corporate
leadership an opportunity to use institutional benefits selectively in ways
that either enhance the careers of certain individuals who are seen as
potential community "leaders" or provide benefits for those social and
civic activities endorsed by the corporate sector.

A continuing interest of corporate leadership will be the level and
quality of political participation among poor and working-class Blacks.
Corporate America could be politically and economically threatened if
this sector were to experience a heightening of political consciousness.
The fear exhibited by the corporate sector of the Black poor was illustrated in the early 1970s when they made numerous suggestions about
physically confining Blacks and Latinos as a way of socially controlling
poor and crime-ridden communities. For example, one proposal called
for building a fence to encircle a Puerto Rican neighborhood in Hartford,
Connecticut. Presumably this fence would help fight crime in that area of
the city. A similar approach to this but without wire fences, "planned
shrinkage," was discussed widely among high-level public officials in New
York City in the mid-1970s. Roger Starr, administrator for housing in this
city, argued that local government should allow municipal services to
deteriorate to unbearable levels as a means of encouraging people to leave
blighted areas; then land would become available for redevelopment
in ways that could ultimately produce more taxes and profits for businesses.[76] Although the avowed reasoning behind these kinds of development suggestions was to control and limit the expansion of crime-ridden
and poverty areas, the target groups involved Blacks and Latinos who
might be most threatening to the political arrangements undergirding the
economic operations of the corporate sector.

In several large cities attempts at population and land control, such
as that suggested by Starr, were not necessary because interests managing

and planning physical development were able to isolate poor Black and Latino residential pockets, removed from white middle-class residents or professional personnel employed by the corporate sector. This geographic segregation was pointed out in one study that focused on urban development in Washington, D.C.:

> Today it is difficult to escape the impression that the primary motivating force for diverting new office construction to the area north and west of the White House was not only to escape the deterioration of the old downtown but also to avoid the black shoppers and pedestrians who were beginning to predominate there. Fear among real estate business people and investors that new offices in the old downtown could not be leased at desired rates of financial return certainly inhibited construction there. Fear of crime was influential too. But the "high-income residential areas" referred to in the plan were the white neighborhoods of Georgetown, the embassy area, and the upper northwest. Proximity to these sections and the buffer provided by the White House in the south created a location for the new downtown to grow and prosper relative 'safe' from what were considered racial and physical deterrents of the old downtown.[77]

The major purpose of development plans for urban design in some large cities seems to have been managing the growth and movement of Blacks and Latinos. Although there may have been other reasons for particular large-scale urban design plans, the management of Black physical movement was many times an unspoken concern of those introducing or approving development plans.

In response to the needs of working-class and poor sectors, Blacks in control of government could push activist programs that infringe on the interests of big business. This presents a confrontational situation to corporate managers because, as Edward S. Herman writes, the "primacy of corporate initiatives derives in large part from the successful preservation of corporate autonomy, corporate dominance over basic economic activities, and weak government."[78] A local, activist Black-controlled government could clash philosophically with corporate-based leadership regarding not only programmatic concerns but also those concerns around the proper role of government. The particular responses of these two sectors to each other have implications not only for race relations but also for the quality of life in urban America—indeed for the future political, social, and economic health of many larger cities in the United States.

This is a major reason why local dominant interests, including the corporate sector, have found it advantageous to integrate some prominent Black individuals into its corporate or foundation bureaucracy to broaden its image and blunt Black criticism. The more sophisticated wing of corporate leadership has attempted to coopt and reward a certain kind of Black leadership in order to discourage the emergence of populist or radical Black leadership.[79] Martin Kilson has identified this as "client-incorporation"; he explains that "the politics of client-incorporation enables politically skillful leaders to carve out a power niche for themselves, but not for their constituency. This power niche produces sizeable personal clout for black leaders, as well as some wealth and business opportunities. But it seldom facilitates effective political incorporation for blacks in general."[80] Incorporating clients has been most effective for those leaders seeking access or rewards from prevailing political and economic arrangements but least effective for Blacks advocating public policies that would effectively redistribute economic benefits from the business sector.

This kind of integration or cooptation dampens Black demands for public policies considered unacceptable by the interests that reflect wealth and power. But this political cooptation results in what Ira Katznelson describes as "unauthentic participation": "Citizens may be invited to participate in an institution in ways that do not challenge the distribution of power and which in fact may reinforce the inequality of choice possibilities. Under conditions of unauthentic participation, there is not meaningful opportunity for participants to shape conditions which affect their lives."[81] The assimilation of potentially threatening individuals or interests was also a major political resource of public service bureaucracies in the 1960s. As Black insurgency increased and made demands for better municipal services, the leadership of the public bureaucracies typically responded by targetting for hire some leaders of insurgency.[82]

Selective integration of individual activists serves a political aim: it separates some Black leaders from the development of a mass-based agenda that might structurally challenge the political and economic status quo of the metropolitan establishment. Greer reported such a pattern in Gary, Indiana: "A variety of small favors were extended to Black professionals and petty bourgeois whose marginal economic position rendered them easily influenced."[83] "Clientage," "interest-group articulation," and cooptation were ways of including Blacks on a token basis in the political corridors of power while ensuring that whites—whether machine supporters or reformers—retained control of the contents of a Black public agenda.

Through white-controlled political machines, local governments have also encouraged Blacks to register and vote in ways that keep whites in power. In fact, one group of researchers found that the 1950s "manipulated Negro vote" in several small Southern towns had been operating for many years in Northern big cities as well: "Our data suggest that the white politician's encouragement of Negro registration was based either on actual or anticipated competition for public office. Organization and manipulation of a Negro vote was conceived of as a means of either obtaining or retaining control of public policy-making positions."[84] This is consistent with Kilson's argument that "as a type of Negro political adaptation to cities, interest group articulation had one feature in common with clientage politics: both required influential white patrons as a major political resource enabling the Negro community, or rather special interests thereof, to derive benefits from the political process."[85] The patterns uncovered by Martin Kilson sought neither change in nor challenge to racial hierarchy in the political arena; thus, the corporate sector white wanted to insure its control of Black political behavior and demands.

Attempts to discredit local Black leaders who advocate policies that threaten the interests of the corporate sector have also proven to be an effective strategy. Consider the campaign against minority leaders who challenged the policies and authority of corporate leaders during New York City's fiscal crisis in the early 1970s.[86] A more recent example of this particular negative strategy was reflected in the *Boston Globe*'s editorial campaign against Black elected officials who either declared their support for the secession of predominantly Black Roxbury or opposed corporation but just supported public debate on the question.[87] It seems that no other issue so aroused emotions in Boston's establishment as did the question of secession. Some voters of Roxbury and parts of Dorchester, Mattapan, and the South End were asked to approve a call for the secession of this area from the municipality of Boston. Although this was a nonbinding referendum, it was treated as a major political threat by the *Boston Globe,* the corporate community, Boston Mayor Raymond Flynn, and several opponents of secession in the Black community. The question was defeated in November 1986 and November 1988; approximately 36,000 voters opposed the referendum, while another 12,000 persons approved it on the first ballot. Approximately half of these voters reside in Black areas; this number represents much less than half the registered electorate in the Black community—perhaps only 15 to 20 percent of the total potential electorate in this community. One might, based on these numbers, argue that the defeat of this referendum did not necessarily reflect the sentiment of the *potential* Black electorate in this city, but merely the wishes of those who were registered and decided to vote. By the time of the second election on this issue, voter support for Mandela had increased considerably.

When first raised, the *Boston Globe*'s response to the Mandela issue verged on hysteria. Rather than taking a stand on this issue and then justifying its opposition to idea of secession to its readers, this newspaper and its corporate partners proceeded to orchestrate a campaign of personal attack and innuendo against the individuals identified as leaders of the secession movement. The proponents of secession were not given equal time to respond fully to the political and personal charges in the editorial pages of the *Boston Globe*. And certain Black elected officials were even castigated for not speaking out against the measure as strongly as this newspaper thought appropriate.

The issue of the secession of Greater Roxbury permitted the *Boston Globe* and corporate leaders to direct a campaign against that component of Black leadership considered too politically independent—for instance, State Representatives Byron Rushing and Gloria Fox and State Senator Bill Owens. The electoral defeat of the measure also provided an excuse for the corporate sector, through its relationship with the *Boston Globe* and other major newspapers, to declare the birth of a new Black leadership, supposedly one that is "cooperative," and not "confrontative." Regarding the Mandela editorials, the *Boston Globe* reflected the wishful thinking of many corporate leaders in anxious proclamation that individuals like activist Mel King were no longer "viable" for the Black community. This newspaper suggested that Blacks who work cooperatively with the corporate sector, or who are hired by this sector, or who even happen to be appointed by the mayor, in fact, better represent the interests of Blacks in Boston.

The pattern exhibited by the *Boston Globe* and corporate leadership during the Mandela episode is consistent with national and historical patterns and responses. Hanes Walton, Jr., stated that the tendency to appoint "leaders" for the Black community was also evident:

> . . . during the 1984 Democratic presidential campaign when several of its commentators and opinion leaders of the news media tried nearly throughout the campaign to discredit Jesse Jackson to black folks and make him appear as a radical and violent leader supposedly not in the tradition of his "mentor" Martin Luther King, Jr. Both electronic and print media were filled with allusions to other "responsible" and more acceptable potential black presidential candidates.[88]

Theodore Cross has described other processes of discrediting Black leaders. He argued that Black leaders seeking power rather than access have been discredited or weakened through "racial defamation, tokenism, and discrediting Black power."[89] Boston's secession episode showed how powerful interests seek to appoint, hire, or otherwise control Black leadership in response to its political and economic agenda. It is in the interests of powerful corporate actors to determine as much as possible the appropriate "leaders" in the Black community so that issues like the Mandela referendum in Boston do not emerge frequently. Dominant interests, representing the owners and managers of wealth, can ill afford to allow the emergence of independent Black political leadership on the basis of electoral victories, community, or religious institutions. As Black communities, characterized by increasing and intensifying social crisis, grow in this nation's central cities, corporate America will continue to seek the annointing of a "new" Black political leadership that major newspapers may describe as "sophisticated," "intelligent," "deracialized," and "nonconfrontative," but somehow "effective." Major corporate institutions praise the "maturity" of Black individuals or organizations that adopt political platforms and behavior sanctioned by— and not threatening to—corporate interests in central cities. Independent Black leaders seeking to empower the Black community by politically and socially challenging those interests with power and wealth are called "visionary," "unrealistic," and ignorant of the complicated nature of government.

CHAPTER SIX

The Changing Black Electorate

The fact that he [Min. Louis Farrakhan] received the greatest reception of any speaker indicates that not only do the people want unity . . . but we are of a far more militant and revolutionary attitude than you would expect.

Rep. Gus Savage (African-American National Summit in New Orleans, April 23, 1989)

Louis Farrakhan's reception at the African-American Summit in New Orleans on April 23, 1989, was far more enthusiastic than it had been for any previous speakers, including Jesse Jackson. This is interesting because a few of the summit's planners and organizers threatened to walk out in protest if Farrakhan was formally invited. In the opinion of one convenor of both the 1989 Summit and the Gary Convention, former mayor Richard Hatcher, Farrakhan had to be invited to legitimize the notion of Black unity. But some Black Republicans took issue with this and threatened to withdraw their support for the summit.[1] Others argued that Farrakhan should be invited to a panel but not to address the entire session. This suggestion, however, was rejected by those who argued that he should be recognized as a legitimate leader; moreover, supporters felt that none of the rooms for the panels could hold the number of people that Louis Farrakhan would attract. Eventually Farrakhan agreed to attend when informally invited by some planners. The informal invitation was extended because participants soundly criticized the steering committee for not inviting Farrakhan in the first place.

By the time this Black leader approached the podium, many leaders holding and representing organizational positions in the Democratic

165

party and the Republican party had left the summit; but many of the rank and file decided to stay for what they considered the highlight of the African-American Summit of 1989. This incident reflected the political bifurcation that exists in the Black community regarding issues of philosophy, values, and organizational relationships to white-dominated political and social mainstream processes within American society. Nevertheless, the African-American Summit effectively muffled this kind of political split; in this sense, it differed significantly from the 1972 National Black Political Convention in Gary, Indiana.

In terms of substantive progress political scientist Robert Smith argues that the last summit featured many similarities with the 1974 New Orleans Convention and the 1972 Gary Convention.

> From its origins to its end, the African-American Summit '89 was, pardon the expression, *deja vu* all over again. Indeed, in conversation with participants and in reviewing clips one might easily confuse the New Orleans summit with the Little Rock convention of 1974. . . . Organizers had indicated that 4,000 delegates were expected but, again reminiscent of Gary, it was said that the four months planning time was not enough to extend invitations and organize the process of widespread participation and that many establishment blacks did not wish to be associated in convention with nationalists like Farrakhan and radicals like Angela Davis.[2]

Although this assessment is generally true, important differences between the 1989 Summit and the Gary Convention should not be overlooked.

Although it occurred almost twenty years earlier, the Gary Convention captured and portrayed certain political dynamics in the Black community that the African-American Summit of 1989 did not. The Gary Convention reflected to a far greater extent than the 1989 Summit a grass-roots mobilization in Black communities in the United States. The planning for the summit, while carried out in part by committed Black activists, was centralized. Perhaps this was necessary to ensure the participation of the conservative sector of Black leadership. A decentralized mobilization, based in local cities and regions, rather than Washington, D.C., may have dampened or even prevented the participation of those calling for some form of accommodation with the two major political parties. Centralized planning, rather than grass-roots mobilization, also produced a relatively small summit—reports indicated approximately 1,000 persons attended the convention. Reported turnout at the Gary Convention ranged from six to seven thousand. The participants at the African-American Summit in 1989 were not as widespread geographically as was the case with the Gary Convention.

One theme of the African-American Summit was political unity. In fact, this tempered unity did not reflect equally various viewpoints in the Black community regarding the range of political philosophy and direction for Blacks. The acknowledgment and acceptance of a broad range of ideologies that was reflected in the Gary Convention in 1972—and which perhaps led to major infighting and mistrust—was not a strong theme at the 1989 Summit.

Another major difference between these two events involved their relationships to the Democratic party. Strong Democratic party partisans ensured that the 1989 meeting would not turn a critical eye to the party. In 1972, both the Democratic and Republican parties were critiqued in the plenary sessions in terms of their responses to the needs of Blacks. The 1989 Summit resulted in a summary statement of resolutions that did not challenge substantively the philosophical and economic underpinnings of mainstream American politics. America realized during and after the Gary Convention that Blacks were angry and seeking ways to ensure the political mobilization of masses of Blacks. What did America politically think of Blacks after the 1989 Summit? The opportunity to show that Blacks were not only angry, but also still seeking effective ways by which to generate a mass mobilization of Blacks and other people of color, was not seized. The summit may not have reflected a growing grass-roots activism in Black America.

Based on a review of the literature and interviews with grass-roots activists across the country, I suggest that Black political activism in support of empowerment and populist public policy agenda are gaining momentum. This development could ultimately change the political relationship and balance between the corporate sector, local government, and the Black community. These three sectors, which have accommodated each other in the past, will become more adversarial given the growingly aggressive political posture of Blacks toward needed economic changes. Furthermore, these changes will generate a split in Black political activism and leadership, where one faction seeks accommodation with the corporate sector and the other faction continues to push for social change. If the latter faction continues to use the local electoral arena, then these developments will occur more rapidly. As the progressive face of Black activism takes hold in the electoral arena it will present public policy initiatives that do not fall neatly into either the liberal or the conservative policy camps.

Some activists argue that access without substantive change in the political and social relationships the Black community has with powerful interest groups may not be enough to resolve economic problems facing Blacks; consequently more community-based activists are beginning to focus on changing or redistributing power in the American city. Many Black leaders and activists interviewed believe that the socioeconomic needs of Blacks require systemic rather than reformist approaches to transform wealth and reallocate its subsequent benefits in this society; that is, the system must change in terms of how money and power are accumulated, managed, and distributed. Increasingly the nature and essence of Black politics in urban America is changing and moving toward structural rather than reformist challenges to the power and wealth status quo.

Reviews about which face of Black activism and political orientation is winning are mixed. The first Black elected governor of Virginia may be an example of the importance of moderate Black leadership that neither politically threatens white voters nor, much more important, upsets white powerful interests. Although many traditionally loyal white voters abandoned their political habits by voting for Douglas Wilder's Republican opponent or his lieutenant governor rather than supporting the Democratic Party gubernatorial nominee, it seems that an alliance was effected in the election of Wilder. The moderate Black leadership joined hands with white power interests to maintain political and economic control of Virginia. This coalition has specific economic orientations regarding development and balancing the budget at both the state and city level. For the most part this orientation deemphasizes the social and economic needs of Blacks and poor people. According to political scientist and activist Charles E. Jones, Governor Wilder "has not moved on issues of importance for Black people; he has not supported D.C. statehood, is against the drawing of congressional lines in order to make it easier to elect a Black representative, and supported the role of the national guard in the brutalizing of young Black college students during the 1988 Virginia Beach disruption."[3] If this perception grows, then it will be interesting to note how long Governor Wilder will be able to count on his base of Black support.

The Virginia case has been repeated in other places. The call for a moderate Black leadership that would reach out to the white power structure by calling for access rather than a social change in the status of Blacks as a people seems to have worked for some mayoral aspirants in Atlanta, Los Angeles, Seattle, and perhaps Detroit. Activist Linda Thurston, working with the American Friends Service Committee in Philadelphia, describes a similar political "understanding" in that city. She notes that Mayor Goode sees himself as a good manager, who can carry out the corporate agenda of cutting social services rather than raise questions about the benefits accruing to the corporate sector.[4] In other places, however, there are indications that the progressive face of Black activism is stronger. Several electoral campaigns and political issues illustrate this face of Black activism. The election of Eddie James Carthan in Tchula, Mississippi, in the early 1980s—as was the case of Black radicals in the 1960s and 1970s running for local office—was perhaps a harbinger of this political development. Barbara Mouton in East Palo Alto, California, Harold Washington in Chicago, Timothy Evans's mayoral effort under the "Harold Washington" party in that city, the mayoral candidacy of Mel King in Boston in 1979 and 1983, the Black and Latino vote for mayoral candidate Frank Barbaro in 1981 in New York City, and the many calls for developing Black political agendas throughout the country are examples of the new activism being described here.

This new Black activism may also be evidenced in both presidential campaigns of Jesse Jackson. His campaigns, based in the Black community with primarily a lower-income, poor and working-class base have, in effect, challenged corporate leadership in this country. Although some white political analysts have attributed the massive Black support received by Jesse Jackson to emotional appeals, in fact, his support is based on articulating issues that collectively call for redistributing wealth in American society as well new relationships of power between in-groups and out-groups or "have and have not" interests.

Jesse Jackson's view of the issues addressing the distribution of power were developed over a long period of time. Paulette Pierce comments on Jackson's genesis:

> Jackson developed many of the themes he and others had articulated more than a decade ago. Regarding issues of power he reiterated: (1) the fundamental relationship to the Democratic Party would have to be renegotiated; (2) blacks were ignored and disrespected in party decision-making and slate-making; (3) blacks should accept nothing less that their proportionate share of power; (4) blacks, poor whites, and other disenfranchised groups would have to be brought into the party or else; (5) real power, including the Presidency, was at hand if only blacks trusted in their collective will.[5]

Jesse Jackson would have been unable either to expand his base of support from 1984 to 1988 or to attract a cadre of Black leftist and nationalist actors into his campaign without adopting a platform pushing social change. In addition, Jackson has attracted first-time voters who may not have been previously involved in the electoral arena. More important, he has appealed to Blacks who have consciously or unconsciously rejected, if not the legitimacy of American political institutions, then certainly the effectiveness of such institutions for resolving deteriorating Black life conditions.

Blacks and the Liberal and Conservative Agendas

Diminishing Black support for a liberal agenda or liberal-based politics does not mean a shift toward a conservative agenda or the Republican party as some have suggested. This notion is sometimes fueled by surveys such as the 1986 study conducted by the Center for Media and Public Affairs; it reported the existence of a gap between Blacks and organization-based leaders on several policy issues.[6] Manning Marable points out that "this curious thesis that Afro-Americans were moving to the ideological right superficially has been reinforced by several gubernatorial and municipal elections. . . . In Cleveland's recent mayoral election, 85% of the Black precincts supported incumbent Republican Mayor George Voinovich. Three out of five New Jersey Black voters endorsed incumbent Republican Governor Thomas Kean."[7] But, Marable explains that this is not a sign of a conservative-oriented attraction but rather disaffection and alienation from an established Black leadership perceived as ineffective, compromising, and individualistic. A shift toward the Republican party on the part of former Democratic party Black loyalists can be explained partially as anger and disillusionment with the Democratic party rather than gravitation toward conservative philosophy. This was the position of several prominent Black journalists and newspaper editors around the country. Journalist Tony Brown argued that Blacks should consider adopting such a strategy primarily to punish the Democrats and teach them a lesson, not to endorse the policy orientation of the Republicans.[8]

State Representative Polly Williams, in another example, endorsed a Republican for the 5th Congressional District in Milwaukee over a Democrat as one way to pursue power, not a conservative agenda.

> The issue is blackness, the issue is empowerment of Black people and the expansion and increase of Black representation at all levels of government. That's what we talk about; getting people from our community to impact on those policies that have to deal with our lives. The only way that we're going to be helped is by us, by one of us. . . . I feel that way because my commitment to blackness transcends my Democratic affiliation.[9]

Black activists and voters are beginning to revolt from the Democratic party at this time because they desire goals broader than the usual patronage limited to a few individuals. Blacks are seeking broader group benefits as a result of increased political participation, but they are finding that the Democratic party and many of its leaders are not always supportive, despite Black party loyalty.

Given the continuing negligence of their economic interests, Black support for the Democratic party is eroding; in fact, one political scientist has observed that "the allegiance of blacks to the Democratic Party may be less strong than is often assumed."[10] Thomas Cavanagh offers further insight, "The other prong for a possible new approach for black leaders to take is independent candidacies, and this option, too, is receiving increased attention. Although the constituency for a separate black party remains fairly limited, . . . independent candidacies launched on a selective basis for tactical reasons might be received more positively."[11] This suggestion is supported by a poll conducted by the National Black Election Study; it reported that in 1984 more than half (57 percent) of Blacks would vote for Jesse Jackson if he ran as an independent.[12]

Growing numbers of Black activists believe that only by operating and mobilizing within an independent political framework and strategy, not tied to the major national parties, can the accumulation and management of wealth and the progrowth ideology of corporate America be challenged effectively. Only by making and mobilizing these kinds of challenges is there any hope of making the American city liveable for everyone, not just for upper middle-class whites and the wealthy. Increasing numbers of Black activists are questioning leadership that is politically tied to dominant power structures.

In earlier periods, but still continuing in some places, political mobilization and activism in the Black community has depended on select individuals whose influence was based on their personal accessibility to powerful and wealthy whites in the public and private sectors. Black individuals assigned the role of "liaisons" or "gatekeepers" by governmental and corporate entities, however, could not provide leadership necessary to mobilize Blacks for massive political participation calling for social change. As Ira Katznelson writes, the major function of these Black gatekeepers was to deliver "voters while avoiding contact with white voters in the area. In return, the 'leader' achieved prestige because of his influence with his white patrons. . . . The black voters which the 'leader' mobilized were awarded a few menial patronage jobs to create an illusion of progress."[13] These individuals were, at times, primarily responsible for keeping more independent Black leaders from gaining influence, but also they were instrumental in ensuring that any Black mobilization unfold only within the existing political and social status quo or arrangements sanctioned by the appointers of Black officials. This system started to change during the 1960s and 1970s as Blacks made major inroads into the electoral arenas of American cities through the election of several mayors and congressional and state legislators. Black elected leaders, however, also found themselves operating within a framework that inhibited their effectiveness in responding to the economic needs of poor and working-class Blacks. This growing realization occurred at the same time that the Black electorate was expanding.

The expansion of the Black electorate continued throughout the early 1980s. According to the Joint Center for Political Studies in Washington, D.C., 600,000 Blacks were registered between 1980 and 1982 alone; and the number of Black elected officials nationwide rose by 8.6 percent between July 1982 and July 1983.[14] One study reporting selected primary results for Blacks between 1980 and 1984 showed that in Alabama Black turnout in 1984 surpassed Black turnout in 1980 by 87.0 percent; in New York the figure more than doubled (127.0), while in New Jersey, North Carolina, and Tennessee the figures surpassed a 50 percent jump.[15] Still another study reported that nationally the increase of Blacks claiming to be registered between 1980 and 1984 grew much faster (6.3 percent) than it did for whites claiming to be registered (1.2 percent); this study also reported figures showing that Blacks claiming to have voted between 1980 and 1984 increased much faster (5.3 percent) than was the case for whites (0.5 percent).

Changes in the Black electorate go beyond the increase in numbers. The Black electorate reflects different factors for its behavior today than it did just a few years ago. Factors explaining black political behavior in the current period are not mentioned, for example, in an essay by Chuck Stone. He offered seven reasons why Blacks supported Jimmy Carter in the 1976 presidential election: continuing high Black unemployment, "hypnotic compulsion" to support the Democratic party, Carter's support of the Humphrey-Hawkins Full Employment bill, an effective get-out-the-vote organization, the attitude of President Ford toward Blacks, Carter's endorsement by Rev. "Daddy" King, and the fact that Carter was a Southerner.[16] The 1980 and 1984 presidential elections reflected a different kind of political thinking on the part of Black America. Not only was there some evidence of increased electoral growth and political mobilization, but there were also some indications that the ideological or "civic" orientation of the Black electorate was changing.

Black electoral growth is occurring during a period in which Black leadership is becoming differentiated along certain attitudinal and even ideological lines. There are examples of a different kind of competition between Black leaders, a competition based more on the particular kind of public policy docket pursued rather than on whether one is elected or appointed. Although one kind of leadership—elected or appointed—

seeks accommodation and access into the corridors of public and private power and supports Yankee Capitalism, another kind of Black leadership is challenging the legitimacy of arrangements that maintain certain political and economic processes in both the public and private sectors. Kenneth M. Dolbeare calls this alternative "economic democracy."[17] This Black leadership is more supportive of a populist public policy agenda that challenges corporate leadership's growth ideology.

Two Kinds of Black Leaders

The competition between these two kinds of Black political leadership—or the two faces of Black politics discussed earlier—is becoming crystalized as a result of demography, worsening socioeconomic conditions for the majority of Blacks in America, and a rising political consciousness. In a city like Chicago, for example, the seeds of this split in leadership—certainly not a new development in the 1990s—was the degree of political alienation many Blacks felt with the Democratic party machine. Gregory D. Squires reported some evidence of this development in his study of the first mayoral victory of Harold Washington:

> In effect, two of the long-standing subcurrents in modern Chicago politics were joining in late 1982. First, black alienation from the politics of the machine was becoming focused, and given the increasing minority proportion of the city's population and the sudden jump in their voter registration— one might say a return to the electoral fold—a major political eruption was in the offing. Second, the growth of community groups, so many of which had serious interest in the policies and service activities of government even as they eschewed politics Chicago-style, served as the fulcrum for the 1982 registration drive. They passed the word, staffed the registration tables, and seem to have taken seriously the prospect of using the upcoming mayoral election to upset the machine's apple cart. The seeds of the regular Democrats' indifference to blacks' and most neighborhood organizations' interests were at last bearing fruit.[18]

Similarly, the president of the National Black United Front in Chicago also described the "battle lines" of Black politicians in the city's post-Washington period:

> The battle lines are clearer between the independent, progressive, Harold Washington allies on one side versus those politicians with the Daley machine who benefitted from the Washington rise—e.g., Wilson Frost who was endorsed by Washington and won a position with the Board of Tax Appeal and Cecil Partee who formerly ran as Treasurer with Washington who

is now a Cook County State Attorney, both of these men are now allied
with the regular party machine with Daley. The battle lines have these people going back to plantation politics and currying favor with Daley.[19]

Another writer referred to the two faces of Black activism when he wrote
that only the leadership empowering the Black community is effective or
worthy of pursuit and support. Bruce Wright points out,

> If the racial atmosphere in America is ever to be improved, the Blacks who
> are called leaders must offer genuine leadership. They cannot simply be the
> tools of the white establishment, for such leadership is ersatz and calculated
> to keep the anger of the Blacks internal and tranquilized. . . . Such leader-
> ship obeys a directed policy but does not make policy. Genuine black lead-
> ership must be muscular and not swayed by those who would neutralize it
> into puppetry. It must address publicly and express exactly what most
> Blacks really think and feel about white American society and why.[20]

Joe Darden and his colleagues cite an example of the early seeds of this
growing bifurcation of Black politics in Detroit during the 1960s. They
describe the competition between the nationalist Interdenominational
Ministries Alliance who urged a Black bullet vote in city council elections
and the more "moderate" Black organization, The Trade Union Leadership Council, that opposed a boycott of white candidates.[21] But as the
authors write, "In the 1960s the threat of radical black politics—or at
least black politics to the left of black moderates in the liberal coalition—
posed problems for the established black politicians, but the threat never
materialized into any substantial challenge."[22] Several things, however,
differ today: This debate is taking place with greater frequency, and Black
support is growing in the electoral arenas of major American cities.
Moreover, conditions exist for a substantial Black-led challenge to the
dominant institutional arrangements supporting liberal and conservative
power structures.

This competition does have historical roots. It reminds one of Harold
Cruse's argument that the major theme in the history of Blacks in America is the conflict between nationalism and integration. At times the
former may be associated with challenges to the social status quo, but it
can also be accommodating to a racially reformed political and economic
status quo.[23] One could use the recent taxonomy of anthropologist John
Brown Childs who argues that Afro-American social thought and political action can be categorized generally into those interests advocating
either a "Vanguard" or a "Mutuality" perspective. The former represents
an elite vision and program for Black political direction, while the latter
focuses on the importance of the involvement of mass-based interests in
the Black community.[24] These positions can be summarized as pushing

either accommodation, albeit with an element of reform, with the structure of wealth and power, or structural challenge to the status quo of power and wealth.

Until recently, the leadership that supported a liberal agenda and sought accommodation rather than development of community-based political structures maintained an important advantage over the more independent Black leadership through its use of the electoral arena. Community-based leadership calling for challenges and changes in the economic and social status quo generally deemphasized activism in the electoral arena. As Black political activism begins to shift from the pursuit of access to more serious systemic challenges an important debate arises in the Black community. Interests pursuing access-oriented strategies and policies—that is, structural accommodation to the power and social status quo—will conflict with those subverting this same status quo. Examples of this may include the debates generated between Jesse Jackson supporters in the 1984 presidential campaign for the Democratic party nomination and those Black individuals supporting Gary Hart or Walter Mondale. These discussions pitted Blacks calling for strategies built upon changing the power status quo within the Democratic party against Blacks calling for access to, or accommodation with, the power status quo. While one faction called for a new direction, perhaps even new values, and consequently different kinds of social relationships between Blacks and the Democratic party, the other faction merely sought to have those with power accommodate or integrate more fully Black interests.

The competition of these two faces of Black activism was also reflected in the Jackson delegates' vociferous criticism of prominent Mondale supporters—Atlanta Mayor Andrew Young and Coretta Scott King in the 1984 Democratic Party National Convention. Robert G. Newby, a sociologist and Jackson delegate during this convention, explained this rift in ideological terms:

> The major distinction between the Jackson delegation and the party as a whole was an ideological difference: the Jackson delegates were twice as likely as the delegates of both Hart and Mondale to consider themselves to be "very liberal," and on the ABC/Washington Post Poll nearly 20 percent of the Jackson delegates rated themselves to be at the most extreme "liberal" point. . . . This difference in political ideology is the difference between mainstream, status quo politics and the politics of change, or "movement politics," with its attendant ideology.[25]

Thus one kind of Black activist seeks to challenge the power status quo, but another seeks access to those interests holding power.

In a city like Boston one can uncover numerous instances of this emerging debate in the Black community. Grass-roots organizations, such as the Black Political Task Force, are continually faced with these theoretical questions. This organization, founded in 1979, has become one of the most influential political interest groups in Boston's Black community today. About thirty-five activists, interested in building a network dedicated to the "empowerment of people of color" by working in the electoral arena, founded the task force. It has been in the forefront of important electoral battles. Members have attempted to both encourage and resolve the debate between activists who focus on access and those who argue that such a focus may ultimately lead Blacks away from empowerment. This theoretical debate is reflected in much of the factionalism found within the organization. Although one mindset supports accommodation with whites in power who may have been racially reformed by arguing that alliance with such powerful whites could result in jobs, contracts, and access to important decision makers, the other mindset supports the development of a Black public policy agenda on the basis of empowerment that confronts the power and wealth status quo.

Significantly this growing debate between the two faces of Black politics portends a changing Black electorate, different from the traditional one pursuing access and accommodation or desegregation. A few years ago David Sears and John McConahay referred to the emergence of "New Urban Blacks" who represented "more than a demographic group. They are persons characterized by a distinctive psychology and a common approach to political life." These researchers referred to this particular category of young Blacks in explaining the attitudes and behavior of individuals who participated in the Watts riot. They found that the New Urban Blacks have "more positive Black identity," "more generalized political disaffection," and had "more political sophistication than older, southern migrant, rural, or less educated Blacks."[26] In general, community activists pursuing changes in power relationships between Blacks and whites target this sector in particular for voter mobilization. The introduction of these "New Urban Blacks" could mean the development of an electorate not familiar to Salisbury's "urban executive coalition."

Urban Managerialism versus Political Activism
The dominant urban executive coalitions approach problems of the cities in ways that neither threaten nor interrupt the distribution or flow of power, money, status, and privilege. Although the broad membership

of the urban executive coalition has changed over the years and the political relationship between the federal government, mayors, unions, the corporate sector, and racial and ethnic groups are continually in flux, the "governing framework" has not changed significantly. This framework, which includes both liberal and conservative policy orientations, continues to maintain a status quo of power and wealth. Local politics currently operates within a managerial or "technocratic" orientation, consistent with this framework; here the specific distribution of power and wealth is not questioned.

The managerial approach to local politics dictates the substance and the style of electoral campaigns. For example, electoral challengers to incumbents usually present themselves as better managers or technicians. Under the old face of local politics, those who seek electoral office offer themselves, not as leaders of the citizenry, but as effective brokers. Thus, the major function of mayors elected within this context is to mediate the needs of various citizens' groups with the wealth and power status quo. In other words, the basic problem faced by these urban managers—the mayors—is how to accommodate the social and economic problems facing Blacks, the poor, and the working class, within the present hierarchy of wealth and power.

Activism in the electoral arena on the part of new Black actors and groups points to an important change in the Black electorate. New actors reflect the change from access and accommodation toward a politics in the electoral arena that seeks to change arrangements maintaining the social and economic status quo. Several electoral developments have emerged during Black politics' shift from a traditional, liberal face to a progressive one. For example, Black activists who had been involved with earlier social protest, desegregation, and community control struggles have begun to use the electoral arena in a more systematic pursuit of power. In many cases, the renewed political surge is led and supported by Blacks who have heretofore rejected electoral activism as a tool for substantive change in the Black community but who, given their heightened sense of Black consciousness, reflect much organizing experience in the arena of social protest. Many who are now participating in progressive electoral campaigns rejected electoral participation in the past. Black intellectuals and activists on the left, as well as many among the Black poor and working class, never fully accepted the use of electoral politics to effect meaningful social change. Understanding that electoral politics was dominated by individuals and groups seeking accommodation into the power and economic status quo rationalized this rejection. More

Blacks today are participating in a kind of electoral activism that presents systemic challenges to the traditional groups and coalitions responsible for making and implementing public policy for cities.

Black Political Radicalization

It has been proposed that the Black electorate is experiencing a radicalization and a greater acceptance of Black nationalism in the form of increasing neighborhood activism and political consciousness. That is, the political choices and behavior of Blacks is beginning to suggest less patience with and faith in the economic values and arrangements of America that this group perceives as responsible for deteriorating social conditions. Chicago offers two examples of radicalization: the 1982 People's Coalition to Boycott Chicagofest and the People Organized for Welfare and Employment Rights (POWER), a coalition of various community groups. The coalition helped lay a foundation for the eventual election of Harold Washington as the first Black and progressive mayor of Chicago in 1983; POWER was responsible for voter registration activities that enrolled hundreds of thousands of new voters.[27] Basil Wilson suggests that in New York City Black nationalists who have rejected access and integration are having a major impact in the local electoral arena. This sector has carried out an insurgency movement against interests led by Ed Koch while he was mayor. Wilson argues that the work of activists like Jitu Weusi and Sonny Carson, along with the Black United Front, ultimately led to Koch's political downfall.[28]

Because some activists in the Black community are concerned or disheartened with both Jesse Jackson's treatment by powerful interests and his developing detente with the Democratic party, a period of increasingly militant Black activism could be in the offing. Some activists felt that, despite the Jackson gains in the 1984 and 1988 primary campaigns, Blacks have been continually snubbed and tokenized within the Democratic party. This sentiment is echoed by Black columnist Earl Caldwell: "The current state of affairs doesn't say much about the future of Blacks in this country. . . . The Black electorate, after false hopes brought about by Jackson's bids, is where it started eight years ago. The feelings of racism throughout the country are as strong as ever—which means that the party will not allow any significant role for Jackson in the future."[29] This was reiterated by another observer of Black activism, Salim Muwakhil, "the African-American crusade for racial justice has now been marginalized by Reagan-era conservatism and hobbled by its own lack of focus."[30]

Despite the election of Ron Brown as chair of the Democratic National Committee many Black activists interviewed felt that this party seeks to disassociate itself from any position that acknowledges the important and critical role of Black voters. Still other Black activists feel that Jackson is becoming too mainstream and comfortable with the Democratic party's centrist leadership to keep calling for the need for fundamental economic and social change in America. Louis Farrakhan, for example, has observed that Jackson's attempt to be accepted by the Democratic party has forced a certain degree of disassociation from a Black agenda that could radically alter race relations and the distribution of power in America and abroad.[31]

These events indicate that Black political activism in the electoral arena is raising important issues about the nature of American capitalism and the welfare of the Black community. The activists who are emerging as advocates for renewed activism in the Black community are beginning to emphasize class issues: they are not confining themselves to the usual conceptual boundaries of local and ethnic politics as described by political scientist Robert A. Dahl in his classic *Who Governs*. In this study Dahl proposed an axiom of local politics: "In allocating rewards to individuals and groups, the existing socioeconomic structure must be taken as given, except for minor details."[32] Black activists are raising new issues; they offer alternative responses to pressing social problems in ways that are not defensive about questioning the American values and economic practices protective of wealth and the kinds of social relationships flowing from these arrangements. As reflected in the emerging calls for "Black agendas" in different parts of the country, many Black activists are now willing to confront the corporate leadership to help define a different relationship between this sector and the Black community and local government.

This observation is questioned by some who argue that Blacks are becoming increasingly similar to whites in political attitudes and behavior, moving together toward what Virginia Governor Douglas Wilder has referred to as "the new mainstream." On the basis of reviewing national election studies as well as general social surveys one researcher concluded that Blacks are not disillusioned with the prevailing social and economic order. According to his interpretation of the data, the political attitudes of Blacks are quite similar to those held by whites.[33] But juxtaposed to this claim is the fact that major differences in social and political attitudes have been reported in several surveys. Based on these surveys, one can conclude that "by the 1970s their increasingly liberal (relative to the population) attitudes on school integration and black welfare placed them equally far from the population on these issues. Blacks also moved substantially further to the left on the issues of the cold war and the scope of government. . . . No other group in American society is as distinctively liberal as American blacks."[34] The suggestion that Blacks and whites are not substantially different in their political attitudes on broad systemic questions invites a major criticism: actual political behavior and activism in the Black community suggest significant differences in social and political orientation and behavior. In light of the argument that there is a new mainstream, how does one explain the Mandela referendum in Boston or the attempt to empower an independent Black school district in Milwaukee? How does one explain the growing popularity of Louis Farrakhan if, in fact, the political attitudes of Blacks "look much like the attitudes held by whites"?

A few developments portend a radicalization of the Black electorate at the same time that some Black mayors and the nation's first Black governor are being elected on the basis of "deracialized" campaign strategies. Black support for economic protest, such as attempts to force extractions from the corporate sector through boycotts, linkage requirements, and plant-closing legislation may be instances of this. The radical trend is also reflected in numerous calls for Black control of land and the public institutions operating within areas numerically dominated by poor and working-class Black residents. Today this major political issue pits the interests of the corporate sector and its government allies against the Black community. Thus, in the 1990s the political saliency of the electoral arena has increased as it becomes a tool by which either to muffle the mobilization and demands of the Black community or to raise demands reflecting the interests of this community. For example, the electoral arena as a focal point in some local political struggles is reflected in the Nation of Islam's decision to run and endorse their own candidates for congressional and school committee positions in Washington, D.C. Consider also the aggressive role that Black nationalists and Black power advocates have been pursuing in the electoral arena, especially evident in Jesse Jackson's campaigns.

The last few years have seen a precipitous infusion of new Black actors into the electoral arena. Many of these new voters with strong nationalist leanings are having major impact on the direction of Black politics. As Lucius J. Barker stated,

> The infusion and activation of new and old voters could bring new and potential candidates for public office. and while black voters tend to vote for

black candidates, it is by no means clear or certain that new or reactivated black voters will vote for a black incumbent over a black challenger. . . . Undoubtedly, this infusion of new black voters and aroused black political interest could affect the nature and structure of black politics and black political leadership.[35]

More aggressive voter registration drives in the Black community, as well as opposition to Reagan public policies, explain some of this increased interest.

The fact that Jesse Jackson was competitive with other Democratic party presidential primary candidates also raised the saliency of electoral politics for many Blacks. But political scientist Michael B. Preston also argues that heightened group consciousness and presentation of pertinent issues were important factors in explaining the presence of new Black actors in the electoral arena.[36] In light of this, the suggestion by journalist John B. Judis is strange; he claims that "by the mid-70s, black power advocates and black nationalists had become politically irrelevant and would remain so until they resurfaced during Jesse Jackson's 1984 presidential campaign. Even now they play a largely rhetorical rather than substantive role, feeding on the already existing impasse in race relations."[37] In fact, the nationalist sector in the Black community had a major influence on how Jesse Jackson presented and molded his campaign issues, especially in the 1984 campaign; this sector also pulled important votes for the Dinkins mayoral campaign in New York City, helped propel Mel King as Boston's first Black mayoral candidate to make the run off election in 1983, provided the philosophical glue to deliver a solid bloc of Black voters to Harold Washington the same year, and have played significant roles in many local elections across the country.

New Black voters and the growing electoral participation of Black social activists and protest leaders indicate an increase in the level of efficacy regarding the electoral arena as a way of addressing an agenda of social change and a medium for mass mobilization directed at social change. But this is also causing the Black electorate to become splintered. The Black electorate is becoming differentiated on the basis of ideological and philosophical issues. Different groups within the Black electorate are expressing a range of political options for the Black community. This is significant for several reasons: (1) the diversity represents a new development for the Black urban electorate; (2) it has implications for the ways in which Blacks are mobilized for voter registration and turnout; and (3) it reflects a rise in political consciousness among certain sectors in Black urban communities. This growing differentiation can also explain some particularities of Black local electoral behavior in various cities.

Differentiation in the Black electorate has been overlooked by much of the literature on Black voting behavior, according to Hanes Walton, Jr., who has reported a tendency "to combine the black electorate with the black voter. Political behavioralists tend to see these groups as synonymous."[38] At least one empirical study, however, shows support for the proposition that the Black electorate is becoming more issue-conscious and differentiated. Paul Carton's study of the effects of personal contact in campaigning among Black voters in Detroit provided "convincing evidence that both party organizational activity and community leadership activity can have a dramatic impact on black voter behavior. Campaigns that desire to increase black voter turnout and later black voter preference for a particular issue or candidate would do well to engage in extensive voter contacting activities within the black community."[39] Personal contact conducted by community leaders in low-income areas can have a significant impact on registration and turnout probably because such contact brings out the "activist" and "alienated" sectors. This development may explain another conclusion of the investigation: "Community leadership activity affected voter behavior exclusively in lower-middle income and low-income black precincts. One of the most interesting findings of this study is that community leadership activity had no effect on voter turnout or preference in upper-middle income black precincts."[40] It seems that different sectors of the Black electorate must be appealed to differently for purposes of electoral mobilization. The appeals involve not only personal contact but also the political and ideological messages regarding issues of race and power and the kinds of economic development strategies advocated for the Black community. It is very likely that appeals based on Black nationalism, the acquisition of power, and control of land in the Black community will attract a different kind of Black voter than those based on traditional, integrationist appeals.

This suggestion is supported by research of Black political patterns at the local level. Preston has suggested that new Black voters in urban America must fit into one of two categories. The first includes the previously registered voters, but the second now includes "the groups that have been the least likely to register and vote; the young, poor, women, and the elderly. They have come to believe, like many of their middle-class brethen, that they can make a difference. This is especially true when the choice presented call into question their ethnic pride or group identity."[41]

In a study of Detroit, Wilbur C. Rich asserts that part of the constituency of a Black mayor is this second group, the nonvoters.

Nonvoters, many of whom are not registered, are a reserved electoral force that can be mobilized on cue by a mayor who is perceived as a race leader. . . . Black mayors are expected to play a "watchman's" role, among others, and this distinguishes them from old-time machine politicians, as well as from their modern-day white counterparts. Hence, their constituency contains both active and reserve electorates, and accordingly, actions by the mayor must be scrutinized for both psychological content and signal intent. Mayoral initiative and leadership are critical to the care and maintenance of the silent reserve voting bloc. Black mayors have tended to treat this group much like a part of their audience, but many have provided uplift rhetoric as well, which encourages the silent voters.[42]

Thus, Rich also found evidence to differentiate the Black electorate and its varying patterns of behavior and participation on the basis of symbolic and political messages received by these sectors. Although certain political messages may motivate one sector, they may not have the same effect on other sectors in the Black electorate. Rich corroborates Preston's observation: the sector that tends to remain nonparticipatory is motivated to a greater extent by race-conscious and nationalist appeals. Such appeals help explain the upsurge of Black political activism in the last several years and the introduction of new kinds of Black voters into urban electoral arenas.

The infusion of new Black actors participating in electoral activism coupled with a strong attraction to populist agenda produces both wide and large voter registration and turnout fluctuations, evident at the local level. In Boston, for example, various elections have elicited different and inconsistent rates of Black participation. One year the turnout may be relatively high, but in the very next year it could be of low and of little interest. In studying Chicago, Preston also uncovered indications of voter fluctuation that had to do with issues and quality of leadership presented to Black voters rather than the social or economic characteristics of Blacks.

The data indicate that increasing numbers of qualified black voters are avoiding the system in mayoral elections. Considering the difference in Democratic support at the polls in national and local elections, the increased or steady machine support in local general elections, and the decreased black turnout, it would seem that many of the black voters who are staying away from the polls are potential anti-machine votes.[43]

Large and inconsistent fluctuation in Black electoral participation at the local level reflects the ideological bifurcation discussed earlier; certain sectors in the Black community are more responsive to political messages with a particular ideological or philosophical content.

The Black electorate is changing not only quantitatively as a result of demographic developments but also qualitatively as a result of new political actors and heightened political consciousness. In fact, the Black electorate of the 1990s seems to be evolving into several components. Fluctuating voter registration rates and the unpredictable change in the level of involvement from one election to the next point to the development of three sectors within the local Black electorate.

One sector consistently remains registered; individuals in this sector need not be reminded to register to vote. Another sector is basically alienated from electoral processes; many Blacks have never voted in local government elections. These "politically divorced," to use political scientist Robert Lane's term, may have consciously considered electoral participation a futile exercise of time and effort; others may want to remain in Charles V. Hamilton's term "functionally anonymous."[44] During the 1980s a third sector has emerged. This sector, with its relatively strong influence on the political behavior and direction of the Black electorate, features a relatively high level of social and political consciousness and uses the electoral processes selectively, depending on the particular issues at stake and their presentation. Activist Conrad Worrill provides an example: "I believe in selectively participating in political elections around candidacies and issues." He argues that the decision regarding entry into the electoral arena by Black grass-roots activists should be based on the protection of their economic interests, with "less emphasis on electoral politics" merely to get someone into office.[45]

Of the three kinds of Black voters—the "politically divorced" voter, the "selective," and the "participatory" voter—the participatory Black voter probably represents the largest sector. Based on voter registration and turnout rates, the size of this sector ranges from 40 and 50 percent. Participatory Blacks not only remain registered but are also competitive with white voters in terms of turnout. The selective and politically divorced sectors each comprise about one-quarter of the Black electorate. The selective Black electorate, perhaps a recent development, is politically active and involved in the public affairs of the community. Unlike participatory Blacks, selective Black actors approach the electoral process not as a civic responsibility but as deliberate political strategy. If the electoral arena is perceived as particularly important for a political issue, then this sector becomes active in this arena; but if electoral activity is not perceived as salient for an issue, then this sector continues to pursue social change through means other than the voting booth.

This analytical framework can help explain the outcome of issues like the Mandela proposal in the Black community in Boston, leadership factionalism, and fluctuating Black voter registration and turnout levels. The "in-out" electoral activism of the activist sector that sometimes pulls the "politically divorced" may explain rapidly changing voter registration and participation patterns. One study points out, for example, that "our previous research had shown that turnout peaked at times of major challenges to conservative coalitions and then fell, even though minority candidates continued to win elections. . . . Peak turnout seemed necessary to successful challenges but not necessary for sustained incorporation. It was as if the issue had been settled, minority representation was accepted, and peak effort to turn out the vote was no longer needed."[46] The selective and politically divorced sectors in the Black electorate basically stay in reserve, until they hear certain kinds of messages or invitations that convince them of the worth of electoral over other forms of community mobilization. Perhaps this explains the easier generation of higher levels of registration and turnout when conservative coalitions are being challenged, as suggested in the study cited earlier.

The Mandela referendum lost in many of Boston's Black precincts, but there are several explanations for this. Certainly the campaign directed against this referendum by the city's corporate leadership added to the "no" votes, but the very way the Black electorate was approached by pro-Mandela organizers influenced the outcome. The contest was decided by what is referred to here as the participatory Black electorate. The politically divorced sector was basically left out of the debate, although the discussion was presumably carried out on their behalf. This sector, in fact, represented an important base for this new experiment in Boston local government.

The organizers and supporters of Mandela approached the Black electorate as if it were monolithic, but the three electoral sectors within this community respond to different messages. The fate of the Mandela referenda was placed in the hands of Black voters who, for the most part, have always been conscientious participants in Boston's electoral contests; these voters, as a result of this participation, were loyal to the notion of participating within the political system and attempting to change that system from within. For a proposal like Mandela to continue as a salient political issue, the typical nonparticipants in the electoral process must be brought into the debate. There is a parallel development at the national level.

The Plight of the Democratic Party

The paradigm offered above is relevant on a national level regarding the developing relationship between Black voters and the Democratic party. Although participatory voters in the Black community may remain loyal to the Democratic party, this is not necessarily the case with either the activist or politically divorced strata. But this does not mean that the latter sections would turn to the Republican party, however. The politically divorced sector, if organized—and this can only occur with certain ideological and philosophical messages—is significant because of the numbers of Blacks who might comprise this sector. Generally alienated from electoral processes, this sector can still have an impact on national elections and politics. The mobilization of this sector was a major reason for Jesse Jackson's success in the 1988 Democratic party primary campaign when he carried most major American cities with significant Black populations.

The splintering of the Black electorate presents a major problem for the Democratic party. Because of the growing demographic and political influence of Blacks in many American cities and the impact that new Black voters can have on local and national elections, this party can remain competitive at the national level if it can count on the loyal support of these sectors. But the Democrats cannot maintain this loyalty without supporting the issues to which activist and politically divorced Blacks respond. Thus, the Democratic party faces what columnist Tom Wicker has called an "identity crisis."[47]

The Democratic party was able to remain in power in the past by holding to the center of the national political spectrum. The strength of the Democratic party in various periods after the New Deal was due in part to its appeal and control of the political and ideological "center." But since the revolt of millions of "Wallace Democrats" in 1968, the party has found it increasingly difficult to hold on to a rapidly disappearing center in the American political spectrum. As sociologist John F. Zipp has written,

> Mondale's sizeable defeat in 1984 means that the traditional liberal center (usually referred to as the "left") of the Democratic Party has been severely weakened. Although there may be attempts to revive it, the struggle could be between the neo-liberals like Hart, Senator Bill Bradley (D.–N.J.), and others, and people like Jesse Jackson. . . . In policy terms, it will be easier then for Democratic candidates to let concern for social justice fall by the wayside: it could more easily be seen as a political albatross, weighing heavily on the necks of any major political candidate.[48]

The defeat of Dukakis in 1988 also reflected, in part, the party's "identity crisis" and failure to mold and hold the political and ideological center. The Republican party has opted to control the right in the American political spectrum, and therefore, they do not face this identity crisis. Although the leadership of the Republican party must also balance certain ideological factions, the general philosophical direction of the Republicans is far more clear-cut and consistent than for the Democrats. At stake for the Republican party is whether to hold the right by adopting an extreme political style in the mode of Reagan or by working with a "gentler" approach.

One can note the intense ideological and philosophical pressures on the Democratic party generated by Black activism even in the international arena. Black activists in the aftermath of several 1988 presidential primary victories for Jackson forced the Democratic Party Platform Committee to declare South Africa a terrorist state. Similarly, the question of Palestinian self-determination and statehood was given a national forum following this activism. In Illinois two hundred supporters of Jackson's presidential campaign "persuaded the Platform Committee to approve a plank endorsing 'the rights of the Palestinian people to safety, self-determination and an independent state.'" As the *New York Times* reported: "These moves, often prompted by the Rev. Jesse Jackson's presidential campaign, raise an issue that threatens the party with a bitter emotional conflict at a time when it is seeking harmony."[49]

The Democratic party is today in another historical political bind. A similar crisis faced the party when the Mississippi Freedom Democratic Party demanded representation at the Atlantic City Convention in 1964. At that time the party leadership temporarily managed the crisis by offering Blacks token access. This kind of response is no longer possible; Blacks want power, not access. But if American liberal leadership acknowledges this and acts upon it, many white voters will continue to abandon the ranks of the Democrats to join the Republican party. The Democratic party maintained majority status in most national elections as long as Blacks not only remained loyal to the party and, as Theda Skocpol points out, also did not question their marginality in the New Deal programs and policies.[50] As Blacks begin to demand a bigger share of power within the party, however, white voters will become increasingly threatened because the demands of the activist and politically divorced sectors in the Black electorate imply major changes in terms of the racial and economic hierarchies of this society. The Democratic party may be unwilling or incapable of responding effectively to such challenges—only forthcoming elections will tell.

Notes

Introduction

1. Lucius J. Barker, *Our Time Has Come* (Chicago: University of Illinois Press, 1988), p. 205.

2. Gil Scott-Heron, "Winter in America" (New York: Arista Records, 1974).

3. John Trice, *From Dependency to Empowerment* (Chicago: Clifton and Lee Publishing Company, 1981), p. 14.

4. C. Ashford Baker, "Revolt of An Underclass: A View of the Jackson Candidacy," *Urban Research Review* 10, no. 1 (1985): 4–6.

5. For a discussion about factors that lead to a rise in Black nationalism, see Robert Allen, *Black Awakening in Capitalist America* (New York: Doubleday, 1969), and also Manning Marable, *Black American Politics* (London: Verso Press, 1985).

Chapter One

1. See *Boston Herald,* January 19, 1986; *Philadelphia Tribune,* April 1, 1988; *Chicago Metro News,* March 5, 1988.

2. *Chicago Defender,* April 6, 1988.

3. *Milwaukee Courier,* April 4, 1988.

4. See *Philadelphia Tribune,* April 1, 1988; *Chicago Defender,* April 5, April 28, 1988.

5. *Atlanta Constitution,* July 17, 1988, for a brief description of the two meetings in Atlanta; see also Cornel West, *Prophetic Fragments* (Grand Rapids, Mich.: William B. Eedermans, 1988), pp. 137–143.

6. Rob Gurwitt, "A Younger Generation of Black Politicians Challenges Its Elders," *Governing* (February 1990): 30.

7. Joseph Darden et al., *Detroit: Race and Uneven Development* (Philadelphia: Temple University Press, 1987), p. 207.

8. Shafik Abu-Pahir, interview, Philadelphia, April 11, 1990.

9. Martin Luther King, Jr., *Where Do We Go From Here: Chaos or Community?* (Boston: Beacon Press, 1968), p. 149.

10. *In These Times,* July 6, 1988.

11. Bayard Rustin, "From Protest to Politics: The Future of the Civil Rights Movement," *Commentary* 39 (February 1965): 25–31.

12. Lucius J. Barker and Ronald W. Walters, *Jesse Jackson's 1984 Presidential Campaign: Challenge and Change in American Politics* (Chicago: University of Illinois Press, 1989), p. 32.

13. See *Black Panther Newspaper,* April 12, 1975; *Milwaukee Courier,* March 10, March 17, 1990.

14. Thaddeus P. Mathis, *The State of Black Philadelphia* (Philadelphia: The Urban League, 1988), p. 32.

15. Basil Wilson, "Race and Politics of New York State: A Tale of Two Cities," paper presented at National Conference of Black Political Scientists, Atlanta, Georgia, March 13–17, 1990.

16. Charles V. Hamilton, "New Elites and Pluralism," in *Power To Govern: Assessing Reform in the United States,* ed. Richard M. Pious (New York: Academy of Political Science, New York, 1981), p. 167.

17. Sheila D. Collins, *The Rainbow Challenge: The Jackson Campaign and the Future of United States Politics* (New York: Monthly Review Press, 1986), p. 29.

18. Hanes Walton, Jr., *Invisible Politics* (Albany: State University of New York Press, 1985), pp. 7–42.

19. Earl Hutchinson, "Misunderstood Legacy of King," *Guardian* (January 21, 1987): 18–19.

20. For a discussion about the impact of Black nationalism and changing relationships between race, class, and community, see James Jennings, "The Politics of Black Empowerment in Urban America: Reflections of Race, Class and Community," in *Dilemmas of Activism,* ed. Joseph Kling and Prudence Posner (Philadelphia: Temple University Press, 1990). See also Huey L. Perry and Alfred Stokes, "Politics and Power in the Sunbelt: Mayor Morial of New Orleans," in *The New Black Politics,* ed. Michael B. Preston, Lenneal J. Henderson, and Paul Puryear (New York: Longman Publishers, 1987), p. 251; in the same collection, see Bruce Ransom, "Black Independent Electoral Politics in Philadelphia and the Election of Mayor W. Wilson Goode," p. 281.

21. Margot Harry, *Attention, Move* (Chicago: Banner Press, 1987), p. 91.

22. Rose Upshaw, interview, Houston, March 16, 1990.

23. Joyce Brooks, interview, Philadelphia, April 16, 1990.

24. W. E. B. Du Bois, *Black Reconstruction in America, 1860–1880* (New York: Atheneum, 1985), chap. 15.

25. James Boggs, *Racism and The Class Struggle: Further Pages From A Black Worker's Notebook* (New York: Monthly Review Press, 1970).

26. Committee on Policy for Racial Justice, "Black Initiative and Governmental Responsibility," (Washington, D.C.: Joint Center for Political Studies, 1987), p. 1.

27. Hanes Walton, Jr., *Black Politics: A Theoretical and Structural Analysis* (Philadelphia: Lippincott, 1972), p. 12.

28. Stephan Thernstrom, *The Other Bostonians: Poverty and Progress in the American Metropolis, 1880–1970* (Cambridge: Harvard University Press, 1973), pp. 204–5.

29. Martin Kilson, "Political Change in the Negro Ghetto, 1900–1940's," *Key Is-*

sues in the Afro-American Experience, ed. Nathan I. Huggins, Martin Kilson, and Daniel M. Fox (New York: Harcourt, Brace, and Jovanovich, 1971), p. 169.

30. Kenneth M. Dolbeare and Murray Edelman, American Politics: Policies, Power and Change (Lexington, Mass: Heath, 1979), p. 29.

31. Peter Steinfels, The Neo-Conservatives: The Men Who Are Changing America's Politics (New York: Simon and Schuster, 1979), p. 34.

32. Joel Lieske and Jan W. Hillard, "The Racial Factor In Urban Elections," Western Political Quarterly 34, no. 4 (December 1984): p. 545.

33. James E. Conyers and Walter L. Wallace, Black Elected Officials: A Study of Black Americans Holding Government Office (New York: Russell Sage Foundation, 1976), p. 31; the 1984 data is based on a survey reported in Gerald D. Jaynes and Robin M. Williams, Jr., A Common Destiny: Blacks and American Society (Washington, D.C.: National Academy Press, 1989), pp. 212, 213.

34. Diane R. Brown and C. Ashford Baker, "Attitude Differentiation at the 1980 Presidential Conventions: Aspects of Race and Party Identification," Urban Research Review 10, no. 1 (1985): 3.

35. Mary Ann Crayton, correspondence with author, April 16, 1989.

36. In These Times, November 25, 1987.

37. Chicago Defender, July 6, 1988.

38. Dennis Gale, Washington, D.C.: Inner City Revitalization and Minority Suburbanization (Philadelphia: Temple University Press, 1987), p. 161. This is also fueled by information released by the government that showed the Internal Revenue Service had developed a "hit list" of influential Black organizations in the 1960s and 1970s. According to Paul Des Fosses, former senior IRS agent and currently president of the National Coalition of IRS Whistleblowers, the purpose of "Operation Bird Dog" was to harass or discredit Black leaders. See Chicago Crusader, February 3, 1990. Another situation that fuels Blacks' sense that powerful white interests intend to resist any kind of political advancement is the case of the Black mayor of Atlantic City, New Jersey. Mayor James L. Usry was indicted and arrested on July 27, 1990, based on the accusation that he had received bribes from an individual later identified as a state informant. But Grand Jury transcripts disclosed that Mayor Usry never asked for money as the state informant had alleged. See Philadelphia Inquirer, February 9, 1990, and City Sun, February 14, 1990.

39. In These Times, November 25, 1987.

40. Philadelphia Tribune, June 14, 1988.

41. Walter W. Morrison, "Racists Terror Tactics Won't Work, Hooks Vows," Crisis (January 1990): I–III.

42. Clarene Royston, interview, St. Louis, April 4, 1990.

43. National Council of Churches, "Harassment of African American Elected Officials," Resolution of Governing Board, New York, N.Y., November 16, 1989.

44. Congressional Record, January 27, 1988, p. H31.

45. For a description of the term "zero sum" and its political and policy implications, see Lester C. Thurow, The Zero Sum Society (New York: Basic Books, 1980); but for specific case study of how white ethnics and Blacks interact within this kind of setting, see Edwin R. Lewinson, Black Politics in New York City (New York: Twayne, 1974).

46. Leonard A. Cole, Blacks in Power: A Comparative Study of Black and White Elected Officials (Princeton: Princeton University Press, 1975), p. 233.

47. Clarence N. Stone, Economic Growth and Neighborhood Discontent (Chapel Hill: University of North Carolina Press, 1976), p. 211.

48. Adolph Reed, Jr., "A Critique of Neo-Progressivism in Theorizing About Local Development Policy: A Case From Atlanta," in *The Politics of Urban Development*, ed. Heywood J. Sanders and Clarence N. Stone (Lawrence: University Press of Kansas, 1987), p. 206.

49. *Atlanta Daily World,* September 10, 1989.

50. Marian Petty, interview, Atlanta, April 2, 1990.

51. Anthony Obershall, *Social Conflict and Social Movement* (New Jersey: Prentice-Hall, 1973), p. 241.

52. Ronald W. Walters, *Black Presidential Politics in America: A Strategic Approach* (Albany: State University Press of New York, 1987), p. 87.

53. Ron Daniels, "Some Reflections on the Ohio Black Political Assembly on the Occasion of Its First Reunion," Speech, Columbus, Ohio, September 17, 1988.

54. Gerald D. Jaynes and Robin M. Williams, Jr., *A Common Destiny: Blacks and American Society,* (Washington, D.C.: National Academy Press, 1989), p. 245.

55. See, for example, William E. Nelson, "Cleveland: The Rise and Fall of the New Black Politics," in *The New Black Politics: The Search for Political Power,* ed. Michael B. Preston et al. (New York: Longman, 1982), where one major theme is the political experimenting by Black activists in the electoral arena. See also Martin Kilson, "Report on Black Politics in Comparative Perspective-A Study in the Politics of Inclusion," paper prepared for the Committee on the Status of Black Americans, National Research Council, Washington, D.C., 1987.

56. *In These Times,* January 18, 1989.

57. Jitu Weusi, interview, New York City, April 3, 1990.

58. *In These Times,* January 18, 1989.

59. Gwen Patton, interview, Birmingham, Ala., April 12, 1990.

60. Harold Cruse, "Plural But Equal," *In These Times,* January 18, 1989.

61. *Baltimore Afro-American,* August 16, 1988.

62. Harry, *Attention, Move,* p. 173.

63. Edward Ransford, *Race and Class in American Society* (Cambridge, Mass.: Schenkman, 1977), p. 7.

64. Ibid., p. 35.

65. Theodore Cross, *The Black Power Imperative: Racial Inequality and the Politics of Non Violence* (New York: Faulkner Books, 1984), p. 15.

66. Mancur E. Olsen, *Power In Societies* (New York: MacMillan, 1970), p. 3.

67. Amos Hawley, "Community Power and Urban Renewal Success," in *Community Structure and Decision Making: Comparative Analyses,* ed. Terry N. Clark (San Francisco: Chandler, 1968), p. 394.

68. King, *Where Do We Go From Here.*

69. Mack H. Jones, "Black Political Empowerment in Atlanta: Myth and Reality," *The Annals* 439 (September 1978), p. 93.

70. See Chuck Stone, *Black Political Power In America* (New York: Dell, 1970), and William R. Keech, *The Impact of Negro Voting: The Role of the Vote in the Quest for Equality* (Westport, Conn.: Greenwood Press, 1981).

71. Charles E. Lindbloom, *Politics and Markets: The World's Political-Economic Systems* (New York: Basic Books, 1977), p. 26.

72. Ralph Miliband, *The State in Capitalist Society: An Analysis of the Western System of Power* (New York: Basic Books, 1964), p. 9; see also Ralph Miliband, *Class Power and State Power* (London: Verso Press, 1983), pp. 63–78.

73. Jones, "Black Political Empowerment," p. 101.

74. Ibid., p. 116.

75. Howard J. Stanback, "Las Transformaciones En Las Relaciones de Clases En La Comunidad Negra" *Seminario Sobre La Situacion de las Comunidades Negra, Chicana, Cubana, India, y Puerterriquena en Estados Unidos* (Cuba: Centro de Estudios Sobre America Editora Politica, 1984), p. 25.

76. Abdul Alkalimat, interview, Chicago.

77. Stanback, *Seminario*.

78. Jitu Weusi, interview.

79. Jones, "Black Political Empowerment," p. 90.

80. Gurwitt, "A Younger Generation," (February 1990), p. 31.

81. *The Nation*, October 16, 1989.

82. Minion K. C. Morrison, *Black Political Mobilization: Leadership, Power and Mass Behavior* (Albany: State University of New York Press, 1987), p. xviii.

83. Gwen Patton, interview.

84. Hanes Walton, Jr., correspondence with author, 1988.

85. Elaine Dillahunt, interview, North Carolina, April 10, 1990.

86. Lucius J. Barker, *Our Time Has Come* (Chicago: University of Illinois Press, 1988), p. 204.

87. Conrad Worrill, interview, Chicago, March 22, 1990.

88. Jitu Weusi, interview, New York.

89. Rufus P. Browning, David Tabb, and Dale Marshall Rogers, *Protest Is Not Enough: The Struggle of Blacks and Hispanics For Equality in Urban Politics* (Berkeley: University of California Press, 1984), p. 76.

90. Ira Katznelson, *City Trenches: Urban Politics and The Patterning of Class in the United States* (Chicago: University of Chicago Press, 1982), p. 6.

91. Roger Friedland, Francis Fox Piven, and Robert Alford, "Political Conflict, Urban Structure and the Fiscal Crisis," in *Comparing Public Policies: New Concepts and Methods* ed. Douglas E. Ashford (Beverly Hills: Sage, 1978), p. 201.

92. There are three cities of the current twenty with the greatest number of Blacks not listed that by the year 2000 may have a smaller proportion of Blacks in the total population. But in Los Angeles, Washington, D.C., and Newark the white population is also declining considerably, while in each of these cities the Latino population is increasing rapidly. See Table 1, "Population Projections For The 20 U.S. Cities With The Greatest Number of Blacks," *Ebony*, April 1989, p. 88.

93. Kenneth M. Dolbeare, *Democracy at Risk: The Politics of Economic Renewal* (New Jersey: Chatham House Publishing, 1986), p. 14.

94. Angelo Falcon, interview, New York City, August 8, 1989.

95. *Call and Post*, June 30, 1988.

96. Friedland, Piven, and Alford, "Political Conflict," p. 199.

97. Stone, *Economic Growth*, p. 15.

98. *The New York Times,* June 5, 1988.

99. David Greenstone and Paul E. Peterson, *Race and Authority in Urban America: Community Participation and the War on Poverty* (New York: Russell Sage Foundation, 1973): see Part II, "Interests, Ideologies, and Participation."

100. Joyce Brooks, interview.

101. Melvin King, "Mandela Proposal," 1987, unpublished paper.

102. Manuel Castells, *The City and The Grassroots* (Berkeley: University of California Press, 1983).

103. Cross, *Black Power Imperative*, p. 77.

104. Ibid., p. 186.

105. Gregory Squires et al., *Chicago: Race, Class and the Response to Urban Decline* (Philadelphia: Temple University Press, 1988), p. 185.

Chapter Two

1. Gerald Horne, *Black and Red: W. E. B. Du Bois and the Afro-American Response to the Cold War, 1944–1963* (Albany: State University of New York Press, 1986).

2. Roger Alford and Robert Friedland, *Power of Theory: Capitalism, the State and Democracy* (London: Cambridge University Press, 1985), p. 412.

3. Ibid., p. 413.

4. Dolbeare, *Democracy at Risk*, p. 7.

5. Ibid., p. 7.

6. Ibid., p. 8.

7. Ibid., p. 9.

8. Darden et al., *Detroit*, p. 253.

9. Ibid., p. 254.

10. Dennis Gale, *Washington, D.C.: Inner City Revitalization and Minority Suburbinization,* (Philadelphia: Temple University Press, 1987), p. 81.

11. Joyce Brooks, interview.

12. *Philadelphia Tribune,* April 15, 1988.

13. *Philadelphia Tribune,* May 10, 1988.

14. Andrew Walker, interview, Milwaukee, October 15, 1988.

15. *Milwaukee Courier,* June 8, 1988.

16. Rose Upshaw, interview.

17. *New York Times,* July 13, 1988.

18. Ibid.

19. Willie Davis, interview, Albany, New York, April 14, 1989.

20. Carl Boggs, *Social Movements and Political Power* (Philadelphia: Temple University Press, 1986), p. 5.

21. Alford and Friedland, *Powers of Theory*, p. 413.

22. Gary Orfield, "Race and the Liberal Agenda: The Loss of the Integrationist Dream, 1965–1974," in *The Politics of Social Policy in the United States,* ed. Margaret Weir, Ann S. Orloff, and Theda Skocpol (Princeton: Princeton University Press, 1988), p. 315. See also Charles V. Hamilton, "New Elites and Pluralism," in *Power to Govern: Assessing Reform in the United States,* ed. Richard Pious (New York: Academy of Political Science, 1981), p. 172; John H. Mollenkopf, "The New Deal and After: The Political Determination of Federal Urban Policy," in *The Contested City* (Princeton: Princeton University Press, 1983).

23. Hamilton, "New Elites," p. 172.

24. Herbert Haines, *Black Radicals and the Civil Rights Mainstream, 1954–1970* (Knoxville: The University of Tennessee Press, 1988), p. 177.

25. Ralf Dahrendorf, *Class and Class Conflict in Industrial Society* (Stanford, Calif.: Stanford University Press, 1959); on this discussion also see Ransford, *Race and Class,* pps. 31–45.

26. Jones, "Black Political Empowerment," p. 92.

27. Gwen Patton, interview.

28. See E. E. Schattschnieder, *The Semi-Sovereign People* (New York: Holt, Rinehart and Winston, 1960); C. W. Mills, *The Sociological Imagination* (New York: Oxford University Press, 1959); Walton, *Invisible Politics.*

29. William Fletcher, interview, April 22, 1990; September 17, 1988.

30. Roger Friedland and William T. Bielby, "The Power of Business in the City," in *Urban Policy Analysis: Directions for Future Research,* ed. Terry N. Clark (Beverly Hills, Calif." Sage, 1981), p. 135.

31. Susan S. Fainstein and Norman I. Fainstein, *Urban Policy Under Capitalism* (Beverly Hills: Sage Publications, 1982), p. 12.

32. Ibid., p. 135.

33. John R. Howard, "A Framework for the Analysis of Black Politics," *The Annals* 439 (September 1978): 8.

34. Joseph P. McCormack, "The Continuing Significance of Race: Electoral Politics in Cleveland, Ohio," paper presented at the American Political Science Association Annual Meeting, Washington, D.C., September 1979.

35. For a brief historical overview at how earlier potential alliances between Blacks and whites failed, see Milton D. Morris, *The Politics of Black America* (New York: Harper and Row, 1975), pp. 198–204, and V. O. Key, *Southern Politics in State and Nation* (New York: Knopf, 1950); see also Robert L. Allen, *Reluctant Reformers: The Impact of Racism on American Social Movement* (Washington, D.C.: Howard University Press, 1983).

36. Susan S. Fainstein, *Reconstructing the City: The Political Economy of Urban Development* (New York: Longman, 1986), p. 185.

37. Jane H. Bayes, *Minority Politics and Ideologies in the United States* (Novato, Calif.: Chandler and Sharp, 1982), p. 21.

38. Greenstone and Peterson, *Race and Authority,* p. 13.

39. Allen, *Black Awakening,* p. 273.

40. Shafik Abu-Pahir, interview.

41. *Manifesto for an American Revolutionary Party* (Philadelphia: National Organization for an American Revolution, 1982), p. 14.

42. Clarence J. Mumford, *Production Relations, Class and Black Liberation: A Marxist Perspective in Afro-American Studies* (Amsterdam: B. R. Grumes Publishing, 1978), p. 49; for a thorough historical study of the relationship and interaction between Marxism and Black political radicalism, see Cedric J. Robinson, *Black Marxism: The Making of the Black Radical Tradition* (London: Zed Press, 1983).

43. William Fletcher, interview.

44. Browning et al., *Protest Is Not Enough,* p. 84.

45. Walton, *Invisible Politics,* p. 29; and also Jaynes and Williams, *A Common Destiny,* pp. 13, 218.

46. Jones, "Black Political Empowerment," p. 91.

47. See Eddie N. Williams, "1986 Joint Center for Political Studies/Gallup Survey," Paper delivered at National Press Club, Washington, D.C., October 14, 1986. See also Howard Schuman, Charlotte Steeh, and Lawrence Bobo, *Racial Attitudes in America* (Cambridge: Harvard University Press, 1985).

48. Reginald E. Gilliam, Jr., *Black Political Development: An Advocacy Analysis* (Port Washington, N.Y.: Kennikat Press, 1978), pp. 3–7.

49. Bayes, *Minority Politics and Ideologies.*

50. Charles P. Henry and Lorenzo Morris, *The Chit'lin Controversy* (Washington, D.C.: University Press of America, 1978), p. 17.

51. Walton, *Invisible Politics,* p. 29.

52. Allen, *Black Awakening,*

53. Memo, Ralph Bunche to Gunnar Myrdal, May 5, 1940, *Ralph Bunche Papers,* Widener Library, Harvard University.

54. Ibid., p. 103.

55. Howard Brotz, ed., *Negro Social and Political Thought, 1850–1920* (New York: Basic Books, 1966).

56. For a concise elaboration and definition of these terms, see Charles V. Hamilton, *The Black Experience in American Politics* (New York, Capricorn Books: 1973), introduction.

57. Gilliam, *Black Political Development*, p. 7.

58. Ibid., p. 8; and Charles V. Hamilton, "The Silent Black Majority," *New York Times Magazine*, May 10, 1970.

59. *In These Times*, November 11, 1987.

60. Chokwe Lumumba, Imari Abubakari Obadele, and Nkechi Taifa, *Reparations Yes*, rev. ed. (Washington, D.C.: Commission for Positive Education, 1989), p. 67.

61. *The Final Call*, May 11, 1989.

62. *In These Times*, October 11–17, 1989.

63. *The Final Call*, August 20, 1988.

64. *The Final Call*, April 12, 1990; see also *In These Times*, September 19–25, 1990.

65. *Call and Post*, April 21, 1988.

66. Adolph Reed, *The Jesse Jackson Phenomenon: The Crisis of Purpose in Afro-American Politics* (New Haven: Yale University Press, 1986).

67. William Fletcher, interview with author.

68. *Facts on File* June 3, 1986; *New York Times,* June 15, 1986.

69. *Facts on File*, June 13, 1986.

70. *The Final Call*, April 21, 1989.

71. Thomas E. Cavanaugh, "The Meaning of the 1984 Election: What the Media Didn't Tell You," *Urban Research Review* 10, no. 1 (1985): 8.

72. Elaine Dillahunt, interview.

73. Gwen Patton, interview.

74. Walters, *Black Presidential Politics*, p. 106.

75. Barker, *Our Time Has Come*, p. 203.

76. David Hatchett, "The Case for a Third Black Party" *Crisis* (January 1990), p. 21.

77. Ibid., p. 23.

78. Ronald E. Brown, "Group Based Determinants of Campaign Participation in the 1984 Presidential Election," Paper presented at the National Conference of Black Political Scientists, Columbus, Ohio, April 23–25, 1985.

79. Gwen Patton, interview.

80. Shafik Abu-Pahir, interview.

81. Conrad Worrill, interview, March 1990.

82. Jitu Weusi, interview.

83. See Constitution, "National Black Independent Political Party," National Black Political Convention, New Orleans, August 21–24, 1980, p. 40; for one discussion of the emergence of the National Black Independent Political party, see Ron Daniels, "National Black Political Assembly: Building Independent Black Politics in the 1980s," *Black Scholar* 11 (March/April 1980): 32–42.

84. "The Pan African Party and the Black Nation," *Black Scholar* 2 (March 1971): 28.

85. *Unity,* February 15, 1988.

86. *Chicago Metro News,* March 5, 1988.

87. *Chicago Defender,* April 13, 1988.

88. *Guardian,* December 30, 1988.

89. Abdul Alkalimat, "Chicago: Black Power Politics and The Crisis of the Black Middle Class," *Black Scholar* 19 March 1988): 48.

90. Marcia Cerda, interview, Chicago, February 19, 1990.

91. Squires et al., *Chicago,* p. 177.

92. *In These Times,* November 25, 1982.

93. Lloyd King, interview, Boston, November 29, 1987.

94. James Jennings, Kwami Sarpeng, and Alice J. Burnette, *Blacks in Boston: A Policy Agenda: Proceedings of the Black Agenda Convention, July 1989* (Boston: William Monroe Trotter Institute, 1990).

95. *Chicago Crusader,* February 13, 1988.

96. Donald I. Warren, *Black Neighborhoods: An Assessment of Community Power* (Ann Arbor: University of Michigan Press, 1975).

97. William Fletcher, correspondence with author, September 5, 1988.

98. Omali Yeshitela, *Not One Step Backward: The Black Liberation Movement from 1971 to 1982* (California: Burning Spear Publications, 1982), p. 79.

99. This is a major theme in Lloyd Hogan, *Principles of Black Political Economy* (Boston: Routledge and Kegan Paul, 1984).

100. *Chicago Defender,* January 13, 1988.

101. *The Crusader,* June 18, 1988.

102. *Chicago Defender,* May 10, 1988.

103. B. J. Widick, *Detroit: City of Race and Class Violence* (Detroit: Wayne State University Press, 1989), p. 260.

104. Jim Schutze, *The Accommodation: The Politics of Race in an American City* (Secaucus, N.J.: Citadel Press, 1986).

105. *Unity,* June 20, 1988.

106. Maria Borrero, interview, Hartford, Conn., February 19, 1990.

107. *Organization for Black Struggle Newsletter* (Summer 1989).

108. Chuck Turner, *Annual Report to Center for Community Change* Boston, Massachusetts, May 1, 1988.

109. "Developing a Latino Voice," Conference Proceedings for the Hispanic Office of Planning and Evaluation, Boston, Massachusetts (October 2, 1987).

110. Joyce Brooks, interview.

111. *New York Times,* July 6, 1989.

112. Panel Discussion, New Sunny Mt. Baptist Church, St. Louis, Mo., February 24, 1990.

113. Gale, *Washington, D.C.,* p. 82.

114. Lawrence J. Hanks, *The Struggle for Black Political Empowerment in Three Georgia Counties* (Knoxville: University of Tennessee Press, 1987), p. xi.

115. Rudolf Heberle, *Social Movements: An Introduction to Political Sociology* (New York: Appleton-Century-Crofts, 1951), p. 6.

116. Clarence W. King, *Social Movements In The U.S.* (New York: Random House, 1956), p. 27.

117. Ralph H. Turner and Lewis M. Killian, *Collective Behavior* (Englewood Cliffs, N.J.: Prentice-Hall, 1957), p. 308.

118. Daniel A. Foss and Ralph Larkin, *Beyond Revolution: A New Theory of Social Movements* (Massachusetts: Bergen and Garvey Publishing, 1986), p. 2.

119. Robert H. Salisbury, "Political Movements In American Politics: An Essay on Concept and Analysis," *National Political Science Review* 1 (1989): 15–30.

120. *Racial Formation in the U.S.: From the 1960s to 1980s* (New York: Routledge, 1986), p. 83.

121. Hanks, *Black Political Empowerment*, p. 45.

122. Ibid.

123. Martin Shefter, *Political Crisis, Fiscal Crisis* (New York: Basic Books, 1985), p. 4.

Chapter Three

1. Ron Daniels, Lecture at the University of Massachusetts/Boston, February 28, 1989; see also Andrew Kopkind, "Black Power in the Age of Jackson" *The Nation* November 26, 1983.

2. Barker and Walters, *Jesse Jackson's 1984 Presidential Campaign: Challenge and Change in American Politics*, p. vii.

3. *Unity*, February 12, 1990.

4. Ira Katznelson, Hollis Gille, and Margaret Weir, "Race and Schooling: Reflections on the Social Bases of Urban Movements," in *Urban Politics Under Capitalism*, ed. Susan S. Fainstein and Norman I. Fainstein (Beverly Hills: Sage Publications, 1982), p. 218.

5. Samuel P. Huntington, *Political Change in Modern Societies* (New Haven: Yale University Press, 1968).

6. Charles V. Hamilton, "Social Policy and the Welfare of Black Americans: From Rights to Resources," *Political Science Quarterly* 101 (June 1986): 239.

7. *Manifesto For An American Revolutionary Party* April 1986, p. 1.

8. Gregory D. Squires, "Capital Mobility Versus Upward Mobility: The Racially Discriminatory Consequences of Plant Closings and Corporate Relocations" in *Sunbelt, Snowbelt: Urban Development and Regional Restructuring*, ed. Larry Sawers and William K. Tabb (New York: Oxford University Press, 1984), p. 159.

9. Speech delivered by McGeorge Bundy, at the 1966 Annual Meeting of National Urban League Philadelphia, August 2, 1966; this citation is from Allen, *Capitalist Awakening*, p. 71.

10. Michael Omi and Howard Winant, *Racial Formation in the U.S.: From the 1960s to 1980s* (New York: Routledge, 1986), p. 90.

11. Fred R. Harris and Roger W. Wilkins, eds., *Quiet Riots: Race and Poverty in the U.S., The Kerner Report Twenty Years Later* (New York: Pantheon Books, 1989); for the Kerner Report see National Advisory Commission on Civil Disorder Report (New York: Dutton, 1968).

12. Paul Robeson, *Here I Stand* (Boston: Beacon Press, 1958), p. 99.

13. "To Fulfill These Rights," June 4, 1965, *Public Papers, LBJ 19654 II*, p. 636.

14. Albert P. Blaustein and Robert L. Zangrando, *Civil Rights and the Black American: A Documentary History* (New York: Trident Press, 1968), p. 470.

15. "A Theory of Black Political Participation in The U.S.," *Social Forces*, September 1977, p. 43.

16. Thomas Sowell, *Civil Rights: Rhetoric or Reality* (New York: William Morrow, 1984), p. 32.

17. Ibid.

18. Keith Jennings, interview, Atlanta, February 9, 1990.

19. William E. Nelson, correspondence to author, March 2, 1989.

20. Charles V. Hamilton, "Social Policy and the Welfare of Black Americans," pp. 239–55.

21. *Education Week*, May 4, 1988; *Chicago Metro News*, March 5, 1988; and *Philadelphia Tribune*, April 1, 1988.

22. Basil Wilson, interview, New York, March 23, 1990.

23. Abdul Alkalimat, interview.

24. Jennifer Helmick and Daniel P. Welch, "Black-led Populism and the Defeat of the Democrats," *Forward Motion* (March 1990), p. 48.

25. *City Sun,* April 13, 1989.

26. *The Guardian,* April 12, 1989.

27. John Brown Childs, *Leadership, Conflict, and Cooperation in Afro-American Social Thought* (Philadelphia: Temple University Press, 1989), p. 146.

28. Abdul Alkalimat, interview.

29. William Fletcher, interview.

30. See "Act for Minority Development Fund" (House Bill #3315) filed by State Representative Gloria Fox in 1986; she again filed the bill in 1988 (House Bill #1649), but it died in the House Ways and Means Committee. And for information about the efforts of the two Black city councillors, see *Bay State Banner,* June 15, 1989.

31. James Jennings and Mel King, *From Access To Power* (Cambridge: Schenkman Books, 1985), p. 24.

32. Ibid., p. 24.

33. Ibid., p. 25.

34. Helmick and Welch, "Black-led Populism," *Forward Motion* 9 (March 1990): 46.

35. David Moberg, "Why Liberal Has Become a Dirty Word," *Utne Reader* (March/April 1989): 72.

36. V. O. Key, *Southern Politics in State and Nation* (Knoxville: University of Tennessee Press, 1984).

37. *W. E. B. Du Bois Speaks: Speeches and Addresses 1890–1920,* ed. Philip S. Foner (New York: Pathfinder Press, 1970), p. 251.

38. William K. Tabb and Larry Sawers, eds., *Marxism and the Metropolis: New Perspectives in Political Economy* (New York: Oxford University Press, 1984), p. 12.

39. Morrison, *Black Political Mobilization,* p. 65.

40. *Boston Globe,* April 3, 1988.

41. Robert L. Allen, *Reluctant Reformers: The Impact of Racism on American Social Reform Movements* (Washington, D.C.: Howard University Press, 1983).

42. Boggs, *Social Movements and Political Power,* p. 165.

43. Ibid., p. 166.

44. Werner Sombert, *Why Socialism Has Failed In The United States* (1906: New York: M. E. Sharpe, 1976).

45. More than one writer has observed that the spark that gave birth to this modern phase of civil rights movement was Asa Philip Randolph's threatened march on Washington in 1941. But even earlier than this numerous marches and demonstrations for civil rights included a 1933 march on Washington, D.C., of about five thousand people who supported a petition for a "Negro Bill of Rights." Many works are available for a summary of civil rights and labor marches and demonstrations before World War II, but see John Hope Franklin, *From Slavery to Freedom, A History of Negro Americans* (New York: Alfred A. Knopf, 1980); Philip S. Foner and Ronald L. Lewis, *Black Workers: A Documentary History From Colonial Times to the Present* (Philadelphia: Temple University Press, 1989); and Manning Marable, *Black American Politics* (London: Verso Press, 1985).

46. William L. Patterson, *We Charge Genocide: The Crime of Government Against the Negro People* (1951; New York: International Publishers, 1970).

47. Paulette Pierce, "The Roots of the Rainbow Coalition," *Black Scholar* 19, no. 2 (March 1988): 3.

48. Anthony Downs, *Who Are The Urban Poor?* (New York: Committee for Economic Development, 1968), p. 57.

49. Katznelson and Kesselman, *Politics of Power,* p. 409.

50. C. Vann Woodward, *The Strange Career of Jim Crow* (New York: Oxford University Press, 1974), p. v.

51. Walters, *Black Presidential Politics,* p. 42.

52. Boggs, *Racism and The Class Struggle,* p. 59.

53. Allen, *Black Awakening,* p. 168, esp. pps. 164–192, for a nationalist and leftist critique of cultural nationalism in the Black community.

54. Katznelson, *City Trenches,* p. 121.

55. Jewell Bellush and Stephen M. David, *Race and Politics In New York City* (New York: Praeger, 1971); see especially their chapter, "Pluralism, Race, and the Urban Political System."

56. Peter Bachrach and Morton S. Baratz, *Power and Poverty: Theory and Practice* (New York: Oxford University Press, 1970), p. 100.

57. Hanks, *Black Political Empowerment,* p. 36.

58. See Joint Center for Political Studies, "Black Elected Officials: A National Roster" (Washington, D.C.: 1985).

59. Hanks, *Black Political Empowerment,* p. 164.

60. Derrick Bell, *And We Are Not Saved: The Elusive Quest for Racial Reform* (New York: Basic Books, 1987), pp. 156–57, and "The Gyroscopic Effect in American Racial Reform: The Law and Race from 1940 to 1986," Paper prepared for the Committee on the Status of Black Americans, National Research Council, Washington, D.C., 1986. See also Manning Marable, "Beyond the Race Dilemma," *Nation* April 11, 1981, pp. 428, 431.

61. Gilliam, *Black Political Development;* see especially his chapter, "Black Population Patterns: The Demography and Physical Environment of the Black Inner City."

62. Harold Cruse, *Plural but Equal: Blacks and Minorities in America's Plural Society* (New York: Morrow, 1987), p. 200.

63. Wilbur C. Rich, Paper delivered at Annual Meeting of the National Conference of Black Political Scientists, Washington, D.C., March 23–27, 1988; and William E. Nelson, Jr., "The Evolution of Black Political Power," in *The New Black Politics: The Search for Political Power,* ed. Michael B. Preston et al. (New York: Longman, 1987), p. 176.

64. Stanley Lieberson, *A Piece of the Pie: Blacks and White Immigrants Since 1880* (Berkeley: University of California Press, 1981), p. 383.

65. Tim Black, interview, Chicago, March 29, 1990.

66. *Guardian,* January 27, 1988.

67. Abdul Alkalimat, "Chicago," p. 54.

68. Roundtable meeting, "The Jesse Jackson Campaign: Consequences For Black America," National Conference of Black Political Scientists, Baton Rouge, La., March 16–18, 1989.

69. West, *Prophetic Fragments,* p. 35.

70. William J. Wilson, *The Truly Disadvantaged* (Chicago: University of Chicago Press, 1987), see pp. 118–124; and Abigail M. Thernstrom, *Whose Votes Count?: Affirmative Action and Minority Voting Rights* (Cambridge: Harvard University Press, 1987), p. 243.

71. *In These Times,* August 3, 1988.

72. Frances F. Piven and Richard Cloward, *Why Americans Don't Vote* (New York: Phantheon Books, 1988), p. xii.

73. Ronnie Moore and Marvin Rich, "When Blacks Take Office," *Progressive,* May 1972.

74. Cole, *Blacks in Power,* p. 222.

75. See Bette Woody, *Managing Black Cities: The New Black Leadership and the Politics of Resource Allocation* (Westport, Conn.: Greenwood Press, 1982).

76. Robert Smith, "Black Power and the Transformation from Protest to Politics," *Political Science Quarterly* 96, no. 3 (Fall 1981): 441.

77. Lindbloom, *Politics and Markets,* p. 345.

78. Ibid., p. 348.

79. Ibid.

80. Howard, "A Framework for the Analysis of Urban Black Politics," p. 2.

81. Sidney M. Wilhelm, *Black In White America* (Cambridge: Schenkman Publishers, 1983), p. 319.

82. Woodward, *The Strange Career,* p. 215.

83. Wilhelm, *Black in a White America,* p. 329; see also Samuel F. Yette, *The Choice: The Issue of Black Survival in America* (Silver Spring, Md.: Cottage Books, 1982); see especially his chapter, "A Plan to Destroy the Obsolete People." For a dramatic expression of this, see the last work by James Baldwin, *The Evidence of Things Not Seen* (New York: Henry Holt and Co., 1985).

84. Cruse, *Plural But Equal,* p. 382.

Chapter Four

1. See Jaynes and Williams, *A Common Destiny,* and also Wornie Reed, ed., *The Status of African-Americans* (Boston: William Monroe Trotter Institute, 1989).

2. See Herbert Hyman, *Political Socialization: A Study in the Psychology of Social Behavior* (Glencoe, Ill.: Free Press, 1959).

3. Thomas E. Cavanaugh, *Inside Black America: The Message of the Black Vote in the 1984 Elections* (Washington, D.C.: Joint Center for Political Studies, 1985), Tables 4 and 5.

4. Michael Hager, "Racial Difference in Voter Registration and Turnout," Paper prepared for the Committee on the Status of Blacks in America, National Research Council, Washington, D.C., 1986, p. 17.

5. Projections of Population of Voting Age for States, U.S. Bureau of Census, November 1988. See also William P. O'Hare, *Redistricting in the 1990s: A Guide for Minority Groups* (Washington, D.C.: Population Reference Bureau, Inc., 1989).

6. Thomas F. Pettigrew, "When a Black Candidate Runs for Mayor: Race and Voting Behavior," in *People and Politics in Urban Society,* ed. Harlan Hahn et al. (Beverly Hills: Sage Publications, 1972), p. 95.

7. John R. Howards, *Awakening Minorities: Continuity and Change* (New Brunswick, N.J.: Transaction Books, 1983), p. 14.

8. Cole, *Blacks in Power.*

9. Burt Neuborne and Charles Simms, "Americans Far Less Free Today than a Year Ago," *Civil Liberties* 350 (Spring/Summer 1984), p. 12.

10. Barker, *Our Time Has Come,* p. 197.

11. William E. Nelson, Jr., correspondence to author, March 2, 1989; this echoes a statement by Nelson in an earlier article, "The upshot . . . [of the election of Black mayors] . . . has been the perpetuation of old patterns of political influence within the formal framework of new politics symbolized by the expansion of black numerical representation in city government." See his article "Cleveland: The Evolution of Black Political Power," in *The New Black Politics,* ed. Michael B. Preston et al. (New York: Longman, 1987), p. 175.

12. Thaddeus P. Mathis, "A Critical Assessment of Black Power and Social Change in Post-Industrial Philadelphia," *The State of Black Philadelphia* (Philadelphia: Urban League of Philadelphia, 1988) vol. vii, p. 25.

13. Kirk E. Harris, "African-American Mayoral Leadership, The African-American Urban Underclass, and Local Economic Development," unpublished paper, June 1989, p. 30.

14. *New York Times,* October 30, 1989.

15. *Guardian,* May 30, 1990.

16. *Boston Globe,* January 25, 1988; see also William P. O'Hare, *Poverty In America: Trends and Characteristics* (Washington, D.C.: Population Reference Bureau, March 1987).

17. William E. Nelson, correspondence with author, March 2, 1989.

18. Gwen Patton, interview.

19. C. Ashford Baker, "Revolt of the Underclass: A View of the Jackson Candidacy," *Urban Research Review* 10, no. 1 (1985): 5.

20. Thaddeus P. Mathis, "A Political Analysis of the So-Called 'MOVE' Tragedy: Preliminary Examination of Black Power and Municipal Decision-Making under Crisis," Paper presented to American Friends Service Committee, Philadelphia, March 21, 1987, p. 3.

21. Jesse L. Jackson, "Three Challenges to Organized Labor" *Freedomways* 12, no. 4 (1972): 310.

22. See James Jennings, "Blacks and Progressive Politics," in *The New Black Vote,* ed. Rod Bush (San Francisco: Synthesis Publications, 1984).

23. Martin Luther King, Jr., wrote that members of the Black Stone Rangers, a Chicago gang, participated in political demonstrations in this city; see *The Trumpet of Conscience* (New York: Harper & Row, 1967).

24. Michael B. Preston, "The 1984 Presidential Primary: Who Voted for Jesse Jackson and Why?" in Barker and Walters, *The 1984 Presidential Campaign* (Chicago: University of Illinois Press, 1989), p. 130.

25. Sheila Collins, *The Rainbow Challenge: The Jackson Campaign and the Future of U.S. Politics* (New York: Monthly Review Press, 1986), p. 53.

26. Robert H. Salisbury, "The New Convergence of Power in Urban Politics," *Journal of Politics* 26 (November 1964): 775–97; see also Mollenkopf, *The Contested City.*

27. Katznelson, *City Trenches,* p. 108.

28. Darden et al., *Detroit,* p. 203.

29. Haines, *Black Radicals,* p. 35.

30. Dan Georgakas and Marvin Surkin, *Detroit – I Do Mind Dying: A Study in Urban Revolution* (New York: St. Martin's Press, 1975), p. 1.

31. Ibid.

32. Eric Lichten, *Class, Power and Austerity: The New York City Fiscal Crisis* (South Hadley, Mass.: Bergin & Garvey, 1986), p. 8.

33. Barbara Ferman, *Governing The Ungovernable City: Political Shell, Leadership and The Modern Mayor* (Philadelphia: Temple University Press, 1985), p. 4.

34. Lyle W. Dorsett, *Franklin D. Roosevelt and the City Bosses* (Port Washington, N.Y.: Kennikat Press, 1977), p. 5.

35. Charles V. Hamilton, "The New Elites and Pluralism," in *Power To Govern: Assessing Reform in the United States,* ed. Richard M. Pious (New York: Academy of Political Science, 1981), pp. 167–168.

36. Edward Greer, *Big Steel: Black Politics and Corporate Power in Gary Indiana* (New York: Monthly Review Press, 1979), p. 32.

37. Kilson, "Political Change in the Negro Ghetto, 1900–1940's," p. 182.

38. Cruse, *Plural But Equal,* p. 202.

39. This was suggested by the FBI when it instructed its field offices in a memo on August 25, 1967, to disrupt any group or activity that might lead to a uniting of various Black insurgents and their organizations; see George Breitman, Herman Porter, and Baxter Smith, *The Assassination of Malcolm X* (New York: Pathfinder Press, 1976), p. 168; see also

Kenneth O'Reilly, *Racial Matters: The FBI's Secret File on Black America, 1960–1972* (New York: Free Press, 1989).

40. Joan Roelofs, "Foundations and Social Change Organizations: The Mask of Pluralism," *The Insurgent Sociologist* 14, no. 2 (Fall 1987): 51.

41. Stone *Economic Growth and Neighborhood Discontent*, p. 214.

42. See Peter Eisinger, *The Politics of Displacement: Race and Ethnic Transition in Three American Cities* (New York: Academy Press, 1980).

43. Floyd Hunter, *Community Power Succession: Atlanta's Policy Makers Revisited* (Chapel Hill: University of North Carolina Press, 1980), p.

44. *Manifesto*, p. 7. For a complete discourse on this idea by two activists, see James Boggs and Grace Lee Boggs, *Revolution and Evolution in the Twentieth Century* (New York: Monthly Review Press, 1974).

45. *Boston Globe*, January 25, 1988.

46. Edward S. Herman, *Corporate Control, Corporate Power* (London: Cambridge University Press, 1982), p. 297.

47. Collins, *Rainbow Challenge*, p. 105.

48. See Stone, *Economic Growth and Neighborhood Discontent*.

49. Joyce Gelb, *Blacks, Blocs and Ballots: The Relevance of Party Politics to the Negro* (Ann Arbor, Mich.: Xerox University Microfilms, 1975), p. 57.

50. Stuart Rothenberg, "The Second Generation of Black Leaders," *Public Opinion* 10, no. 2 (July/August 1987): 43.

51. Clarence N. Stone, "Citizens and the New Ruling Coalition," in *Urban Governance and Minorities,* ed. Herrington J. Bryce (New York: Praeger Publishers, 1976), p. 165.

52. See William P. O'Hare, *Poverty in America: Trends and New Patterns,* p. 16.

53. *The Atlanta Voice,* January 16, 1988.

54. Ibid.

55. *The Atlanta Constitution,* September 22, 1983.

56. Joyce Brooks, interview.

57. Abdul Alkalimat, interview.

58. *The Atlanta Voice,* March 19, 1988.

Chapter Five

1. Fiona Williams, *Social Policy: A Critical Introduction* (Cambridge, Eng.: Polity Press, 1989), p. 35.

2. Roger Friedland, "Corporate Power and Urban Growth: The Case of Urban Renewal," *Politics and Society* 10, no . 2 (1980): 213.

3. G. William Domhoff, *Who Rules America Now?* (New York: Simon and Schuster, 1983), p. 56.

4. Mollenkopf, *Contested City.*

5. Morris Zeitlin, "Transnational Corporations and Urban Decline," *Political Affairs* 62, no. 1 (January 1983): 36.

6. Susan S. Fainstein and Norman I. Fainstein, "Regime Strategies, Communal Resistance, and Economic Forces," in *Restructuring the City,* ed. Susan S. Fainstein et al. (New York: Longman, 1986), p. 273.

7. Harold M. Baran "The Political Economy of Race and Class," *Review of Radical Political Economies* 17, no. 3 (Fall 1985).

8. Ira Katznelson, Kathleen Gille, and Margaret Weir, "Race and Schooling: Reflections on the Social Bases of Urban Movements," in *Urban Policy Under Capitalism* (Beverly Hills: Sage Publications, 1982), p. 216.

9. Norman I. Fainstein and Susan S. Fainstein, "Restructuring the City: A Comparative Perspective," in Fainstein and Fainstein, *Urban Policy Under Capitalism* (Beverly Hills: Sage, 1982), p. 172.

10. This is a major theme developed in James Boggs, *Racism and the Class Struggle* (New York: Monthly Review Press, 1970).

11. Peter Murrell, interview with author, Milwaukee.

12. Ferman, *Governing the Ungovernable City,* p. 177.

13. David Rogers, *The Management of Big Cities* (Beverly Hills: Sage, 1971), p. 23.

14. Norman I. Fainstein and Susan S. Fainstein, "Regime Strategies: Communal Resistance and Economic Forces," in Fainstein and Fainstein, *Restructuring the City: The Political Economy of Urban Redevelopment* (New York: Longmans, 1986), p. 251; for a theoretical discussion of the relationship between class and state from a Marxist perspective, see Bob Jessup, "Marx and Engels on the State," in *Politics, Ideology and the State,* ed. Sally Hibbin (London: Lawrence and Wishart, 1978).

15. Todd Swanstrom, *The Crisis of Growth Politics: Cleveland Kucinich, and The Challenge of Urban Populism* (Philadelphia: Temple University Press, 1985), p. 4.

16. See Litchen, *Class, Power and Austerity.*

17. Fainstein and Fainstein, "Regime Strategies," p. 253.

18. Lichten, *Class, Power, and Austerity,* p. 2.

19. Squires et al., *Chicago: Race, Class, and The Response to Urban Decline,* p. 12.

20. Gale, *Washington, D.C.,* p. 80.

21. Ibid.

22. Ibid., p. 201.

23. Squires et al., *Chicago: Race, Class, and The Response to Urban Decline,* p. 24.

24. Ibid., p. 58.

25. *Chicago Defender,* January 14, 1988.

26. Panel Discussion, National Conference of Black Political Scientists, Atlanta, Georgia, March 15, 1990.

27. Joyce Brooks, interview.

28. Gus Newport, interview, Boston.

29. Richard C. Hill, "Crisis in the Motor City: The Politics of Economic Development in Detroit," in *Restructuring the City,* ed. Susan S. Fainstein et al. (New York: Longman, 1986), pp. 116–119.

30. Harry Braverman, *Labor and Monopoly Capital: The Degradation of Labor in the Twentieth Century* (New York: Monthly Review Press, 1974), p. 67, but see especially the chapter, "The Origin of Management."

31. Fainstein and Fainstein, "Regime Strategies," p. 258.

32. Freidland and Bielby, "The Power of Business in The City, p. 314.

33. Ibid., p. 144.

34. Larry Sawers, "New Perspectives for The Urban Political Economy," in *Marxism and the Metropolis,* ed. William Tabb and Larry Sawers (New York: Oxford University Press, 1984), p. 5.

35. Michael Useem, *The Inner Circle: Large Corporations and the Rise of Business Political Activity in the United States and the United Kingdom* (New York: Oxford University Press, 1984), p. 5.

36. John Kenneth Galbraith, *The Industrial State* (Boston: Houghton Mifflin, 1985), p. xv.

37. Michael Useem, "Corporations and the Corporate Elite," in *Annual Review of Sociology,* ed. Alex Inkeles, Neil J. Smelsner, and Ralph Turner (Palo Alto: Annual Reviews, 1980), p. 60.

38. Harry C. Boyte, *The Backyard Revolution: Understanding The New Citizen Movement* (Philadelphia: Temple University Press, 1980), p. 15.

39. Domhoff, *Who Rules America Now,* p. 56.

40. Boyte, *The Backyard Revolution,* p. 14.

41. Useem, *The Inner Circle,* p. 150.

42. Herman, *Corporate Control and Corporate Power,* p. 248.

43. Piven and Cloward, *Why Americans Don't Vote,* p. 213.

44. Adolph Reed, Jr., "The Black Revolution and the Reconstruction of Domination," in *Race, Politics, and Culture* (Westport, Conn.: Greenwood Press, 1986), p. 66.

45. Jack Bloom, *Class, Race & The Civil Rights Movement* (Bloomington: Indiana University Press, 1987), p. 216.

46. Manning Marable, *Race, Reform and Rebellion: The Second Reconstruction in Black America, 1945–1982* (Jackson: University Press of Mississippi, 1984), p. 95.

47. Shefter, *Political Crisis, Fiscal Crisis,* p. 208.

48. Alex Poinsett, *Black Power, Gary Style: The Making of Mayor Richard G. Hatcher* (Chicago: Johnson Publishing Co., 1970), p. 162.

49. Fainstein and Fainstein, "Restructuring the American City," p. 163; see also *The Washington Afro-American,* November 24, 1987.

50. See Rufus P. Browning, Dale R. Marshall, and David H. Tabb, eds., "Has Political Incorporation Been Achieved? Is It Enough?" *Racial Politics in American Cities* (New York: Longman, 1990), pp. 212–30.

51. Ibid., p. 212.

52. *The Municipal Year Book, 1986* (Washington, D.C.: International City Management Association), vol. 53, p. 7.

53. Squires et al., *Chicago: Race, Class and The Response to Urban Decline,* p. 184.

54. Ibid.

55. Friedland, Piven, and Alford, "Political Conflict," in Ashford, *Comparing Public Policies,* p. 200.

56. Lichten, *Class, Power, and Austerity,* p. 23.

57. For several case studies of this relationship, see Greer, *Big Steel;* Swanstrom, *The Crisis of Growth Politics;* and Jack Newfield and Paul Dubrul, *The Permanent Government: Who Really Runs New York?* (New York: Pilgrim Press, 1981).

58. Collins, *The Rainbow Challenge,* p. 31.

59. Conyers and Wallace, *Black Elected Officials,* p. 31.

60. This information from the 1984 General Social Survey is reported in Jaynes and Williams, *A Common Destiny,* 1989, p. 213.

61. This table is derived from 1982 General Social Survey, reported in Richard Seltzer and Robert C. Smith, "Race and Ideology: A Research Note Measuring Liberalism and Conservatism in Black America," *Phylon* 46 (June 1985): 100, 104.

62. See *New York Times,* January 17–24, 1989, for a review of disturbances in Miami, and *New York Times,* September 4–7, 1989, for a review of Virginia Beach.

63. Huntington, *The Crisis of Democracy.*

64. Jim Chapin, "Who Rules New York Today?" *Dissent* 34 (Fall 1987): 478.

65. Useem, *The Inner Circle,* p. 76.

66. Shefter, *Political Crisis, Fiscal Crisis,* p. 24.

67. Many times these kinds of efforts are carried out through the establishment of "good government" committees such as the "Committee for Better Government" and also the "Friends of Good Government" in Boston. One purpose of these groups is to provide campaign funds to cooperative incumbents and challengers. See *Boston Globe,* January 8, 1988.

68. *In These Times,* March 15, 1989; for a more systematic study of how corporate money influences city politicians and public policy, see Jack Newfield and Paul Dubrul, *The Permanent Government;* Shefter, *Political Crisis, Fiscal Crisis.*

69. Freidland, "Corporate Power," p. 207.

70. During the May 21, 1987, Annual Luncheon of the Greater Boston Chamber of Commerce, the president of this organization, Harold Hestnes, stated that the business community selected the superintendent and continued to support him despite the concerns of the Black school committee members.

71. Clarene Royston, interview.

72. Squires et al., *Chicago: The Response of Urban Decline,* 70.

73. Edward Greer, "Air Pollution and Corporate Power: Municipal Reform Limits In A Black City," *Politics and Society* 4, no. 4 (1974) 484.

74. See Stone, *Economic Growth and Neighborhood Discontent.*

75. Georgakas and Surkin, *Detroit – I Do Mind Dying,* p. 2.

76. Roger Starr, "Making New York Smaller," *New York Times Magazine,* November 14, 1976; see also *New York Post,* November 25, 1977, and Jay W. Forrester, *Urban Dynamics* (Cambridge: MIT Press, 1969).

77. Gale, *Washington, D.C.,* p. 36.

78. Herman, *Corporate Control, Corporate Power,* p. 295.

79. Martin Kilson, "The Weakness of Black Politics," *Dissent* vol. 34, no. 4 (Fall 1987): p. 527.

80. Ibid., p. 527.

81. Ira Katznelson, "Antagonistic Ambiguity: Notes in Reformism and Decentralization," *Politics & Society* 2, no. 3 (1972): 329.

82. Richard A. Cloward and Francis F. Piven, "The Professional Bureaucracies: Benefit Systems as Influence Systems," *The Politics of Turmoil* (New York: Vintage, 1974.

83. Greer, *Big Steel,* p. 37.

84. Alfred B. Clubok, John M. Degune, and Charles D. Fareses, "The Manipulated Negro Vote: Some Pre-Conditions and Consequences," *Journal of Politics* 26 no. 1 (1964): 117.

85. Kilson, "Political Change in the Negro Ghetto, 1900–1940's," p. 177.

86. For a study highlighting alternative ideas that are considered neither legitimate nor allowable as part of certain kinds of policy discussions, see Jack Newfield and Paul Dubrul, *The Permanent Government: Who Really Runs New York?* (New York: The Pilgrim Press, 1981).

87. For a review of the various political actors involved with the Mandela campaign, see Charles Kenny, "The Politics of Turmoil," *Boston Globe Magazine,* April 12 and 19, 1987.

88. Walton, *Invisible Politics,* p. 266.

89. Cross *The Black Power Imperative,* p. 155.

Chapter Six

1. *The Philadelphia New Observer,* April 12, 1989.

2. Robert Smith, "On The Failure To Learn The Lessons of History: An Anatomy of the National Black Political Convention, 1972–1980," Paper presented at the National Conference of Black Political Scientists, Atlanta, Georgia, March 14–19, 1990, p. 112. Also see Harold W. Cruse, "The Little Rock National Black Political Convention," *Black World* 23, no. 12 (October 1974): 10–17.

3. Charles E. Jones, interview, Richmond, Virginia.

4. Linda Thurston, interview, Philadelphia, February 26, 1990.

5. Pierce, "The Roots of the Rainbow Coalition," p. 13.

6. Robert Lichter and Linda Lichter "Who Speaks for Black America," Center for Media and Public Affairs (Washington, D.C.: American Enterprise Institute, August/September 1985), pp. 41–44.

7. Manning Marable, "The Contradictory Contours of Black Culture," in *The Year Left 2: Toward a Rainbow Socialism* ed. Mike Davis, Manning Marable, Fred Pfeil, and Michael Sprinker (London: Verso Press, 1987), p. 7.

8. *Washington Informer,* October 20, 1988.

9. *Milwaukee Courier,* October 22, 1988.

10. Cavanagh, *Inside Black America,* p. 40.

11. Ibid., p. 68.

12. Ronald E. Brown, "Group-Based Determinants of Campaign Participation in the 1984 Presidential Election," Paper presented at the National Conference of Black Political Scientists Columbus, Ohio, April 10–13, 1985, p. 9.

13. Ira Katznelson, *Black Men, White Cities* (New York: Oxford University Press, 1973), p. 68.

14. *Inside Black America;* for a thorough descriptive analysis of Black electoral gains at the national level in the early 1980s, see Linda Williams, "Black Political Progress in the 1980s: The Electoral Arena," in *The New Black Politics,* ed. Michael Preston et al. (New York: Longman, 1987).

15. Barker, *Our Time Has Come,* p. 105.

16. Piven and Cloward, *Why Americans Don't Vote,* p. 205; also see, Chuck Stone, "Black Political Power in the Carter Era," *Black Scholar* 8 (January 1977): 6–16.

17. Dolbeare, *Democracy At Risk.*

18. Squires et al., *Chicago: Race, Class, and the Response to Urban Decline,* p. 131.

19. Conrad Worrill, interview.

20. Bruce Wright, *Black Robes, White Justice* (New Jersey: Lyle Stuart, 1987), p. 188.

21. Darden et al., *Detroit,* p. 204.

22. Ibid., p. 206.

23. Cruse, *Plural but Equal.*

24. Childs, *Leadership, Conflict, and Cooperation.*

25. Roger Newby, "The 'Naive' and the 'Unwashed': The Challenge of the Jackson Campaign at the Democratic Party National Convention," in Barker and Walters, p. 174.

26. David Sears and John McConahy, *The Politics of Violence* (Boston: Houghton Mifflin Co., 1973), pp. 70–90. Another survey of Black college students found evidence of increasing nationalism and ideological preference for collective action and protest as a political response to poor living conditions; see Patricia Gurin and Edgar Epps, *Black Consciousness, Identity, and Achievement: A Study of Students in Historically Black Colleges* (New York: John Wiley, 1975), pp. 193–234.

27. Squires et al., *Chicago: Race, Class, and the Response to Urban Decline,* p. 87.

28. Basil Wilson, "Race and Politics of New York State: A Tale of Two Cities," paper presented at the National Conference of Black Political Scientists Annual Meeting, Atlanta, Georgia (March 14–17, 1990).

29. *City Sun,* November 16, 1988.

30. *In These Times,* January 18, 1989.

31. Louis Farrakhan, "The Black Agenda," speech delivered in Atlanta, Georgia, July 14, 1988.

32. Robert Dahl, *Who Governs: Power in An American City* (New Haven: Yale Uni-

versity Press, 1961), p. 94. But see also Dianne M. Pinderhughes, *Race and Ethnicity in Chicago Politics: A reexamination of Pluralist Theory* (Chicago: University of Illinois Press, 1987); she rejects pluralist theory based on the historical and political experiences of Blacks in the city of Chicago.

33. James M. Glaser, "The Paradox of Black Participation and Other Observations on Black Activism, 1952–1984," Paper prepared for the Committee on the Status of Black Americans, National Research Council, Washington, D.C., 1987.

34. Norman Nie, Sydney Verba, and Joan Petrocik *The Changing American Voter* (Cambridge: Harvard University Press, 1979), p. 255.

35. Barker, "Jesse Jackson's Candidacy in Political Social Perspective: A Contextual Analysis," in *The 1984 Presidential Campaign* ed. Barker and Walters, p. 20.

36. Preston, "The 1984 Presidential Primary Campaign."

37. *In These Times,* May 16, 1990.

38. Walton, *Invisible Politics,* p. 77.

39. Paul Carton, *Mobilizing The Black Community: The Effects of Personal Contact Campaigning among Black Voters* (Washington, D.C.: Joint Center for Political Studies, 1984), p. 24.

40. Ibid., p. 20.

41. Michael B. Preston, "The Election of Harold Washington: An Examination of the SES Model in the 1983 Chicago Mayoral Election," in *The New Black Politics* (New York: Longman, 1987), p. 141.

42. Wilbur C. Rich, *Coleman Young and Detroit Politics* (Detroit: Wayne State University Press, 1989), p. 30.

43. Michael B. Preston, "Black Politics in the Post-Daley Era," in *After Daley: Chicago Politics in Transition* ed. Samuel K. Gove and Louis H. Masotti (Champaign, Ill.: University of Illinois Press, 1982), p. 99.

44. Charles V. Hamilton, "Race and Class in American Politics," Lecture, School of Journalism, Columbia University, New York, October 9, 1978.

45. Conrad Worrill, interview.

46. Browning, Marshall, and Tabb, *Protest Is Not Enough,* p. 78.

47. *New York Times,* November 25, 1984.

48. John F. Zipp, "Did Jesse Jackson Cause A White Backlash Against the Democrats?" in *The 1984 Presidential Campaign,* ed. Barker and Walters, p. 224.

49. *New York Times,* June 23, 1988.

50. Theda Skocpol, "The Limits of the New Deal System and the Roots of Contemporary Welfare Dilemmas," in *The Politics of Social Policy in the United States,* ed. Margaret Weir, Ann S. Orloff, and Theda Skocpol (Princeton: Princeton University Press, 1983), p. 302.

Selected
Bibliography

Books and Articles

Alford, Roger, and Robert Friedland. *Power of Theory: Capitalism, the State and Democracy.* London: Cambridge University Press, 1985.

Alkalimat, Abdul. "Chicago: Black Power Politics and the Crisis of the Black Middle Class." *Black Scholar* 19, no. 3. (March 1988): 45–54.

Alkalimat, Abdul, and Doug Gills. "Black Power vs. Racism: Harold Washington Becomes a Mayor." In *The New Black Vote,* ed. Rod Bush. San Francisco: Synthesis Publications, 1984.

Allen, Robert L. *Black Awakening in Capitalist America: An Analytic History.* New York: Doubleday, 1969.

———. *Reluctant Reformers: The Impact of Racism on American Social Reform Movements.* Washington, D.C.: Howard University Press, 1983.

Anderson, Susan. "Black Leadership Gap: Eyes on the Prize, Not the People." *The Nation* (October 16, 1989).

Ashford, Douglas E. *Comparing Public Policies: New Concepts and Methods.* Beverly Hills: Sage, 1978.

Bachrach, Peter, and Morton Baratz. *Power and Poverty: Theory and Practice.* New York: Oxford University Press, 1970.

Baker, C. Ashford. "Revolt of an Underclass: A View of the Jackson Candidacy." *Urban Research Review* 10, no. 1 (1985): 4–7.

Baldwin, James. *The Evidence of Things Not Seen.* New York: Henry Holt and Co., 1985.

Banfield, Edward C. *The Unheavenly City.* Boston: Little Brown and Co., 1973.

Baran, Harold M. "The Political Economy of Race and Class." *Review of Radical Political Economies* 17, no. 3 (Fall 1985).

209

Barker, Lucius J. *Our Time Has Come*. Chicago: University of Illinois Press, 1988.

Barker, Lucius J., and Ronald Walters. *Jesse Jackson's 1984 Presidential Campaign: Challenge and Change in American Politics*. Chicago: University of Illinois Press, 1989.

Bayes, Jane H. *Minority Politics and Ideologies in the United States*. Novata, Cal., Chandler and Sharp, 1982.

Bell, Derrick. *And We Are Not Saved: The Elusive Quest for Racial Reform*. New York: Basic Books, 1987.

Bellush, Jewell, and Stephen M. David. *Race and Politics In New York City*. New York: Praeger, 1971.

Blackwell, James E. *The Black Community: Diversity and Unity*. New York: Harper and Row, 1985.

Blaustein, Albert P., and Robert L. Zangrando. *Civil Rights and the Black American: A Documentary History*. New York: Trident Press, 1968.

Bloom, Jack. *Class, Race and The Civil Rights Movement*. Bloomington: Indiana University Press, 1978.

Boggs, Carl. *Social Movements and Political Power*. Philadelphia: Temple University Press, 1986.

Boggs, James. *Racism and The Class Struggle: Further Pages From a Black Worker's Notebook*. New York: Monthly Review Press, 1970.

Boggs, James, and Grace L. Boggs. *Revolution and Evolution in the Twentieth Century*. New York: Monthly Review Press, 1974.

Boyte, Harry C. *The Backyard Revolution: Understanding the New Citizen Movement*. Philadelphia: Temple University Press, 1980.

Braverman, Harry. *Labor and Monopoly Capital: The Degradation of Labor in the Twentieth Century*. New York: Monthly Review Press, 1974.

Breitman, George, Herman Porter, and Baxter Smith. *The Assassination of Malcolm X*. New York: Pathfinder Press, 1976.

Brotz, Howard, ed. *Negro Social and Political Thought, 1850–1920*. New York: Basic Books, 1966.

Browning, Rufus P., Dale R. Marshall, and David H. Tabb. *Protest Is Not Enough: The Struggle of Blacks and Hispanics For Equality in Urban Politics*. Berkeley: University of California Press, 1984.

———. eds. *Racial Politics in American Cities*. New York: Longman, 1990.

Bryce, Herrington J. *Urban Governance and Minorities*. New York: Praeger Publishers, 1976.

Bunche, Ralph, Memo to Gunnar Myrdal on Black Ideologies, May 5, 1940. Ralph Bunche Papers, Harvard University.

Carton, Paul. *Mobilizing the Black Community: The Effects of Personal Contact Campaigning among Black Voters*. Washington, D.C.: Joint Center for Political Studies, 1984.

Castells, Manuel. *The City and The Grassroots*. Berkeley: University of California Press, 1983.

Cavanaugh, Thomas. *Inside Black America: The Message of the Black Vote in the 1984 Elections*. Washington, D.C.: Joint Center for Political Studies, 1985.

Childs, John Brown. *Leadership. Conflict, and Cooperation in Afro-American Social Thought*. Philadelphia: Temple University Press, 1989.

Clubok, Alfred B., John M. Dequne, and Charles D. Fareses. "The Manipulated Negro Vote: Some Pre-conditions and Consequences." *Journal of Politics* 26 (1964): 112–29.

Cole, Leonard A. *Blacks in Power: A Comparative Study of Black and White Elected Officials*. Princeton: Princeton University Press, 1975.

Collins, Sheila D. *The Rainbow Challenge: The Jackson Campaign and the Future of United States Politics*. New York: Monthly Review Press, 1986.

Conyers, James E., and Walter L. Wallace. *Black Elected Officials: A Study of Black Americans Holding Governmental Office.* New York: Russell Sage Foundation, 1976.

Cross, Theodore. *The Black Power Imperative.* New York: Faulkner Books, 1984.

Cruse, Harold W. "The Little Rock National Black Political Convention." *Black World* 23, no. 12 (October 1974): 10–17.

———. *Plural But Equal: Blacks and Minorities in America's Plural Society.* New York: Morrow and Co., 1987.

Dahl, Robert. *Who Governs: Power in an American City.* New Haven: Yale University Press, 1961.

Dahrendorf, Ralf. *Class and Class Conflict in Industrial Society.* Stanford: Stanford University Press, 1959.

Daniels, Ron. "The National Black Political Assembly: Building Independent Black Politics in the 1980s." *Black Scholar* 11, no. 4 (March/April 1980): 32–42.

Darden, Joseph, Richard C. Hill, June Thomas, and Richard Thomas. *Detroit: Race and Uneven Development.* Philadelphia: Temple University Press, 1987.

Dolbeare, Kenneth M. *Democracy at Risk: The Politics of Economic Renewal.* New Jersey: Chatham House Publishing, 1986.

Dolbeare, Kenneth M., and Murray Edelman. *American Politics: Policies, Power and Change.* Lexington, Mass.: Heath Co., 1979.

Domhoff, G. William. *Who Rules America Now?* New York: Simon and Schuster, 1983.

Dorsett, Lyle W. *Franklin D. Roosevelt and the City Bosses* Port Washington, N.Y.: Kennikat Press, 1977.

Downs, Anthony. *Who Are the Urban Poor?* New York: Committee for Economic Development, 1968.

Du Bois, W. E. B. *Black Reconstruction in America 1860–1880.* New York: Atheneum, 1985.

———. *W. E. B. Du Bois Speaks: Speeches and Addresses.* Ed. Philip S. Foner. New York: Pathfinder Press, 1970.

Dubrul, Paul and Jack Newfield. *The Permanent Government: Who Really Runs New York?* New York: The Pilgrim Press, 1981.

Eisinger, Peter. *The Politics of Displacement: Race and Ethnic Transition in Three American Cities.* New York: Academy Press, 1980.

Fainstein, Susan S., and Norman I. Fainstein. *Reconstructing the City: The Political Economy of Urban Development.* New York: Longman, 1986.

———. *Urban Policy Under Capitalism.* Beverly Hills: Sage Publications, 1982.

Ferman, Barbara. *Governing The Ungovernable City: Political Shell, Leadership and The Modern Mayor.* Philadelphia: Temple University Press, 1985.

Foner, Philip S., and Ronald L. Lewis *Black Workers: A Documentary History From Colonial Times To The Present.* Philadelphia: Temple University Press, 1989.

Forrester, Jay W. *Urban Dynamics.* Cambridge: MIT Press, 1969.

Foss, Daniel A., and Ralph Larkin. *Beyond Revolution: A New Theory of Social Movements.* Massachusetts: Bergen and Garvey Publishing, 1986.

Franklin, John Hope. *From Slavery to Freedom, A History of Negro Americans.* New York: Alfred A. Kopf, 1980.

Freeman, Richard. *The Black Elite.* New York: Carnegie Foundation, 1976.

Friedland, Roger. "Corporate Power and Urban Growth: The Case of Urban Renewal." *Politics and Society* 10, no. 2 (1980): 203–22.

Friedland, Roger, Francis Fox Piven, and Robert Alford. "Political Conflict, Urban Structure and the Fiscal Crisis." In *Comparing Public Policies,* ed. Douglas C. Ashford. Beverly Hills: Sage, 1978.

Galbraith, John Kenneth. *The Industrial State.* Boston: Houghton Mifflin, 1985.

Gale, Dennis. *Washington, D.C.: Inner City Revitalization and Minority Suburbanization.* Philadelphia: Temple University Press, 1987.

Gelb, Joyce. *Blacks, Blocs, and Ballots: The Relevance of Party Politics to the Negro.* Ann Arbor, Mich.: Xerox University Microfilms, 1975.

Georgakas, Dan, and Marvin Surkin. *Detroit – I Do Mind Dying: A Study in Urban Revolution.* New York: St. Martin's Press, 1975.

Gilliam, Reginald, Jr. *Black Political Development: An Advocacy Analysis.* Port Washington, N.Y.: Kennikat Press, 1978.

Gove, Samuel K., and Louis H. Masotti. *After Daley: Chicago Politics in Transition.* Champaign: University of Illinois Press, 1982.

Green, Charles, and Basil Wilson. *The Struggle for Black Empowerment in New York City: Beyond the Politics of Pigmentation.* New York: Praeger, 1989.

Greenstone, David, and Paul E. Peterson. *Race and Authority in Urban America: Community Participation and the War on Poverty.* New York: Russell Sage Foundation, 1973.

Greer, Edward. *Big Steel: Black Politics and Corporate Power in Gary Indiana.* New York: Monthly Review Press, 1979.

Gurin, Patricia, and Edgar Epps. *Black Consciousness, Identity, and Achievement: A Study of Students in Historically Black Colleges.* New York: John Wiley, 1975.

Gurwitt, Rob. "A Younger Generation of Black Leaders Challenges Its Elders." *Governing* (February 1990): 28–33.

Hahn, Harlan, et al. *People and Politics in Urban Society.* Beverly Hills: Sage, 1972.

Hagen, Michael G. "Racial Difference in Voter Registration and Turnout." Paper prepared for the Committee on the Status of Blacks in America, National Research Council, Washington, D.C., 1988.

Haines, Herbert. *Black Radicals and the Civil Rights Mainstream, 1954–1970.* Knoxville: University of Tennessee Press, 1988.

Hamilton, Charles V. *The Black Experience in American Politics.* New York: Capricorn Books: 1973.

––––––. "Social Policy and the Welfare of Black American: From Rights to Resources." *Political Science Quarterly* 101, no. 2 (June 1986): 239–55.

Hamilton, Charles V., and Stokely Carmichael. *Black Power: The Politics of Liberation in America.* New York: Vintage, 1967.

Hanks, Lawrence J. *The Struggle for Black Political Empowerment in Three Georgia Counties.* Knoxville: University of Tennessee Press, 1987.

Harris, Kirk E. "African-American Mayoral Leadership, the African-American Urban Underclass, and Local Economic Development." Unpublished paper, June 1989.

Harry, Margot. *Attention, Move.* Chicago: Banner Press, 1987.

Hatchett, David. "The Case For A Third Party." *Crisis.* January 1990.

––––––. "The State of Race Relations" *Crisis.* November 1989.

Heberle, Rudolf. *Social Movements: An Introduction to Political Sociology.* New York: Appleton-Century-Crofts, 1951.

Helmick, Jennifer, and Daniel P. Welch. "Black-led Populism and the Defeat of the Democrats." *Forward Motion* 9 (March 1990):

Henry, Charles P., and Lorenzo Morris. *The Chit'lin Controversy.* Washington, D.C.: University Press of America, 1978.

Herman, Edward S. *Corporate Control, Corporate Power.* London: Cambridge University Press, 1982.

Hibbin, Sally, ed. *Politics, Ideology, and the State.* London: Lawrence and Wishart, 1978.

Hogan, Lloyd. *Principles of Black Political Economy.* Boston: Routledge and Kegan Paul, 1984.

Howards, John R. *Awakening Minorities: Continuity and Change.* New Brunswick, N.J.: Transaction Books, 1983.

Huggins, Nathan I., Martin Kilson, and Daniel M. Fox, eds. *Key Issues in the Afro-American Experience.* New York: Harcourt, Brace, and Jovanovich, 1971.

Hunter, Floyd. *Community Power Succession: Atlanta's Policy Makers Revisited.* Chapel Hill: University of North Carolina Press, 1980.

Huntington, Samuel P. *Political Change in Modern Societies* New Haven: Yale University Press, 1968.

Hutchinson, Earl. "Misunderstood Legacy of King." *Guardian* (January 27, 1987): 18–19.

Hyman, Herbert. *Political Socialization: A Study in the Psychology of Social Behavior.* Glencoe, Ill.: Free Press, 1959.

Jackson, Jesse L. "Three Challenges to Organized Labor." *Freedomways* 12, no. 4 (1972), pp. 307–15.

Jaynes, Gerald D., and Robin M. Williams. *A Common Destiny: Blacks and American Society.* Washington, D. C.: National Academy Press, 1989.

Jennings, James. "Blacks and Progressive Politics". In *The New Black Vote,* ed. Rod Bush. San Francisco: Synthesis Publications, 1984.

———. "Politics of Black Empowerment: Reflections of Race, Class, and Community." In *Dilemmas of Activism,* ed. Joseph Kling and Prudence Posner. Philadelphia: Temple University Press, 1990.

———. "Race and Political Change in Boston." In *The Emerging Black Community of Boston,* ed. Philip Clay. Boston: William Monroe Trotter Institute, 1987.

———. "Race, Class, and Politics in the Black Community of Boston." *Review of Black Political Economy* 12, no. 1 (Fall 1982): 47–64.

Jennings, James, and Mel King. *From Access to Power.* Cambridge: Schenkman Books, 1985.

Jennings, James, Kwami Sarpong, and Alice J. Burnette. *Blacks in Boston: A Policy Agenda, Proceedings of the Black Agenda Convention, July 1989.* Boston: William Monroe Trotter Institute, University of Massachusetts, 1990.

Johnson, Lyndon B. "To Fulfill These Rights, June 4, 1965." Public papers, LBJ 1965 II, pp. 635–40.

Jones, Mack H. "Black Political Empowerment in Atlanta: Myth and Reality" *The Annals.* 439 (September 1978): 90–117.

———. "A Frame of Reference for Black Politics." In *Black Political Life in the United States,* ed. Lenneal J. Henderson. San Francisco: Chandler, 1972.

Katznelson, Ira. *Black Men, White Cities.* New York: Oxford University Press, 1973.

———. *City Trenches: Urban Politics and The Patterning of Class in the United States.* Chicago: University of Chicago Press, 1982.

Katznelson, Ira, and Mark Kesselman. *Politics of Power: A Critical Introduction to American Government.* New York: Harcourt, Brace and Jovanovich, 1975.

Katznelson, Ira, Kathleen Gille, and Margaret Weir. "Race and Schooling: Reflections on the Social Bases of Urban Movements." In *Urban Policy Under Capitalism,* ed. Norman I. Fainstein and Susan S. Fainstein. Beverly Hills: Sage Publications, 1982.

Keech, William R. *The Impact of Negro Voting: The Role of the Vote in the Quest for Equality.* Westport, Conn.: Greenwood Press, 1981.

Key, V. O. *Southern Politics in State and Nation.* New York: Knopf, 1950.

Kilson, Martin. "Political Change in the Negro Ghetto." In *Key Issues in the Afro-American Experience,* ed. Nathan I. Huggins, Martin Kilson, and Daniel M. Fox. New York: Harcourt, Brace, and Jovanovich, 1979.

———. "The Weakness of Black Politics." *Dissent* (Fall 1987): 523–29.

King, Clarence W. *Social Movements in the U.S.* New York: Random House, 1956.

King, Martin Luther, Jr. *The Trumpet of Conscience.* New York: Harper and Row, 1967.

———. *Where Do We Go from Here: Chaos or Community.* Boston: Beacon Press, 1968.

King, Melvin. "Mandela Proposal." Unpublished paper, Boston.

Kling, Joseph, and Prudence Posner. *Dilemmas of Activism.* Philadelphia: Temple University Press, 1990.

Lichten, Eric. *Class, Power & Austerity: The New York City Fiscal Crisis.* South Hadley, Mass.: Bergin & Garvey, 1986.

Lieberson, Stanley. *A Piece of the Pie: Blacks and White Immigrants since 1880.* Berkeley: University of California Press, 1981.

Lindbloom, Charles E. *Politics and Markets: The World's Political-Economic Systems.* New York: Basic Books, 1977.

Lumumba, Chokwe, Imari Abubakari Obadele, and Nkechi Taifa. *Reparations Yes.* Washington, D.C.: Commission for Positive Education, 1989.

Marable, Manning. *Black American Politics.* London: Verso, 1985.

———. "The Contradictory Contours of Black Political Culture." In *The Year Left 2: Towards a Rainbow Socialism,* ed. Mike Davis, Manning Marable, Fred Pfeil, and Michael Sprinker. London: Verso, 1987.

———. *Race, Reform and Rebellion: The Second Reconstruction in Black America, 1945– 1982.* Jackson: University Press of Mississippi, 1984.

McCormack, Joseph P. "The Continuing Significance of Race: Electoral Politics in Cleveland." Paper presented at the American Political Science Association, Washington, D.C., September 1979.

Mathis, Thaddeus P. "A Critical Assessment of Black Power and Social Change in Post-Industrial Philadelphia." In *The State of Black Philadelphia.* Philadelphia: Urban League of Philadelphia, 1988.

———. "A Political Analysis of the So-called 'MOVE' Tragedy: Preliminary Examination of Black Power and Municipal Decision-Making under Crisis." Paper presented to American Friends Service Committee, Philadelphia, March 21, 1987.

Miliband, Ralph. *The State in Capitalist Society: An Analysis of the Western System of Power.* New York: Basic Books, 1964.

Mills, C. W. *The Sociological Imagination.* New York: Oxford University Press, 1959.

Moberg, David. "Why Liberal Has Become a Dirty Word." *Utne Reader* (March/April 1989):

Mollenkopf, John H. *The Contested City.* Princeton: Princeton University Press, 1983.

Moore, Ronnie, and Marvin Rich. "When Blacks Take Office." *Progressive* 36, no. 5 (May 1972): 30–33.

Morris, Milton D. *The Politics of Black America.* New York: Harper and Row, 1975.

Morrison, Minion K. C. *Black Political Mobilization: Leadership, Power and Mass Behavior.* Albany: State University of New York Press, 1987.

Mumford, Clarence J. *Production Relations, Class and Black Liberation: A Marxist Perspective in Afro-American Studies.* Amsterdam: B. R. Grumes Publishing, 1978.

National Organization for an American Revolution. *Manifesto for an American Revolutionary Party.* Philadelphia: National Organization for an American Revolution, 1982.

Newby, Roger. "The 'Naive' and the 'Unwashed': The Challenge of the Jackson Campaign at the Democratic Party Convention." In *Jesse Jackson's 1984 Presidential Campaign: Challenge and Change in American Politics.* ed. Lucius J. Barker and Ronald Walters. Chicago: University of Illinois Press, 1989.

Nie, Norman, Sydney Verba, and Joan Petrocik. *The Changing American Voter.* Cambridge: Harvard University Press, 1979.

Oberschall, Anthony. *Social Conflict and Social Movements.* New Jersey: Prentice-Hall, 1973.

O'Hare, William P. *Poverty in America: Trends and Characteristics.* Washington, D.C.: Population Reference Bureau, March 1970.

———. Redistricting in the 1990s: A Guide for Minority Groups. Washington, D.C.: Population Reference Bureau, July 1989.

Olsen, Marcus E. *Power in Societies.* New York: MacMillan, 1970.

Omi, Michael, and Howard Winant. *Racial Formation in the United States: From the 1960s to 1980s.* New York: Routledge, 1986.

O'Reilly, Kenneth. *Racial Matters: The FBI's Secret File on Black America, 1960–1972.* New York: Free Press, 1989.

Patterson, William L. *We Charge Genocide: The Crime of Government Against the Negro People.* New York: International Publishers, 1970.

Perry, Huey L., and Alfred Stokes. "Politics and Power in the Sunbelt: Mayor Morial in New Orleans." In *The New Black Politics,* ed. Michael B. Preston et al. New York: Longman Publishers, 1987.

Peterson, Paul E. *City Limits.* Chicago: University of Chicago Press, 1981.

Pierce, Paulette. "The Roots of the Rainbow Coalition." *Black Scholar* 19, no. 2 (March/April 1988): 2–16.

Pinderhughes, Dianne. *Race and Ethnicity in Chicago Politics: A Reexamination of Pluralist Theory.* Chicago: University of Illinois Press, 1987.

Pious, Richard M. *Power to Govern: Assessing Reform in the United States.* New York: Academy of Political Science, 1981.

Piven, Frances F., and Richard Cloward. *Why Americans Don't Vote.* New York: Pantheon Books, 1988.

Poinsett, Alex. *Black Power, Gary Style: The Making of Mayor Richard G. Hatcher.* Chicago: Johnson, 1970.

Preston, Michael B., Lenneal J. Henderson, and Paul Puryear. *The New Black Politics: The Search for Political Power.* New York: Longmans, 1982.

Ransford, H. Edward. *Race and Class In American Society* Cambridge: Schenkman, 1977.

Ransom, Bruce. "Black Independent Electoral Politics in Philadelphia and the Election of Mayor W. Wilson Goode." In *The New Black Politics,* ed. Michael B. Preston et al. 1987.

Reed, Adolph, Jr. *The Jesse Jackson Phenomenon: The Crisis of Purpose in Afro-American Politics.* New Haven: Yale University Press, 1986.

———. Race, Politics, and Culture. Westport, Conn.: Greenwood Press, 1986.

Rich, Wilbur C. Paper presented at the Annual Meeting of the National Conference of Black Political Scientists. Washington, D.C., March 23–27, 1988.

———. Coleman Young and Detroit Politics: From Social Activist to Power Broker. Detroit: Wayne State University Press, 1988.

Robeson, Paul. *Here I Stand.* Boston: Beacon Press, 1958.

Robinson, Cedric J. *Black Marxism: The Making of the Black Radical Tradition.* London: Zed Press, 1983.

Roelofs, Joan. "Foundations and Social Change Organizations: The Mask of Pluralism." *The Insurgent Sociologist* 14, no. 3 (Fall 1987): 31–72.

Rogers, David. *The Management of Big Cities.* Beverly Hills: Sage, 1971.

Rustin, Bayard. "From Protest to Politics." *Commentary,* February 1965.

Salisbury, Robert H. "The New Convergence of Power in Urban America." *Journal of Politics* 26 (November 1964): 775–97.

———. "Political Movements in American Politics: An Essay on Concept and Analysis." *The National Political Science Review* 1 (1989):

Sanders, Heywood J., and Clarence N. Stone. *The Politics of Urban Development.* Lawrence: University Press of Kansas, 1987.

Schattschnieder, E. E. *The Semi-Sovereign People.* New York: Holt, Rinehart and Winston, 1960.

Schuman, Howard, Charlotte Steeh, and Lawrence Bobo. *Racial Attitudes in America.* Cambridge: Harvard University Press, 1985.

Schutze, Jim. *The Accommodation: The Politics of Race in an American City.* Secaucus, N.J.: Citadel Press, 1986.

Sears, David, and John McConahy. *The Politics of Violence.* Boston: Houghton Mifflin, 1973.

Shefter, Martin. *Political Crisis, Fiscal Crisis.* New York: Basic Books, 1985.

Sombert, Werner. *Why Socialism Has Failed in the United States.* New York: M. E. Sharpe, 1976.

Sowell, Thomas. *Civil Rights: Rhetoric or Reality.* New York: William Morrow, 1984.

Smith, Robert. "On The Failure to Learn the Lessons of History: An Anatomy of the National Black Political Convention, 1972–1980." Paper presented at the Annual Meeting of the National Conference of Black Political Scientists, March 12–19, 1990, Atlanta, Georgia.

Squires, Gregory D., Larry Bennett, Kathleen McCourt, and Philip Nyden. *Chicago: Race, Class and the Response to Urban Decline.* Philadelphia: Temple University Press, 1987.

Steinfels, Peter. *The Neo-Conservatives: The Men Who Are Changing America's Politics.* New York: Simon and Schuster, 1979.

Stone, Chuck. *Black Political Power in America.* New York: Dell Publishing, 1970.

Stone, Clarence N. *Economic Growth and Neighborhood Discontent.* Chapel Hill: University of North Carolina Press, 1976.

Swanstrom, Todd. *The Crisis of Growth Politics: Cleveland Kucinich, and the Challenge of Urban Populism.* Philadelphia: Temple University Press, 1985.

Tabb, William and Larry Sawers, eds. *Marxism and the Metropolis: New Perspectives in Political Economy.* New York: Oxford University Press, 1984.

Thernstrom, Abigail M. *Whose Votes Count?: Affirmative Action and Minority Voting Rights.* Cambridge: Harvard University Press, 1987.

Thernstrom, Stephan. *The Other Bostonians: Poverty and Progress in the American Metropolis, 1880–1970.* Cambridge: Harvard University Press, 1973.

Turner, Ralph H., and Lewis M. Killian. *Collective Behavior.* Englewood Cliffs, N.J.: Prentice-Hall, 1957.

Useem, Michael. "Corporations and the Corporate Elite." In *Annual Review of Sociology,* ed. Alex Inkeles, Neil J. Smelsner, and Ralph Turner. Palo Alto: Annual Reviews, 1980.

———. *The Inner Circle: Large Corporations and the Rise of Business Political Activity in the United States and the United Kingdom.* New York: Oxford University Press, 1984.

Walters, Ronald W. *Black Presidential Politics in America: A Strategic Approach.* Albany: State University Press of New York, 1987.

Walton, Hanes, Jr. *Black Politics: A Theoretical and Structural Analysis.* Philadelphia: Lippincott, 1972.

———. *Invisible Politics.* Albany: State University Press of New York, 1985.

Warren, Donald I. *Black Neighborhoods: An Assessment of Community Power.* Ann Arbor: University of Michigan Press, 1975.

Weir, Margaret, Ann S. Orloff, and Theda Skocpol, eds. *The Politics of Social Policy in the United States.* Princeton: Princeton University Press, 1983.

West, Cornel. *Prophetic Fragments.* Grand Rapids, Mich.: William B. Eerdmans, 1988.

Widick, B. J. *Detroit: City of Race and Class Violence.* Detroit: Wayne State University Press, 1989.

Wilhelm, Sidney H. *Black In White America.* Cambridge: Schenkman, 1983.

Williams, Fiona. *Social Policy: A Critical Introduction.* Cambridge, U.K.: Polity Press, 1989.

Wilson, William J. *The Declining Significance of Race.* Chicago: University of Chicago Press, 1980.

_____. *The Truly Disadvantaged.* Chicago: University of Chicago Press, 1987.

Woodward, C. Vann. *The Strange Career of Jim Crow.* New York: Oxford University Press, 1974.

Woody, Bette. *Managing Black Cities: The New Black Leadership and the Politics of Resource Allocation.* Westport, Conn.: Greenwood Press, 1982.

Wright, Bruce. *Black Robes, White Justice.* Secaucus, N.J.: Lyle Stuart, 1987.

Yeshitela, Omali. *Not One Step Backward: The Black Liberation Movement from 1971 to 1982.* California: Burning Spear Publications, 1982.

Yette, Samuel F. *The Choice: The Issue of Black Survival in America.* Silver Spring, Md.: Cottage Books, 1982.

Zeitlin, Morris. "Transnational Corporations and Urban Decline." *Political Affairs* 62, no. 1 (January 1983): 30–37.

Interviews

Shafik Abu-Pahir
Abdul Alkalimat
Tim Black
Maria Borrero
Joyce Brooks
Doris Bunte
Maria Cerda
Israel Colon
Mary Ann Crayton
Tony Crayton
Ron Daniels
Willie Davis
Barbara Day
Elaine Dillahunt
Diane Dujon
Angelo Falcon
William Fletcher
Marilyn Frankenstein
Sadiki Gabon

Ricardo Guthrie
Richard Hatcher
Keith Jennings
Albert Johnson
Charles E. Jones
Mack Jones
Lloyd King
Melvin King
Meizhu Lui
Manning Marable
Thaddeus P. Mathis
Mackie McCloud
Joseph P. McCormack
William Joseph Moore
Vivien Morris
Peter Murrell
William E. Nelson
Eugene Newport
Gwen Patton
Georgia Persons
Marian Petty
Ricky Pringle
Seth Racusen
Eugene Rivers
Jamala Rogers
Clarene Royston
Walter Stafford
Dorothy Stevens
April Taylor
Robert Terrell
Linda Thurston
Charles Quincy Troupe
Chuck Turner
Rose Upshaw
Ken Wade
Andrew Walker
Ronald Walters
Stan Watkins
Jitu Weusi
Hosea Williams
Basil Wilson

Carter Wilson
Conrad Worrill
William Worthy

Newspapers

Amsterdam News
Atlanta Constitution
Atlanta Voice
Baltimore Afro-American
Bay State Banner
Boston Globe
Boston Globe Magazine
Boston Herald
Call and Post
Chicago Defender
Chicago Metro News
City Sun
Crusader
Final Call
Guardian
In These Times
Militant
Milwaukee Courier
New York Times
Philadelphia Observer
Philadelphia Tribune
Roxbury Community News
Unity
Washington Informer
Washington Afro-American

Index

Books in the African American Life Series